Java™ Pitfalls: Time-Saving Solutions and Workarounds to Improve Programs

Michael C. Daconta
Eric Monk
J Paul Keller
Keith Bohnenberger

Wiley Computer Publishing

John Wiley & Sons, Inc.

NEW YORK · CHICHESTER · WEINHEIM · BRISBANE · SINGAPORE · TORONTO

Publisher: Robert Ipsen
Editor: Robert M. Elliott
Managing Editor: Marnie Wielage
Text Design & Composition: Publishers' Design and Production Services, Inc.

Published by John Wiley & Sons, Inc.

Published simultaneously in Canada.

Library of Congress Cataloging-in-Publication Data:

ISBN 0-471-36174-7

Printed in the United States of America.

10 9 8 7 6 5 4 3 2 1

This book is dedicated to programmers around the world who love what they do.

Keep the torch lit...

Contents

Acknowledgments

Many special people have contributed to the completion of this book. I would first like to thank my wife Lynne who supports me in everything. I thank my children, CJ, Greg, and Samantha for the frolicking joy we share. I thank my brother Frank for our weekly chats and shared love of technology. I thank all my family and friends for their warm thoughts, good advice, and encouragement. I thank my editor Bob Elliott and his assistant, Emilie Herman, for shepherding us yet again through this process. Bob is that rare editor with both an understanding of technology and a knack for business. I would also like to thank my professional colleagues who have enriched my consulting life, specifically: Danny Proko, Patrice Isbell, Andy Whittington, Jim Finn, Mike and Susan Saltzman, Erin Flanagan, Jodi Johnson, Kevin Moran, Susan Hansen, Fuad Ahmed, and Vaughn Bullard. Finally, I would like to thank our readers without whose support none of this would be possible. Thanks.

Michael C. Daconta

First I would like to thank my wife Audra, whose hard work and tireless support caring for our family allowed me to focus on writing this book. I would also like to thank my children Madeline, Cameron, and Jonathan whose patience during evenings and weekends gave me the extra time I needed to complete this book. Second, I would like to thank Mike Daconta for getting me started in Java and letting me share in the joy of writing about Java as it continually matures. I would also like to thank J Keller and Keith Bohnenberger for contributing their expertise in Java to make this an excellent book, and for keeping me motivated when progress was slow. Third, I would like to thank Bob Elliott, Emilie Herman, and the rest of the John Wiley & Sons staff for all of their hard work and for making this book possible.

Eric Monk

I would like to thank my wife Julie and son Jason for supporting me, even though I missed a lot of weekends with them. I would like to thank my associates at Sterling Software, especially Steve Bowlds, for reviewing early versions of the book. I'd like to thank Mike Daconta for giving me the opportunity to help with this book, and for his encouragement over the last year. Finally, I would like to thank my father who had the foresight to insist that I study computer science long before it was obvious to me.

J Paul Keller

I would like to thank my wife Patty and my daughter Kirsten for all their love and support. I would like to thank Keith Nonaka, J Keller, Steve Bowlds, Nancy Flaherty, Sumeet Erry, and Greg Davis for all of their technical support. I would also like to thank Larry Schneider for supporting our decision to write our system in Java. Lastly, I would like to thank Mike Daconta for including me in this effort.

Keith Bohnenberger

Introduction

Study after study shows that the very best designers produce structures that are faster, smaller, simpler, cleaner, and produced with less effort. The differences between the great and the average approach an order of magnitude.

−FREDERICK P. BROOKS, *THE MYTHICAL MAN-MONTH*

True effectiveness is a function of two things: what is produced and the producing asset or capacity to produce.

−STEPHEN R. COVEY, *THE 7 HABITS OF HIGHLY EFFECTIVE PEOPLE*

An effective program is one that achieves a desired result, decisively and consistently, in the most straightforward and efficient manner. Effective programming is the discipline of consistently producing effective programs on time and under budget. The key idea that I am stressing is that effectiveness cannot be measured just by the end product; it is also measured by how that end product was achieved. In other words, we need to produce effective programs effectively.

Java as a Silver Bullet

For decades, Information Technology (IT) managers have searched for a magical remedy, a silver bullet, to destroy the unforeseen monsters (like werewolves) that plague software projects. Is Java a silver bullet? Even though Frederick Brooks and most others believe that no single technique can be a silver bullet, Java is proving to substantially boost programmer productivity. In

1998, the International Data Corporation (IDC) conducted a study of nine companies transitioning from C++ to Java and found that Java averaged a savings of 25 percent for the entire project and 40 percent during the coding phase[1]. These types of productivity gains are often credited to Java's automatic memory management, its large set of cross-platform packages, and its pure object oriented stance.

Therefore, doesn't Java make me more productive and effective just by using it? Yes, if you are transitioning from C++ to Java. With Java now over five years old, you must compare your effectiveness against that of other Java developers. Furthermore, although Java enjoys general success as a programming platform, it still has its share of project failures. Even Java projects suffer from systemic problems like unrealistic schedules, lack of experienced developers, and the plethora of new technology choices. This book helps you tackle those obstacles to effectiveness that the Java language could not solve.

Specifically, this book is a collection of effective solutions to specific problems encountered when programming in Java. This book is designed to save you time. It is the fruit of thousands of hours of programming effort from experienced Java programmers working on real-world systems. The book is also designed to illuminate problem areas in the Java language and APIs: areas in the platform that are complex and not intuitive, spots in which you need to tread carefully to be more effective. Last, this book strives to be straightforward. It offers practical solutions to common problems without getting caught up in a theoretical morass.

Our Approach to Effective Java

Just as many training styles are used to create an effective athlete, many approaches are used to create an effective programmer. Our approach leans toward the practical and the concrete. We examine 50 specific problems and demonstrate each in code. After we present the problem, we discuss and code the solution. We selected the problems carefully from our experience in developing real-world solutions. The problems we selected had to fit certain criteria as stumbling blocks to effectiveness. The criteria funneled problems into one of three groups: a pitfall, a confusing or misleading API, or the best approach among many. Pitfalls are the largest group, with confusing APIs second and best approaches third. Each group of problems has its own characteristics:

A pitfall is code that compiles fine but when executed produces unintended and sometimes disastrous results. Pitfalls are the bane of

---

[1]"Java Pays—Positively," by Evan Quinn and Chris Christiansen, IDC Bulletin #W16212, May 1998. See www.idcresearch.com/.

beginning programmers who rely heavily on the blessing of compilation. Some examples of these items are: the Z-order of components when trying to draw one on top of the other (Item 30), hiding instance data members (Item 6), Java is strongly typed (Item 3), when is an overridden method not overridden (Item 1), and declaring a method with the same name as your constructor (Item 4).

What makes an API confusing? Many factors contribute to a difficult API, but the chief ones are size, too many layers, poor documentation, poor design, poor method names. Most of the time, all of these relate to the designer's either using the wrong abstractions or making the API try to do too much. Some examples of these items are: the exception hierarchy and OutOfMemoryError (Item 17), sending serialized objects over sockets (Item 25), stacking items vertically (Item 40), and how to properly use the *GridBagLayout* (Item 33).

Best approach. When schedule pressure exists (which is always), too many implementation options are a bad thing. Having walked a lot of development paths (and some blind alleys), we demonstrate the most effective approach to some common dilemmas. Some examples of these items are: method dispatching with reflection, interfaces and anonymous classes (Item 16), object pools for excessive object creation (Item 44), using *StringBuffer* versus '+' for *String* concatenation inside a loop (Item 47), and handling huge collections with persistent caching (Item 19).

Some of the items fit into more than one category, and a few are best characterized as useful tips. Regardless of how the item is categorized, one feature connects them all: inevitability. You will run into all of these problems in your career as a Java programmer. After reading this book, you will tackle them like a pro.

Organization of the Book

This book is composed of 50 specific items organized into 8 parts. The part categories are as follows:

Part One, Language Syntax. Includes 10 items that relate to properly using the language.

Part Two, Language Support. Includes 7 items from the java.lang package and its subpackages (like reflection).

Part Three, Utilities and Collections. Includes 5 items from the java.util package.

Part Four, Input/Output. Includes 5 items from the java.io package.

Part Five, GUI Presentation. Includes 8 items that relate to visually presenting a graphical user interface on the screen, including both AWT and Swing topics.

Part Six, GUI Control. Includes 7 items that relate to controlling (behind-the-scenes operations) graphical user interfaces.

Part Seven, Performance. Includes 5 items that relate to improving the performance of Java programs.

Part Eight, Miscellaneous. Includes 3 items that did not fit well into any of the aforementioned parts.

Comments Welcome

This book is written by programmers for programmers. All comments, suggestions, and questions from the entire computing community are greatly appreciated. In the past, feedback from our readers has improved the quality of our work more than any editor or technical reviewer. I'd like to thank those who have shared in the past and those who will do so in the future. As the open source community will attest, there is strength in numbers.

I can be reached via e-mail at mdaconta@aol.com or via regular mail:

Michael Daconta
c/o Robert Elliott
John Wiley & Sons, Inc.
605 Third Avenue
New York, NY 10158

Best wishes,

Mike Daconta
Bealeton, VA

Language Syntax

Programmers are always surrounded by complexity . . . If our basic tool, the language in which we design and code our programs, is also complicated, the language itself becomes part of the problem rather than part of its solution.

—C.A.R. HOARE, "THE EMPEROR'S OLD CLOTHES"

The Java language is a derivative of the C++ language with some features borrowed from Objective C, Eiffel, Smalltalk, Mesa, and Lisp. While programmers migrating from other languages to Java quickly recognize some features of and similarities to their former favorite language, those same programmers often assume that a similar feature behaves exactly the same way that it does in the older language, which is rarely the case. This phenomenon is especially true for C++ programmers. This part highlights some pitfalls and language behavior that often trip up new Java programmers.

This part contains the following 10 items:

Item 1, "When Is an "Overriden" Method Not Really Overridden?," explains the subtle difference between the dispatching of static methods and instance methods for subclasses.

Item 2, "Usage of String equals( ) Method versus the "==" Operator," examines the different methods for comparing Strings and how the constant pool confuses the issue.

Item 3, "Java Is Strongly Typed," examines the rules concerning primitive type conversions and promotions. This Item is especially important for C and C++ programmers switching to Java.

Item 4, "Is That a Constructor?," presents a classic, yet simple, pitfall. When training new Java students, this Item always causes an astonished outburst like "the compiler doesn't catch that?" You will chuckle only if you have never been bitten by this one.

Item 5, "Cannot Access Overridden Methods," takes another look at method dispatching in Java. After reading this Item, you will fully understand the issues involved.

Item 6, "Avoid the "Hidden Field" Pitfall," discusses the most common pitfall that should be covered in every introductory Java course and is usually followed by a discussion of the *this* reference.

Item 7, "Forward References," is a short Item demonstrating what forward references are and why you should avoid them.

Item 8, "Design Constructors for Extension," is based on many hours of hard-won experience. This Item is a must read for every programmer interested in developing reusable Java classes.

Item 9, "Passing Primitives by Reference," is especially useful for C and C++ programmers transitioning to Java. This Item tackles the issue of pass by reference in Java.

Item 10, "Boolean Logic and Short-Circuit Operators," covers another common pitfall using logical operators. This Item also demonstrates a clear case of when to use short-circuit operators.

Item 1: When Is an "Overridden" Method Not Really Overridden?

OK, so I admit it. The question posed in the title of this item is really a trick question. The goal of this item, though, is not to trick you, but rather to help you understand the concept of overriding methods. I'm sure that you have picked up a book or two that began explaining Java by pointing out the three main concepts of object-oriented programming: encapsulation, inheritance, and polymorphism. Understanding these three concepts is crucial to understanding the Java language. Understanding method overriding is crucial because it is a key part of inheritance.

Overriding an instance method is covered in Item 5. This item covers overriding static methods. If you didn't know there was a difference, then this item (as well as Item 5) is for you. If you have started breaking out into a sweat and find yourself screaming "You can't override a static method!," then you may want to relax a bit and move on to the next item. But first, see if you can figure out what the output of the following example will be.

This example is taken from the Java Language Specification, section 8.4.8.5:

```
01:  class Super
02:  {
03:      static String greeting()
04:      {
05:          return "Goodnight";
06:      }
07:
08:      String name()
09:      {
10:          return "Richard";
11:      }
12:  }
```

```
01:  class Sub extends Super
02:  {
03:      static String greeting()
04:      {
05:          return "Hello";
06:      }
07:
08:      String name()
09:      {
10:          return "Dick";
11:      }
12:  }
```

```
01:  class Test
02:  {
03:      public static void main(String[] args)
04:      {
05:          Super s = new Sub();
06:          System.out.println(s.greeting() + ", " + s.name());
07:      }
08:  }
```

The output from running class Test is:

```
Goodnight, Dick
```

If you came up with the same output, then you probably have a good understanding of method overriding. If you didn't, let's figure out why. We will start by examining each class. Class *Super* consists of the methods greeting and name. Class *Sub* extends class *Super* and also has the greeting and name methods. Class *Test* simply has a main method.

In line 5 of class *Test*, we create an instance of class *Sub*. Make sure that you understand that even though variable *s* has a data type of class *Super* it is still an instance of class *Sub*. If that's a bit confusing, then you can think of it this way: Variable *s* is an instance of class *Sub* that is cast to type *Super*. The next line (6) displays the value of the returned by s.greeting(), followed by the string "," and the value returned by s.name(). The key question is "Are we calling the methods of class *Super*, or are we calling the methods of class *Sub*?" Let's first figure out if we are calling class *Super*'s name method or class *Sub*'s name method. The name method in both the *Super* class and the *Sub* class is an instance method, not a static method. Because class *Sub* extends class *Super* and has a name method with the same signature as its parent class, the name method in class *Sub* overrides the name method in class *Super*. Because variable *s* is an instance of class *Sub* and class *Sub*'s name method overrides class *Super*'s name method, the value of s.name() is "Dick."

We are half way there. Now we need to figure out if the greeting method is being called by class *Super* or by class *Sub*. Notice that the greeting method in both the *Super* class and the *Sub* class is a static method, also known as a "class" method. Despite the fact that the greeting method of class *Sub* has the same return type, the same method name, and the same method parameters, it does not override the greeting method in class *Super*. Because variable *s* is cast as type *Super* and the greeting method of class *Sub* does not override the greeting method of class *Super*, the value of s.greeting() is "Goodnight." Still confused? Follow this rule: "Instance methods are overridden, static methods are hidden." If you were the reader who was screaming "You can't override a static method!," you are absolutely right.

Now you may be asking this: "What is the difference between hiding and overriding?" You may have not recognized it, but we actually just covered the difference in the *Super/Sub* class example. Using a qualified name can access hidden methods. Even though variable *s* is an instance of class *Sub* and the greeting method of class *Sub* hides the greeting method of class *Super*, we can still access the hidden greeting method by casting variable *s* to class *Super*. Overridden methods differ because they cannot be accessed outside of the class that overrides them. That is why variable *s* calls class *Sub*'s name method and not class *Super*'s name method.

This item is a short explanation of a sometimes confusing aspect of the Java language. Perhaps the best way for you to understand the difference between hiding a static method and overriding an instance method is for you to create a few classes similar to class *Sub* and class *Super*. Remember, instance methods are overridden and static methods are hidden. Overridden methods cannot be accessed outside of the class that overrides them. Hidden methods can be accessed by providing the fully qualified name of the hidden method.

Now that we understand that the answer to the question posed by the title of this item is "never," I have a few more tidbits for you to keep in mind:

- It is illegal for a subclass to hide an instance method of its super class with its own static method of the same signature. This will result in a compiler error.

- It is illegal for a subclass to override a static method of its super class with its own instance method of the same signature. This will also result in a compiler error.

- Static methods and final methods cannot be overridden.

- Instance methods can be overridden.

- Abstract methods must be overridden.

Item 2: Usage of String equals() Method versus the "==" Operator

Those of you who come from a C++ background will no doubt be confused when it comes to the *equal to* operator, ==, when used with class *String*. The main area of confusion centers around the fact that the `String.equals(...)` method and the == operator are not the same even though they sometimes produce the same result. Consider the following example:

```
01: public class StringExample
02: {
03:     public static void main (String args[])
04:     {
05:         String s0 = "Programming";
06:         String s1 = new String ("Programming");
07:         String s2 = "Program" + "ming";
08:
09:         System.out.println("s0.equals(s1): " + (s0.equals(s1)));
10:         System.out.println("s0.equals(s2): " + (s0.equals(s2)));
11:         System.out.println("s0 == s1: " + (s0 == s1));
12:         System.out.println("s0 == s2: " + (s0 == s2));
13:     }
14: }
```

The example contains three variables of type *String*, two of which are assigned the constant expression "Programming" and one of which is assigned an instance of a new *String* whose value is "Programming". Performing the comparisons using the `equals(...)` method and the "==" operator yields the following output:

```
s0.equals(s1): true
s0.equals(s2): true
s0 == s1: false
s0 == s2: true
```

Using the equals (...) method to compare strings will perform a character-by-character comparison on the strings and return a true if the strings are equal. In this case, all three strings are equal so when comparing the string *s0* to either *s1* or *s2* we get a *true* return value. When the "==" operator is used, the references to the string instances are compared. In this case *s0* is not the same instance as *s1*, but *s0* and *s2* are the same object. How can *s0* and *s2* be the same object? The answer to this question comes from the Java Language Specification in the section on String Literals. In this example "Programming," "Program," and "ming" are all string literals[1] and are computed at compile time. When a string is formed by concatenating many string literals, such as *s2*, the result is also computed at compile time to be a string literal. Java ensures that there is only one copy of a string literal so when "Programming" and "Program" + "ming" are determined to have the same value, Java sets both variable references to the same literal reference. Java tracks string literals in the "constant pool."

The "constant pool" is something that is computed at compile time and stored with the compiled *.class* file. It contains information on methods, classes, interfaces, ..., and string literals. When the JVM loads the *.class* file and the *s0* and *s2* variables are resolved, the JVM does something called *constant pool resolution*. The process of constant pool resolution for string follows these steps, as taken from the *Java Virtual Machine Specification (5.4)*:

- If another constant pool entry tagged CONSTANT_String[2] and representing the identical sequence of Unicode characters has already been resolved, then the result of resolution is a reference to the instance of class String created for that earlier constant pool entry.

- Otherwise, if the method intern has previously been called on an instance of class *String* containing a sequence of Unicode characters identical to that represented by the constant pool entry, then the result of resolution is a reference to that same instance of class *String*.

- Otherwise, a new instance of class *String* is created containing the sequence of Unicode characters represented by the *CONSTANT_String* entry; that class instance is the result of resolution.

What this says is that the first time a string is resolved from the constant pool, an instance of the string is created on the Java heap. Any other subsequent references to the same literal in the constant pool always returns the reference of the string instance that was already created. When the JVM processes line 6 it creates a copy of the string literal "Programming" into another instance

---

[1]From the Java Language Specification: "A *string literal* consists of zero or more characters enclosed in double quotes. Each character may be represented by an escape sequence."

[2]This is used internal to the .class file to identify string literals.

of class *String*. So when the references to *s0* and *s1* are compared the result is false because they are not the same object. This is why the behavior *s0 == s1* will sometimes be different from the behavior of *s0.equals(s1)*. The first compares the object reference values; the second actually does a character-by-character comparison.

The "constant pool" that exists in the *.class* file is loaded into memory by the JVM and can be extended at runtime. The method `intern()` mentioned previously serves this purpose for instances of class *String*. When the `intern()` method is called on an instance of *String* it will follow the same rules previously outlined for constant pool resolution, except for step 3. Because the instance already exists there is no need to create another one, so the existing instance reference is added to the constant pool. Let's look at another example.

```
01: import java.io.*;
02:
03: public class StringExample2
04: {
05:     public static void main (String args[])
06:     {
07:         String sFileName = "test.txt";
08:         String s0 = readStringFromFile(sFileName);
09:         String s1 = readStringFromFile(sFileName);
10:
11:         System.out.println("s0 == s1: " + (s0 == s1));
12:         System.out.println("s0.equals(s1): " + (s0.equals(s1)));
13:
14:         s0.intern();
15:         s1.intern();
16:
17:         System.out.println("s0 == s1: " + (s0 == s1));
18:         System.out.println("s0 == s1.intern(): " +
19:                                         (s0 == s1.intern()));
20:     }
21:
22:     private static String readStringFromFile (String sFileName)
23:     {
24:         //...read string from file...
25:     }
26: }
```

This example does not set the values of *s0* and *s1* to string literal values. Instead it reads strings from a file at runtime and assigns the instances created from the method `readStringFromFile(...)` to the variables. After line 9 is processed two new string instances will have been created that have identical character values. When you look at the output that results from line 11 and 12 you will notice once again that the objects are not the same, but the contents of the objects are. Here is the output:

```
s0 == s1: false
s0.equals(s1): true
s0 == s1: false
s0 == s1.intern(): true
```

What line 14 does is add the reference of the *String* instance stored by *s0* into the constant pool. When line 15 is processed, the call to `intern()` simply brings back a reference to *s0*. So the output from lines 17 and 18 is what we expected—there are still two distinct instances of class *String*, so *s0 == s1* is false, and because a call to `s1.intern()` brings back the value from the constant pool (which is *s0*), the expression *s0 == s1.intern( )* is true. If we wanted *s1*'s instance to be in the constant pool, we would have to first set *s0* to null, then run the garbage collector to reclaim the string instance that was pointed to be *s0*. After *s0* was reclaimed a call to `s1.intern()` would add it to the constant pool.

In summary, you should always use the `String.equals(...)` method for doing equality comparisons, not the == operator. If your heart is set on using the == operator you can do so with the help of the `intern()` method. The `n.equals(m)` method returns the same result as the *n.intern( ) == m.intern( )* statement, where *n* and *m* are references to instances of class *String*. The `intern()` method is at your disposal if you determine that you will benefit from using the constant pool.

Item 3: Java Is Strongly Typed

Every Java developer needs a good understanding of the primitive types Java supports. What are the pitfalls? How are they different from the language you used to use? Like many languages, Java is strongly typed, supporting eight primitive data types. These primitives are the building blocks from which objects are constructed. By strictly checking the usage of these types, the Java compiler is able to catch many simple errors early in the development process.

Most developers are familiar with data types and the values and operations associated with them. There are a few subtleties in Java you should be aware of. Unlike when using other languages, because Java's primitive types are always represented consistently in the JVM, you can write code that relies on that representation without affecting portability. This makes bit-manipulation safer to perform.

Also, *boolean* types are not convertible. Unlike C or C++, Java does not let you write code that converts between *boolean* and non-*boolean* types. If you've used either of those languages, you've probably written some "elegant" code hacks that relied on *boolean* false being equal to zero or true being nonzero.

In C, you could write code that checks the return value of a function like this:

```
value = get_value();
if (value) do_something;
```

Similar code will fail to compile in Java. The conditional statement is expecting a *boolean*, so you must give it one:

```
value = getValue();
if (value != null) doSomething;
```

Type Conversion

Because conversion of primitive types can happen implicitly in Java, you need to understand when and how it works. Conversion of non-*boolean* types is logical, and generally the compiler will warn you if your code could result in a loss of precision.

Arithmetic operations in Java are subject to the same potential problems as other languages. Most developers have written code that results in the accidental truncation of data. For example, line 10 in the Truncation class will print out "2.0" instead of the "2.4" output produced by lines 11 and 12.

```
01: public class Truncation
02: {
03:     static void printFloat (float f)
04:     {
05:         System.out.println ("f = " + f);
06:     }
07:
08:     public static void main (String[] args)
09:     {
10:         printFloat (12 / 5);       // data lost!
11:         printFloat ((float) 12 / 5);
12:         printFloat (12 / 5.0f);
13:     }
14: }
```

Because 12 and 5 are both integers, the result of the expression in line 10 is an integer; therefore the fraction is lost. The fact that the `printFloat` method is expecting a *float* does not matter; the truncation has already been done. The fix is simple: As long as either value in the expression is a *float*, the other will be promoted to a *float* also. So, lines 11 and 12 both work fine.

Widening

As long as your values can be converted without loss of magnitude, this conversion will happen automatically. In these cases, the conversion is referred to

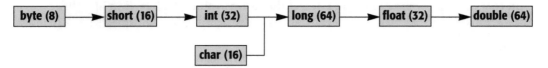

Figure 3.1   Widening conversions.

as *widening* because the types are being converted into a type capable of storing larger values. The automatic conversion is called *promotion*.

For example, you can assign a byte value into an *int* variable because this cannot result in a loss of magnitude or precision. The widening conversions are shown in Figure 3.1. The number of bits used to store each type is shown in parentheses. As long as you convert to a type with more bits, you will not lose any information.

Note that if you convert an *int* or *long* into a *float*, or a *long* into a *double*, you might lose some precision. In other words, some of the least significant bits may be lost. This kind of promotion can happen implicitly. The output from this example (−46) shows a loss of precision that occurs without any compiler warning.

```
public class LostPrecision
{
    public static void main (String[] args)
    {
        int orig = 1234567890;
        float approx = orig;
        int rounded = (int) approx; // lost precision
        System.out.println (orig - rounded);
    }
}
```

Widening is described in more detail in section 5.1.2 of the JLS: "The resulting floating-point value will be a correctly rounded version of the integer value, using IEEE 754 round-to-nearest mode. Despite the fact that loss of precision may occur, widening conversions among primitive types never result in a run-time exception."

Narrowing

Narrowing conversions (any conversion other than a left-to-right trace on Figure 3.1) can result in a loss of information. For example, if you try to convert a floating-point type to an integer, or when you risk overflow by converting a *long* to a *short*, you'll get a compiler error. You can avoid this error by including an explicit cast, which essentially tells the compiler "I know what I'm doing and accept the risk."

Implicit Type Conversion

Implicit conversion means a conversion that happens automatically, without requiring an explicit cast operator. This happens only in the case of widening conversions, with one exception. For convenience, narrowing conversions may be implicit if the variable is a *byte, short,* or *char,* and the expression is a constant *int* value that will fit into the variable.

For example, the assignment in line 7 of the TypeConversion program will compile because 127 can be stored as a byte (range –128 to +127), but line 8 will not because 128 is too large.

```
01: public class TypeConversion
02: {
03:     static void convertArg (byte b) { }
04:
05:     public static void main (String[] args)
06:     {
07:         byte b1 = 127;
08:         // byte b2 = 128;        // won't compile
09:
10:         // convertArg (127);     // won't compile
11:         convertArg ((byte)127);
12:
13:         byte c1 = b1;
14:         // byte c2 = -b1;        // won't compile
15:         int i = ++b1;            // overflow
16:         System.out.println ("i = " + i);
17:     }
18: }
```

Implicit type conversion can happen in three situations: assignments, method calls, and arithmetic operations. Assignment statements store the value from the right-hand expression into a variable, and conversion is necessary if the types are different.

Similarly, when you make a method call, your arguments may need to be converted. For example, the `Math.pow()` method requires its arguments to be *double*s, and you may wish to use integer values. Because that's a widening conversion, you don't have to explicitly cast your arguments. Note that unlike assignment statements, implicit narrowing conversions are not supported for method calls. So, line 10 will not compile, but line 11, which is an explicit cast, will compile fine.

The third case is called *arithmetic promotion,* and it happens whenever you perform arithmetic operations using values with different types—for example, if you want to add an *int* and a *float,* or when you want to compare a *short* and a *double.* In these cases, the narrower type is converted to the wider type.

Also, all *byte*, *short*, and *char* values are always promoted into *int* values (at least). This is true for most (but not all) unary operators, such as the unary minus operator (–) in line 14. If you uncomment line 14 and try to compile the program, you'll get this error message:

```
TypeConversion.java:14: possible loss of precision
found    : int
required: byte
```

The compiler promoted *b1* to an *int*, and then it warned you that the *int* value might not fit into the *byte* variable. Based on that, you might expect (and hope) that the *byte* value in line 15 would be automatically promoted to an integer as it was incremented and that line 16 would print out "i = 128." Instead, an overflow occurs, and the output shows a negative number: "i = –128."

Item 4: Is That a Constructor?

Did you ever have a bug that was caused by a simple mistake, yet it took you all day to figure out? The nature of this type of bug is such that you may discover it in a minute or you may anguish over it for hours. The following code contains one of these bugs. Let's see how long it takes you to figure it out.

```
01:  public class IntAdder
02:  {
03:       private int x;
04:       private int y;
05:       private int z;
06:
07:      public void IntAdder()
08:      {
09:      x = 39;
10:      y = 54;
11:      z = x + y;
12:      }
13:
14:      public void printResults()
15:      {
16:          System.out.println("The value of 'z' is '" + z + "'");
17:      }
18:
19:      public static void main (String[] args)
20:      {
21:          IntAdder ia = new IntAdder();
22:          ia.printResults();
23:      }
24:  }
```

The *IntAdder* class is rather simple. It has three private field members named *x*, *y*, and *z*, a constructor, an instance method named `printResults`, and a static `main` method. Let's step through the code. On line 21, we instantiate an *IntAdder* object named *ia*. The *IntAdder* constructor on line 7 sets the value of field members *x* and *y*, and then it adds them together, storing the results in field member *z*. On line 22, we call the `printResults` method, which prints the value of *z* to the screen. The output from running the *IntAdder* class should be:

```
The value of 'z' is '93'
```

Do you agree with the expected output? If so, you missed the bug. The actual output is:

```
The value of 'z' is '0'
```

Take another look and see if you can find the problem. Still stumped? Let's take a closer look at the code. On line 21, we instantiate an *IntAdder* object name *ia*. The *IntAdder* constructor on line 7 sets the value of field members *x* and *y*, and then it adds them together, storing the results in field member *z*. Or does it? If we take a closer look at line 7 we see that *IntAdder* is actually a method, not a constructor. I mistakenly added a return type of "void" to what I intended to be my constructor. The "void" return type turned my constructor into a method. If the `IntAdder` method on line 7 is not my constructor, then what constructor is getting called when I instantiate my object? Because there is no constructor, Java provides the *IntAdder* class with a default no-argument constructor. The default no-argument constructor has no implementation. The default constructor acts as if I typed in the following constructor:

```
public IntAdder() { }
```

Therefore, the object that gets created on line 21 still has *x*, *y*, and *z* values of 0. When the `printResults` method gets called on line 22, we see the following output:

```
The value of 'z' is '0'.
```

There are a couple of key issues with this "simple" little bug. First, we notice that we did not get a compiler error or a runtime error even though we had a method with the same name as our class name. It is legal to have a method named the same as your class, but it certainly is not advised. Constructors must have the same name as the class. This makes them easy to find. Therefore, only constructors should have the same name as the class. If you have methods with the same name as the class you are likely to confuse your fellow programmers. Also, naming methods the same as the class contradicts standard conventions.

Method names are generally verbs or verb phrases and have the first character of the first word in lowercase and the first character of subsequent words in uppercase. Class names are generally nouns or noun phrases with the first character of every word in uppercase. See section 6.8 of the Java Language Specification for further information on naming conventions. The second issue we notice in this example is that if we do not have a constructor in our class, Java will provide us with a default constructor with no implementation. This happens only if we do not include a constructor. If we have a constructor with any number of arguments then Java does not provide a default no-argument constructor.

Item 5: Cannot Access Overridden Methods

Imagine that you are maintaining an application that contains a third-party Java text editor. The text editor in your application currently supports RTF and has a spelling and grammar checker. In the program code of the application itself, you can create new documents or open new documents by accessing the editor's *DocumentManager* object. Each time one of these methods is called, a *Document* object is returned, which provides instance methods for spell checking, grammar checking, and so on. One day, you get a call from your client, who tells you that the text editor in the application needs to support HTML display and editing in addition to RTF. You feel confident you can fulfill this request because you know the third-party vendor that supplies your text editor just upgraded it to support HTML display and editing. Furthermore, the vendor guaranteed backward compatibility because all new functionality was placed in a subclass of *Document*, called *HTMLDocument*, and the Document code did not change. The new version could be plugged in immediately with no code changes, and the new features of *HTMLDocument* could be accessed by casting the *Document* object returned from the *DocumentManager* to an *HTML-Document*. Wanting to please your client and being a little overzealous, you get the new version, add some code to take advantage of the new HTML features, and tell your client that the new functionality will be available in a month (just enough time for QA).

Feeling good about yourself, you are surprised to see a report from QA indicating a problem with the spell checker. You confirm that the spell checker is broken in the *HTMLDocument*, but thinking you're a smart Java programmer, you believe you can trick the *HTMLDocument* into using the spellCheck() method from the *Document* object instead. After all, the vendor stated that the *Document* code did not change. You try everything to invoke the spellCheck() method from *Document*—not casting *Document* to *HTML-Document*, declaring a local *Document* variable and setting it to the *Document* object passed in, using reflection to access the spellCheck() method in

Document—but nothing works. After many frustrated calls to the vendor support line, which claims that the *Document* object code did not change, you finally consult the *Java Language Specification (8.4.6.1)* and see this:

> An overridden method can be accessed by using a method invocation expression that contains the keyword *super*. Note that a qualified name or a cast to a superclass type is not effective in attempting to access an overridden method; . . .

Finally, it all makes sense! The third-party Java text editor library always creates an object of type *HTMLDocument* when you get a document from the *DocumentManager*. No matter what you try to do to the *HTMLDocument* (casting, reflection, and so forth), you will always call the spellCheck() method of *HTMLDocument* and not the spellCheck() method of *Document*. In fact, when you have a subclass that overrides instance methods of a superclass, the only way to access those overridden methods is by using *super* from within the subclass. Any external classes utilizing the subclass can never get to the overridden instance methods of the superclass. The source code that follows demonstrates this concept.

```
01: class DocumentManager
02: {
03:     public Document newDocument()
04:     {
05:         return (new HTMLDocument());
06:     }
07: }
08:
09: class Document
10: {
11:     public boolean spellCheck()
12:     {
13:         return (true);
14:     }
15: }
16:
17: class HTMLDocument extends Document
18: {
19:     public boolean spellCheck()
20:     {
21:         System.out.println("Trouble checking these darn hyperlinks!");
22:         return (false);
23:     }
24: }
25:
26: public class OverridingInstanceApp
27: {
28:     public static void main (String args[])
29:     {
30:         DocumentManager dm = new DocumentManager();
```

```
31:            Document d = dm.newDocument();
32:            boolean spellCheckSuccessful = d.spellCheck();
33:            if (spellCheckSuccessful)
34:                System.out.println("No spelling errors where found.");
35:            else
36:                System.out.println("Document has spelling errors.");
37:        }
38: }
```

Line 32 is where we attempt to call the spellCheck() method on what we think is a plain *Document* object. It, however, is really an instance of *HTML-Document* so the spellCheck() method call we make calls the one defined in the *HTMLDocument* class. The output produced from this example is this:

```
Trouble checking these darn hyperlinks!
Document has spelling errors.
```

Note that the inability to access overridden superclass methods applies only to instance methods—those methods in a class that are not static. Methods in a class that are *static* can be accessed even if they are overridden by a subclass. This can be accomplished by casting to the superclass. By changing line 11 and 19 to the following line, we change the spellCheck() method call to be static.

```
public static boolean spellCheck(Document d)
```

And by changing line 32 to the following line we can make the call to the static method.

```
boolean spellCheckSuccessful = d.spellCheck(d);
```

Running the modified example will produce the following output:

```
No spelling errors where found.
```

You may be wondering if the example described here has actually occurred. This example is fictitious, but cases do exist where an upgrade of a class has occurred in this manner. Any classes that currently support the old object (superclass) still think they are getting an instance of the old class, when in fact they are getting an instance of the new class (subclass with new functionality). A good example of this is Javasoft's introduction of the *Graphics2D* object when Java 2D was introduced into the JDK. All AWT methods that were passed *Graphics* objects (such as paint(...) and update(...)) in the older version of the JDK were actually being passed *Graphics2D* objects in the new version of the JDK. And yes, *Graphics2D* overrides instance methods in *Graphics* (example: `draw3DRect()`). If `draw3DRect()` contained a bug in the *Graphics2D* class but worked fine in the *Graphics* class, guess what—you were stuck with the method provided by *Graphics2D*.

Even though nothing can be done to access an overridden superclass instance method from outside of a subclass, it is good to know that this can be a source for errors. If you suspect that an object you are using is actually an instance of a subclass you can always call `getClass().getName()` on the object to determine its true identity. And if you are the programmer adding new functionality by subclassing, make sure that extensive compatibility tests are performed or ensure that any new functionality is performed by adding new methods and not by overriding superclass methods.

Item 6: Avoid the "Hidden Field" Pitfall

Understanding how field members are hidden in the Java language is just as important as understanding how methods get overridden. If you think you understand how field members get hidden because you understand how methods get overridden, then you better read the rest of this item. Unintentionally hiding a field member or mistakenly thinking that you have "overridden" a field member can cause undesirable results in your program.

```
01:  public class Wealthy
02:  {
03:      public String answer = "Yes!";
04:      public void wantMoney()
05:      {
06:          System.out.println("Would you like $1,000,000? > "+ answer);
07:      }
08:      public static void main(String[] args)
09:      {
10:          Wealthy w = new Wealthy();
11:          w.wantMoney();
12:      }
13:  }
```

Output:

```
Would you like $1,000,000? > Yes!
```

In this example, class *Wealthy* has an instance variable named *answer*, a `wantMoney` method, and a `main` method. The `main` method creates instance *w* of class *Wealthy*. Instance *w* calls its `wantMoney` method, which prints a question and responds with the value of the instance variable *answer*. The previous example answers the question correctly; now let's take a look at an example that does not answer the question correctly.

```
01:  public class Poor
02:  {
03:      public String answer = "Yes!";
04:      public void wantMoney()
05:        {
06:        String answer = "No!"; // hides instance variable answer
07:        System.out.println("Would you like $1,000,000? > " + answer);
08:      }
09:      public static void main(String[] args)
10:      {
11:          Poor p = new Poor();
12:          p.wantMoney();
13:      }
14:  }
```

Output:

```
Would you like $1,000,000? > No!
```

Notice in the output of this example the response to the question has changed to "No!". The local variable *answer* hides the instance variable *answer*; therefore, the response is the value of the local variable. In an example this simple it is obvious that the local variable *answer* hides the instance variable *answer*, producing an undesired result. In larger, more complex programs, though, it can be difficult to find a problem caused by a field member that is hidden by accident. To avoid problems with data hiding it is important to understand the following:

- The different kinds of Java variables
- The scope of a variable
- Which kinds of variables can be hidden
- How those kinds of variables get hidden
- How to access a hidden variable
- How hidden variables differ from overridden methods

Kinds of Java Variables

The six kinds of variables are class variables, instance variables, method parameters, constructor parameters, exception-handler parameters, and local variables. Class variables are static data fields declared in a class declaration as well as static or nonstatic data fields declared in an interface declaration. Instance variables are nonstatic variables declared in a class declaration. The term "field members" refers to both class variables and instance variables. Method parameters are arguments passed to a method. Constructor parameters are arguments passed to a constructor. Exception-handler parameters are arguments passed to the catch block of a try statement. Finally, local variables are variables declared in a block of code or in a "for" statement.

This example declares a variable of each type:

```
01:   public class Types
02:   {
03:       int x;              // instance variable
04:       static int y;       // class variable
05:       public Types(String s)   // s is a constructor parameter
06:       {
07:           // constructor code f.
08:       }
09:       public createURL(String urlString) //urlString is a method parameter
10:       {
11:           String name = "example";   // name is a local variable
12:           try
13:           {
14:               URL url = new URL(urlString);
15:           }
16:           catch(Exception e)      // e is a exception-handler parameter
17:           {
18:               // handle exception
19:           }
20:       }
21:   }
```

Variable Scope

Variable scope is defined as the block of code in which the variable can be referred to by its simple name. A simple name is a single identifier for a variable. The instance variable x on line 3 has a simple name of "x." Instance variables and class variables have a scope of the entire the class or interface in which the variable was declared. The scope of field members x and y is the entire body of the Types class. Method parameters have a scope of the entire body of the method. Constructor parameters have a scope of the entire body of the constructor. Exception-handler parameters have a scope of the entire body of the catch statement. The scope of a local variable is the entire block of code in which it was declared. The local variable *name*, which is declared in the createURL method on line 11, has a scope of the entire body of the createURL method.

Which Kinds of Variables Can Be Hidden?

Instance variables and class variables can be hidden. Local variables and parameters can never be hidden. Attempting to hide a parameter with a local variable of the same name results in a compiler error. Similarly, attempting to hide a local variable with another local variable of the same name results in a compiler error.

```
01:   class Hidden
02:   {
03:       public static void main(String[] args)
04:       {
05:           int args = 0;        // illegal - results in a compiler error
06:           String s = "string";
07:           int s = 10;          // illegal - results in a compiler error
08:       }
09:   }
```

In this example, the local variable *args* cannot be named the same as the method parameter *args*. The local variable *s* on line 7 will also cause a compiler error because it cannot have the same name as another local variable in the same scope.

How Instance Variables and Class Variables Get Hidden

Field members can be hidden in part of their scope by local variables or parameters of the same name. Field members can also be hidden by a subclass's field member of the same name or through multiple inheritance. A local variable with the same name as a field member will hide that field member in the scope in which the local variable was declared. A method parameter with the same name as a field member will hide that field member in the scope of the body of the method. A constructor parameter with the same name as field member will hide that field member in the body of the constructor. And an exception-handler parameter with the same name as a field member will hide that field member in the scope of the catch block.

```
01:   public class Bike
02:   {
03:       String type;
04:       public Bike(String type)
05:       {
06:           System.out.println("type =" + type);
07:       }
08:   }
```

In this example, the constructor parameter *type* hides the instance variable *type*. The value of the *type* variable displayed by the `System.out.println` method will be the value of the constructor parameter *type*, not the instance variable *type*.

A subclass's field member will hide a parent class's field member of the same name.

```
01:   public class Bike
02:   {
03:       String type = "generic";
04:   }
```

```
01:   public class MountainBike extends Bike
02:   {
03:       String type = "All terrain";
04:   }
```

In this example, the instance variable *type* in class *Bike* is hidden by its subclass's instance variable *type*. A subclass's class variable will hide its superclass's class variable or instance variable of the same name. Similarly, a subclass's instance variable will hide its superclass's instance variable or class variable of the same name.

Multiply inherited field members will, in effect, hide each other. This in itself does not cause a compiler error; however, any reference by simple name to the hidden field members will cause a compiler error. Fields are considered to be "multiply inherited" if two or more fields with the same name are inherited from two or more interfaces, or from an interface and superclass.

```
01:   public interface Stretchable
02:   {
03:       int y;
04:   }
```

```
01:   public class Line
02:   {
03:       int x;
04:   }
```

```
01:   public class MultiLine extends Line implements Stretchable
02:   {
03:       public MultiLine()
04:       {
05:           System.out.println("x = " + x);
06:       }
07:   }
```

This example will compile error free. If a variable named x was added to the *Stretchable* interface, then class *MultiLine* would fail to compile because it attempts to refer to the multi-inherited variable x by its simple name.

How to Access a Hidden Field Member

Most field variables can be accessed using the variable's qualified name as opposed to its simple name. The "this" keyword will qualify an instance variable that is being hidden by a local variable. The "super" keyword will qualify an instance variable that is being hidden by its subclass. A class variable can also be qualified by placing the class name and a "." before the class variable's simple name.

```
01:  public class Wealthy
02:  {
03:      public String answer = "Yes!";
04:      public void wantMoney()
05:      {
06:          String answer = "No!";
07:          System.out.println("Do you want to give me $1,000,000? > " +
08:          answer);
09:          System.out.println("Would you like $1,000,000? > " +
10:          this.answer);
11:      }
12:      public static void main(String[] args)
13:      {
14:          Wealthy w = new Wealthy();
15:          w.wantMoney();
16:      }
17:  }
```

Output:

```
Do you want to give me $1,000,000 > No!
Would you like $1,000,000? > Yes!
```

In this example, class *Wealthy* has an instance variable *answer*. The want-Money method declares a local variable named *answer* that hides the instance variable *answer*. In order to give the correct response to each of the questions in the wantMoney method we need to access the local variable *answer* as well as the instance variable *answer*. By using the "this" keyword to qualify the instance variable we can tell the compiler that we want the instance variable and not the local variable. As is shown in the output, the response to the first question is given by the value of the local variable *answer*. The response to the second question is given by the value of the instance variable *answer*, which is qualified by the "this" keyword.

This example shows how to qualify a hidden instance variable of a parent class:

```
01:  public class StillWealthy extends Wealthy
02:  {
03:      public String answer = "No!";
```

```
04:        public void wantMoney()
05:        {
06:            String answer = "maybe?";
07:            System.out.println("Did you see that henway? > " + answer);
08:            System.out.println("Do you want to give me $1,000,000? > " +
09:            this.answer);
10:            System.out.println("Would you like $1,000,000? > " + super.answer);
11:        }
12:        public static void main(String[] args)
13:        {
14:            Wealthy w = new Wealthy();
15:            w.wantMoney();
16:        }
17:    }
```

Output:

```
Did you see that henway? > maybe?
Do you want to give me $1,000,000 > No!
Would you like $1,000,000? > Yes!
```

Notice from the output that the response to the question on line 7 is given by the value of the local variable. The response to the question on line 8 is given by the value of the *StillWealthy* subclass's instance variable, which is qualified by using the "this" keyword. The response to the question on line 10 is given by the value of the superclass's instance variable, which is qualified by using the "super" keyword.

How Hidden Variables Differ from an Overridden Method

Hidden variables differ from overridden methods in several ways. Perhaps the most important difference is that an instance of a class cannot access its superclass's overridden method by using a qualified name or by casting the instance to that of its superclass.

```
01:  public class Wealthier extends Wealthy
02:  {
03:      public void wantMoney()
04:      {
05:          System.out.println("Would you like $2,000,000? > " + answer);
06:      }
07:      public static void main(String[] args)
08:      {
09:          Wealthier w = new Wealthier();
10:          w.wantMoney();
11:          ((Wealthy)w).wantMoney();
12:      }
13:  }
```

Output:

```
Would you like $2,000,000? > Yes!
Would you like $2,000,000? > Yes!
```

In this example, class *Wealthier* extends class *Wealthy* and overrides the method wantMoney. The main method creates an instance *w* of class *Wealthier* and calls w.wantMoney(). Notice by the first line in the output that the $2,000,000 question is asked. The main method then casts the instance variable *w* to its parent class and once again calls the wantMoney method. Notice by the second line in the output that the $2,000,000 question is still asked. The previous example shows that from an instance of a subclass, the superclass's overridden method cannot be accessed by casting the instance to the superclass.

This example shows that a hidden variable differs from an overridden method because it can be accessed by casting an instance of the subclass to its superclass.

```
01:    public class Poorer extends Wealthier
02:    {
03:        String answer = "No!";
04:        public void wantMoney()
05:        {
06:            System.out.println("Would you like $3,000,000? > " + answer);
07:        }
08:        public static void main(String[] args)
09:        {
10:            Poorer p = new Poorer();
11:            ((Wealthier)p).wantMoney();
12:            System.out.println("Are you sure? > " + ((Wealthier)p).answer);
13:        }
14:    }
```

Output:

```
Do you want $3,000,000? ? No!
Are you sure? > Yes!
```

Class *Poorer* extends class *Wealthier*; the main method creates an instance *p* of class *Poorer*. The main method then casts instance *p* to its superclass. As was explained in the previous example, because the wantMoney method is overridden, the superclass's wantMoney method cannot be accessed by casting to the superclass. Therefore, the wantMoney method of class *Poorer* gets called, which responds with the answer "No!". The main method then asks the question "Are you sure? >". The answer is the value of the superclass's variable, not the value of the subclass's variable. This occurs because the subclass just hides the superclass's field member so casting the instance to its superclass allows access to its superclass's field members. Another difference between data hiding and method overriding is that a static method cannot override a superclass's instance method. A static variable, however, can hide a superclass's instance variable of the same name. Similarly, an instance method cannot override a superclass's method of the same name but different signature. A field member can hide a superclass's field member of the same name even if it is of a different type.

Avoiding the "hidden field" pitfall by understanding the points discussed in this item will help you achieve the desired results of your application as well as save you countless hours debugging complex programs.

Item 7: Forward References

Class variables and static initializers are executed when a class is loaded into the JVM. Section 8.5 of the Java Language Specification notes that "static initializers and class variable initializers are executed in textual order and may not refer to class variables declared in the class whose declarations appear textually after the use...." In other words, these statements are processed in the order in which they appear in the code. Normally, the compiler will catch any forward references. Consider the following code:

```
1: public class ForwardReference
2: {
3:    int first = second;  // this will fail to compile
4:    int second = 2;
5: }
```

Attempting to compile this class will result in an error:

```
ForwardReference.java:3: Can't make forward reference to second in class
ForwardReference.
```

So, even though both *first* and *second* are in the same scope, the language specification disallows this kind of invalid initialization, and the compiler will catch this.

It is possible, though, to circumvent this protection. Java allows method calls to be used to initialize class variables, and accesses of class variables by methods are not checked in this way. The program that follows will compile cleanly.

```
01: public class ForwardReferenceViaMethod
02: {
03:    static int first = accessTooSoon();
04:    static int second = 1;
05:
06:    static int accessTooSoon()
07:    {
```

```
08:        return (second);
09:    }
10:
11:    public static void main (String[] args)
12:    {
13:        System.out.println ("first = " + first);
14:    }
15: }
```

Executing it, however, results in accessing the default value of *second* (which is 0) before it gets initialized to 1. So, *first* is assigned the value of 0 instead of 1.

There's no simple solution to this problem. If you use method calls to initialize static variables, you have to ensure that those methods don't depend on other static variables that are declared later in the file.

Item 8: Design Constructors for Extension

Perhaps the most significant advantage of object-oriented languages in general, and Java in particular, is that code can be easily reused. One of the most common ways to reuse a class is to extend it, and then add or change the functionality to meet your requirements. Unfortunately, many inexperienced developers do not write code that is easily extensible.

There are many situations in the process of software development in which you must make trade-offs between multiple goals. For example, optimizing often results in code that is more complex, harder to maintain, and less portable. When it comes to extensibility, however, you don't usually lose anything when you make your code more extensible.

When you develop a class, you can encounter many pitfalls that discourage, or even prevent, extensibility. Avoiding these pitfalls as you design or implement your code is often easy, if you're aware of them.

One of the most common pitfalls I've seen is in the implementation of constructors. No matter how well designed your methods are, if you don't provide the right constructors, other developers will have trouble extending your class. Because you can't override constructors, you have to work with whatever the base class provides.

If your constructor tries to do too much, it may require any subclass to do things that are not possible for it to do. This is especially true if the developer writing the subclass doesn't have access to the source code. For example, consider the following classes that provide a simple multiple-choice menu object.

```
01: import java.awt.*;
02: import java.awt.event.*;
03: import java.io.*;
04: import java.util.*;
```

```
05:
06: import javax.swing.*;
07: import javax.swing.event.*;
08:
09: public class ListDialog extends JDialog
10: implements ActionListener, ListSelectionListener
11: {
12:     JList model;
13:     JButton selectButton;
14:     LDListener listener;
15:     Object[] selections;
16:
17:     public ListDialog (String title,
18:                        String[] items,
19:                        LDListener listener)
20:     {
21:         super ((Frame)null, title);
22:
23:         JPanel buttonPane = new JPanel ();
24:         selectButton = new JButton ("SELECT");
25:         selectButton.addActionListener (this);
26:         selectButton.setEnabled (false); // nothing selected yet
27:         buttonPane.add (selectButton);
28:
29:         JButton cancelButton = new JButton ("CANCEL");
30:         cancelButton.addActionListener (this);
31:         buttonPane.add (cancelButton);
32:
33:         this.getContentPane().add (buttonPane, BorderLayout.SOUTH);
34:
35:         this.listener = listener;
36:         setModel (items);
37:     }
38:
39:     void setModel (String[] items)
40:     {
41:         if (this.model != null)
42:             this.model.removeListSelectionListener (this);
43:         this.model = new JList (items);
44:         model.addListSelectionListener (this);
45:
46:         JScrollPane scroll = new JScrollPane (model);
47:         this.getContentPane().add (scroll, BorderLayout.CENTER);
48:         this.pack();
49:     }
50:
51:     /** Implement ListSelectionListener. Track user selections. */
52:
53:     public void valueChanged (ListSelectionEvent e)
54:     {
55:         selections = model.getSelectedValues();
```

```
56:            if (selections.length > 0)
57:                selectButton.setEnabled (true);
58:        }
59:
60:        /** Implement ActionListener.  Called when the user picks the
61:         * SELECT or CANCEL button. Generates the LDEvent. */
62:
63:        public void actionPerformed (ActionEvent e)
64:        {
65:            this.setVisible (false);
66:            String buttonLabel = e.getActionCommand ();
67:            if (buttonLabel.equals ("CANCEL"))
68:                selections = null;
69:            if (listener != null)
70:            {
71:                LDEvent lde = new LDEvent (this, selections);
72:                listener.listDialogSelection (lde);
73:            }
74:        }
75:
76:        public static void main (String[] args) // self-testing code
77:        {
78:            String[] items = (new String[]
79:                {"Forest", "Island", "Mountain", "Plains", "Swamp"});
80:            LDListener listener =
81:                new LDListener()
82:                {
83:                    public void listDialogSelection (LDEvent e)
84:                    {
85:                        Object[] selected = e.getSelection ();
86:                        if (selected != null) // null if user cancels
87:                            for (int i = 0; i < selected.length; i++)
88:                                System.out.println (selected[i].toString());
89:                        System.exit (0);
90:                    }
91:                };
92:
93:            ListDialog dialog =
94:                new ListDialog ("ListDialog", items, listener);
95:            dialog.show ();
96:        }
97: }
```

For completeness, here are the *LDListener* and *LDEvent* classes:

```
01: public interface LDListener
02: {
03:     public void listDialogSelection (LDEvent e);
04: }
```

```
01: import java.util.EventObject;
02:
```

```
03: public class LDEvent extends java.util.EventObject
04: {
05:     Object source;
06:     Object[] selections;
07:
08:     public LDEvent (Object source, Object[] selections)
09:     {
10:         super (source);
11:         this.selections = selections;
12:     }
13:
14:     public Object[] getSelection()
15:     {
16:         return (selections);
17:     }
18: }
```

The *ListDialog* class appears to be fairly well written, but it will turn out to be rather difficult to extend. Let's try. Suppose you have a requirement to develop a menu that will present a list of audio files to the user. You want the user to be able to hear each sound as she clicks on the audio file in your interface. Because you don't want to force your clients to specify all of the audio files, you decide to provide a simple API that accepts a directory name and determines the list of audio files in that directory.

This would seem to be a simple extension of the *ListDialog* class. You know you'll need to listen for *ListSelectionEvents*, so you can play the selected sound. This is easy because you have access to the model, and you can simply call addListSelectionListener (...), as shown in line 7 in the code that follows. If the model had been *private* with no accessor method, you would have been unable to add your listener, and you would have had to start from scratch. So far, so good.

When you try to extend *ListDialog*, however, its only constructor (line 17 in the first listing) requires that you send an array of *String* items—which you don't yet have. And, because the call to super (...) must be the first thing your constructor does, there's no way for you to get the list of items and then create the *ListDialog*.

But don't give up yet; there's got to be a workaround. You look at the *javadoc* documentation and notice that there's a setModel (...) method that sounds promising. So, you first try to implement your constructor by instantiating the *ListDialog* with a *null* value for the *items* argument, and then you call setModel (...) after you've determined your list of files (lines 4–6).

```
01: public SoundDialog (String title, LDListener listener,
02:                     String path)
03: {
04:     super (title, null, listener);
```

```
05:     String[] items = getItems (path);
06:     setModel (items);
07:     model.addListSelectionListener (this);
08:     model.setSelectionMode (ListSelectionModel.SINGLE_SELECTION);
09: }
```

This seems reasonable, but when you try to run your class, you get the following error:

```
Exception occurred during event dispatching:
java.lang.NullPointerException
    . . .
  at java.awt.Window.pack(Window.java:259)
  at ListDialog.setModel(ListDialog.java:48)
  at ListDialog.<init>(ListDialog.java:36)
  at SoundDialog.<init>(SoundDialog.java:18)
  at SoundDialog.main(SoundDialog.java:89)
```

Examining this stack trace, you realize the *ListDialog* is calling its `setModel(...)` method from its constructor, and that is producing these undesirable results. After some debugging, you determine that the *NullPointerException* is caused by the empty model (trying to call `pack()` on a *JList* with no items).

Now what? Well, lucky for you, *ListDialog*'s `setModel(...)` method isn't *private*, so you can override it with your own, safer version. Notice that you had to move your *SoundDialog*'s calls, which change the model into your version of `setModel` (lines 27–28) because it's possible for one of your clients to use this *public* method, too. Here's the working version:

```
01: import java.applet.*;
02: import java.awt.*;
03: import java.io.*;
04: import java.net.*;
05:
06: import javax.swing.*;
07: import javax.swing.event.*;
08:
09: public class SoundDialog extends ListDialog
10: implements FilenameFilter, ListSelectionListener
11: {
12:     String selection;
13:
14:     public SoundDialog (String title, LDListener ldl, String path)
15:     {
16:         super (title, null, ldl);
17:         String[] items = getItems (path);
18:         setModel (items);
19:     }
```

```
20:
21:    public void setModel (String[] items)
22:    {
23:       if (items != null)
24:       {
25:          super.setModel (items);
26:          model.addListSelectionListener (this);
27:          model.setSelectionMode
28:            (ListSelectionModel.SINGLE_SELECTION);
29:       }
30:    }
31:
32:    public String[] getItems (String path)
33:    {
34:       File file = new File (path);
35:       File soundFiles[] = file.listFiles (this);
36:       String[] items = new String [soundFiles.length];
37:       for (int i = 0; i < soundFiles.length; i++)
38:          items[i] = soundFiles[i].getName();
39:       return (items);
40:    }
41:
42:    // implement FilenameFilter
43:    public boolean accept (File dir, String name)
44:    {
45:       return (name.endsWith (".aiff") ||
46:               name.endsWith (".au")   ||
47:               name.endsWith (".midi") ||
48:               name.endsWith (".rmf")  ||
49:               name.endsWith (".wav"));
50:    }
51:
52:    // implement ListSelectionListener
53:    public void valueChanged (ListSelectionEvent e)
54:    {
55:       super.valueChanged (e);
56:       JList items = (JList) e.getSource();
57:       String fileName = items.getSelectedValue().toString();
58:       if (!fileName.equals (selection))
59:       {
60:          selection = fileName;
61:          play (selection);
62:       }
63:    }
64:
65:    private void play (String fileName)
66:    {
67:       try
68:       {
69:          File file = new File (fileName);
70:          URL url = new URL ("file://" + file.getAbsolutePath());
```

```
71:            AudioClip audioClip = Applet.newAudioClip (url);
72:            if (audioClip != null)
73:                audioClip.play();
74:        }
75:        catch (MalformedURLException e)
76:        {
77:            System.err.println (e + ": " + e.getMessage());
78:        }
79:    }
80:
81:    public static void main (String[] args) // self-test
82:    {
83:        LDListener listener =
84:            new LDListener()
85:            {
86:                public void listDialogSelection (LDEvent e)
87:                {
88:                    Object[] selected = e.getSelection();
89:                    if (selected != null) // null if user cancels
90:                        for (int i = 0; i < selected.length; i++)
91:                            System.out.println (selected[i].toString());
92:                    System.exit (0);
93:                }
94:            };
95:        SoundDialog dialog =
96:            new SoundDialog ("SoundDialog", listener, ".");
97:        dialog.show();
98:    }
99: }
```

All of these workarounds would have been unnecessary if the original version of *ListDialog* had only provided the appropriate constructors. If you find yourself implementing a constructor that calls a `private` method or requires numerous arguments, make sure you consider the implications. Constructors with lots of arguments can be appropriate, especially if you're providing them as a convenience in addition to other, less burdensome constructors. But if it's your only constructor, consider adding additional versions that accept variations.

If you provide a no-argument constructor and the right additional methods to instantiate your class, you'll be fine. This does require some extra work, in that you have to be careful in your other methods not to use variables that haven't been initialized yet.

If your bare-bones constructor doesn't have enough information to fully instantiate your class, consider restricting access to it. You can do this by leaving off the "public" keyword. This will still allow any subclasses to call it, but you won't have to worry as much about other developers using it to create invalid objects.

Notice that (like most Swing components) the *JList* class we've been using in this example does provide a no-argument constructor, even though an empty *JList* is not really valid. If you use this constructor, you need to call `setList-Data(...)` or `setModel(...)` before using the *JList*. Obviously, the Swing components were designed to be easy to extend.

Item 9: Passing Primitives by Reference

If you are a C or C++ programmer you may have been a little disappointed to learn that Java exposes no concept of a pointer to a programmer. The lack of pointers in Java prevents at least two things you may be accustomed to doing with pointers: performing pointer arithmetic and returning multiple values from a function. As it turns out, only the first one is not allowed in Java. The second, returning multiple values from a Java method, is possible by passing arguments by reference instead of by value. All instantiated objects in Java are accessed by using a reference. Variable types that refer to classes, interfaces, arrays, and objects are all classified as *reference* types. Java also provides another type called a *primitive*. Primitives are used to store a specific type of information, such as a number or character. Java provides the following primitive types: *boolean, byte, short, int, long, char, float,* and *double.* An important concept to get across is that primitive types are not objects and therefore cannot be passed by reference.

Did you just read what you thought you did? Then what is the point of this section if primitives cannot be passed by reference? And why would you want to pass a primitive by reference anyway?

Even though primitives cannot be passed by references directly, they can be passed indirectly. What this implies is that you must use a reference type to wrap a primitive if you want to pass a primitive by reference. I can think of at least two cases where passing a primitive by reference is desired:

- Returning multiple primitive values from a function
- Passing primitive values to methods that accept objects only as arguments (for example, `Hashtable`)

Let's look at an example of doing these two cases the wrong way. Take a look at the *PassPrimitiveByReference1* source listed in the code that follows. This class tries to accomplish both of the desired objectives previously listed, but you can see that there are two major problems. The first problem you see is that the program will not compile because we are trying to pass primitive types to the `Hashtable.put()` method. This particular method accepts only objects as arguments. The second problem you see is code in the `getPersonInfo()` method. The intent of the method is to be able to return multiple values to the method caller by assigning values to the method arguments. The problem here is that primitive types are passed only by value, which means when they are passed to a method call, a copy of the primitive type is made for the exclusive use of the method. When the getPersonInfo() method assigns new values to the method arguments, it changes only the copies of the variables available to the method; it does not change the original variables.

```
01: import java.util.Hashtable;
02:
03: public class PassPrimitiveByReference1
04: {
05:     public static void main (String args[])
06:     {
07:         String   name = null;
08:         int      age = 0;
09:         float    weight = 0f;
10:         boolean isMarried = false;
11:
12:         getPersonInfo(name, age, weight, isMarried);
13:
14:         System.out.println("Name: " + name +
15:                            "\nAge: " + age +
16:                            "\nWeight: " + weight +
17:                            "\nIs Married: " + isMarried);
18:
19:         storePersonInfo(name, age, weight, isMarried);
20:     }
21:
22:     private static void getPersonInfo (String name, int age,
23:                             float weight, boolean isMarried)
24:     {
25:         name = "Robert Smith";
26:         age = 26;
27:         weight = 182.7f;
28:         isMarried = true;
29:     }
30:
31:     private static void storePersonInfo (String name, int age,
32:                             float weight, boolean isMarried)
33:     {
34:         Hashtable h = new Hashtable();
35:         h.put("name", name);
36:         h.put("age", age);              // produces compile time error
37:         h.put("weight", weight);        // produces compile time error
38:         h.put("isMarried", isMarried);  // produces compile time error
39:     }
40: }
```

Now let's look at the solution to the problems. The *PassPrimitiveByReference2* class listed in the code that follows solves both problems presented in the *PassPrimitiveByReference1* example. The problem with the *Hashtable* has been corrected by using the Java class equivalents of the primitive types. In the java.lang package, you will find corresponding classes to all the primitive types. In this example, we used *Integer* for *int*, *Float* for *float*, and *Boolean* for *boolean*. The Java class equivalent of a given primitive type serves to encapsulate the primitive type and provides various utility methods. This could have been the solution to our second problem as well, but the Java primitive class equivalents are immutable (they contain no set (...) method). Instead, we solve the second problem by creating a one-dimensional array of a given type and passing the array to the method. Remember that earlier I mentioned that arrays are reference types. In this particular case, it comes in handy because now I can set the values of primitive types in the getPersonInfo() method, and they are available to the calling method.

```
01: import java.util.Hashtable;
02:
03: public class PassPrimitiveByReference2
04: {
05:     public static void main (String args[])
06:     {
07:         String[]  name = new String[1];
08:         int[]     age = new int[1];
09:         float[]   weight = new float[1];
10:         boolean[] isMarried = new boolean[1];
11:
12:         getPersonInfo(name, age, weight, isMarried);
13:
14:         System.out.println("Name: " + name[0] +
15:                             "\nAge: " + age[0] +
16:                             "\nWeight: " + weight[0] +
17:                             "\nIs Married: " + isMarried[0]);
18:
19:         String  name2 = name[0];
20:         Integer age2 = new Integer(age[0]);
21:         Float   weight2 = new Float(weight[0]);
22:         Boolean isMarried2 = new Boolean(isMarried[0]);
23:
24:         storePersonInfo(name2, age2, weight2, isMarried2);
25:     }
26:
27:     private static void getPersonInfo (String[] name, int[] age,
28:                             float[] weight, boolean[] isMarried)
29:     {
30:         name[0] = "Robert Smith";
31:         age[0] = 26;
32:         weight[0] = 182.7f;
33:         isMarried[0] = true;
34:     }
```

```
35:
36:      private static void storePersonInfo (String name, Integer age,
37:                               Float weight, Boolean isMarried)
38:      {
39:          Hashtable h = new Hashtable();
40:          h.put("name", name);
41:          h.put("age", age);
42:          h.put("weight", weight);
43:          h.put("isMarried", isMarried);
44:      }
45: }
```

Running *PassPrimitiveByReference2* will produce the following output:

```
Name: Robert Smith
Age: 26
Weight: 182.7
Is Married: true
```

This demonstration of passing primitives by an array reference by no means advocates its use. I could have easily created a class that contained the primitives I wanted as instance variables and passed the object to the getPerson-Info() method to have the values set. Encapsulating things in an object is usually the better way to do it, but you may run into situations where passing primitives by an array reference is the only option.

Item 10: Boolean Logic and Short-Circuit Operators

Like C++ (and C), Java supports *bitwise operators* (& and |) for bit-masking operations. Unlike C++, Java supports both *boolean logical operators* (& and |) and *conditional and/or operators* (&& and ||). This can lead to some problems if you're not careful.

If you were to program a line like this in C++, many compilers would warn you.

```
if (ptr != null & ptr->count > 1)   // wrong operator!
```

For example, the Gnu C compiler produces the warning:

```
warning: suggest parentheses around comparison in operand of &
```

Although this is legal code, it's probably not what you want. If the *ptr* variable is null, you'll attempt to dereference a null pointer in the right-hand comparison (and the program will crash). The compiler can make the assumption that you probably did not want to do a bitwise AND there.

In Java, however, the compiler can't make that assumption. If both sides of the expression are *boolean* values, then the "&" operator will be treated as a *boolean* logical operator, not a bitwise AND (see JLS 15.21.2). Let's say you want to check if a *Vector* object has any elements before you use it. You might unintentionally code it this way:

```
if ((v != null) & (v.size() > 0))   // wrong operator!
```

The compiler won't produce a warning because that may very well be what you intended. The code will still throw a *NullPointerException* if *v* is null.

What you want, of course, is the *short-circuit* operator. The *boolean* logical and conditional operators provide similar functionality, with one significant difference. The conditional operators (&& and ||) will short-circuit. That is, if the result of the first (left) expression is enough to determine the result of the conditional operation, then the second (right) expression will not be evaluated. Here's the correct line:

```
if ((v != null) && (v.size() > 0))
```

The same behavior holds true for the OR operators, though these are much less problematic than the common *null*-check described previously. The "|" operator with *boolean* operands will be treated as a logical operator, returning true if either operand is true. Both operands will be evaluated, even if the first one is true. The "||" conditional operator will short-circuit instead. You're not likely to get in trouble using the "|" operator, unless your operands produce some side-effect you weren't counting on.

The simple solution is to always use the conditional operators && and ||. They're safer and more efficient because fewer operands need to be evaluated. If you need to ensure both operands are evaluated, make sure you comment your use of the logical & or | operator.

PART

Two

Language Support

A passenger in an airplane does not usually want to be aware of the levels of fuel in the tanks, or the wind speeds, or how many chicken dinners are to be served, or the status of the rest of the air traffic around the destination—this is all left to employees on different levels of the airlines hierarchy, and the passenger simply gets from one place to another. Here again, it is when something goes wrong—such as his baggage not arriving—that the passenger is made aware of the confusing system of levels underneath him.

—DOUGLAS R. HOFSTADTER,
GODEL, ESCHER, BACH: AN ETERNAL GOLDEN BRAID

Designed as an object-oriented language from the ground up, Java has a layer of classes that are part of the language definition. These are grouped in the java.lang package and are always implicitly imported. Existing at the base of Java's object pyramid, these support classes require a deep understanding. The items in this part are as follows:

Item 11, "Reclaiming References When Using SoftReference Objects," covers how to effectively use the *SoftReferences* to interact with the garbage collector.

Item 12, "Causing Deadlock by Calling a Synchronized Method from a Synchronized Method," is a detailed examination of how to avoid deadlock in multithreaded code.

Item 13, "**Properly Cloning an Object,**" is a tutorial on properly cloning an object that demonstrates the problems caused by not doing so.

Item 14, "**Overriding the equals Method,**" discusses a pitfall to avoid when creating classes that act as keys in a Hashtable.

Item 15, "**Avoid Using a Constructor for Implementing clone( ),**" discusses how to avoid a reusability trap by carefully constructing clones of your object.

Item 16, "**Method Dispatching with Reflection, Interfaces, and Anonymous Classes,**" is an extensive discussion and demonstration of method dispatching options in Java to assist you in choosing the best approach for this technique.

Item 17, "**Handling Exceptions and OutOfMemoryError,**" is an overview of an often avoided subject: good exception handling. It includes the API pitfall concerning the fairly common OutOfMemoryError.

Item 11: Reclaiming References When Using SoftReference Objects

Up until the release of Java 2 there was no way to interact with the garbage collector of the JVM except for one tool in the programmer's arsenal: System.gc(). The lack of interaction with the garbage collector was both a strong point of Java and a weak point at the same time. On one hand, it enforced the concept of Java as a "safe" programming language, where all memory cleanup would be handled automatically, therefore reducing memory leaks from errant code that did not free memory it had allocated. On the other hand, it did not provide enough flexibility to allow those who wanted to manage their own memory to do so in a programmer-friendly way. In the release of Java 2 a new package was included, *java.lang.ref*, which provided several classes that allow some interaction with the garbage collector. If you think of System.gc() as a hammer (or more like a rubber mallet), you can think of the java.lang.ref package as adding an adjustable wrench to your collection of tools. The capability it provides will meet the needs of many problems that were difficult to solve without it. This item focuses on the use of one of the classes available in the java.lang.ref package: the *SoftReference* class. Before we are done, you will learn the purpose of the *SoftReference* class and know how to use it.

A Word about Garbage Collection

The JVM contains a memory area called the *heap*, where the memory needed for arrays and instantiated classes (objects) resides. Whenever you instantiate an object using the "new" keyword, it allocates the necessary memory on the *heap* to hold the data for the object. There is no converse keyword to explicitly deallocate memory that has been allocated. The deallocation (reclaiming) of memory is the role of the garbage collector.[1] The garbage collector runs periodically as a separate thread to check if any objects are eligible for reclamation. If there are, it will perform the necessary steps required to free the objects (such as run *finalization*). The final stages of reclaiming an object results in the object being destroyed and its memory being released back to the *heap*.

Even though there is no explicit way of deallocating memory, one technique is widely used to free memory: set the reference of an object to null and then call System.gc(). Once all of the references to an object are set to null, or all chains of references to the object end in null, the object can be reclaimed by the garbage collector. Calling the System.gc() method will ask the JVM machine to invoke the garbage collection process. It is then up to the JVM[2] to follow through with the garbage collection process. Figure 11.1 illustrates some objects allocated on the heap. On the left side we have a tree of references anchored by

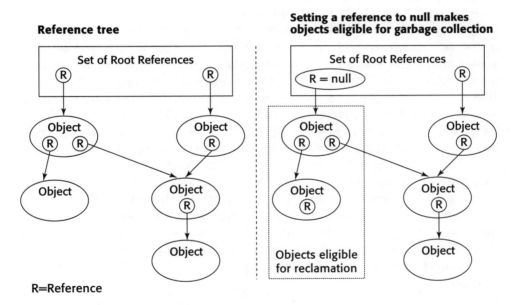

Figure 11.1   Candidates for garbage collection.

---

[1]The garbage collector is used in Javasoft's implementation of its JVMs, but the automatic reclamation of memory is dependent on the implementation of the JVM.

[2]Calling System.gc() does not guarantee that the garbage collector will run immediately or even guarantee that it will run at all. The JVM accepts this call as a suggestion and then determines if and when the garbage collector will run.

a root set of references. None of these objects is eligible for reclamation. On the right side is the same tree of references, except one of the object references has been set to null. Now the two left-most objects of the tree are eligible for reclamation because no valid references to these objects exist anymore.

The java.lang.ref package included with Java 2 introduced a few more constructs to deal with references in relation to garbage collection. The abstract *Reference* class was introduced, along with its three concrete subclasses: *SoftReference, WeakReference*, and *PhantomReference*. This item focuses on using the *SoftReference*, which is the strongest of the three new references; however, most of the same concepts apply to the other new reference classes as well. The reference classes store the reference value to an object. The object whose reference is stored by the reference class is known as the *referrent*. These classes are treated in a special way by the garbage collector. When the garbage collector runs, it evaluates reference trees like the one seen in Figure 11.2 to determine how "reachable" an object is. Before Java 2 there were only two states for an object: *reachable* and *unreachable*. With the release of Java 2, now there are five states: *strongly reachable, softly reachable, weakly reachable, phantom reachable*, and *unreachable*. When an object is deemed to be in any state except *strongly reachable* it is eligible for garbage collection.

How do we determine the reachability of an object? The garbage collector traces back all reference chains from an object. It then looks at the weakest link in each chain. The reachability of an object is determined by the weakest link of the strongest chain. Figure 11.2 shows an example of how using a *SoftReference* affects the reachability of an object. On the left side is a reference tree in which the left-most objects are attached via a *SoftReference*. This makes them eligible for garbage collection. Before the objects are garbage collected the *SoftReference* lets us access them and rescue them if we want (more on this later). On the right side is the same reference tree, but the right-most chain has been disconnected by setting its reference to null. Now you can see that the right-most objects are softly reachable as well. You can determine the reachability of object X by looking at both of its chains and seeing which is the strongest. The one with the *SoftReference* is the strongest because the other chain leads to an unreachable state. Taking the weakest link in this chain yields the reachability of the object. Because the *SoftReference* is the weakest link, Object X is softly reachable.

The SoftReference Class

The *SoftReference* class enables a programmer to mark an object as something that can be garbage collected, but it will allow for retrieval of the object until it actually gets reclaimed by the garbage collector. In a physical-world analogy, it is similar to putting a document in a recycling bin instead of shredding it. Any

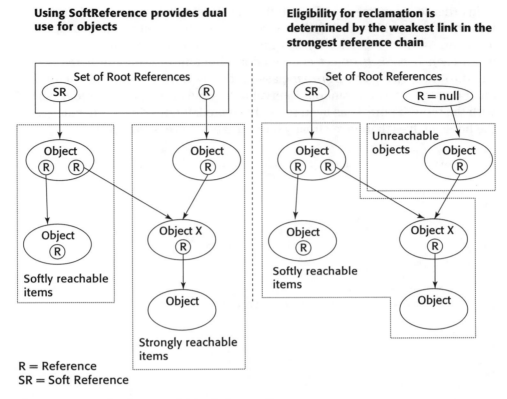

Using SoftReference provides dual use for objects

Eligibility for reclamation is determined by the weakest link in the strongest reference chain

R = Reference
SR = Soft Reference

Figure 11.2 SoftReferences in the Reference Tree.

object that is softly reachable is guaranteed to be reclaimed by the garbage collector before the JVM will throw an *OutOfMemory* error. An object is softly reachable if all reference chains to it have a *SoftReference* as its weakest link (see the previous section). One of the primary uses for the *SoftReference* class is to implement a memory-sensitive cache. Such a cache could be used for caching images from Web pages, caching large data objects from a server, caching multimedia, and so forth.

To demonstrate the *SoftReference* functionality let's use an example that does not use the *SoftReference* object and will produce an *OutOfMemory* error (assuming you keep the default JVM maximum heap size[3]). Then we will modify the example to use the *SoftReference* class to automatically reclaim memory when we need it. Let's look at the first example.

---

[3]This example was run against a JVM with a max heap size of 64 million bytes. If you are using the Javasoft JVM you can set your max heap size to this value with the following command: `java -Xmx64m <class name>`.

In order to eat up memory I created some classes that would simulate storing information for a library. The *BookShelf* class is composed of 100 *Book*s, which are composed of 100 *TextPage*s, which are composed of 300 characters. So when each *BookShelf* object is created a minimum of 6 million bytes is allocated to the object. The *Library* class randomly assigns topics to each *Book-Shelf* created. At some random interval a check will be made to see if a shelf with the topic "Sports" has been recently created. It does this by checking all of the book shelves that have already been created. Here is the code:

```
01: import java.util.Random;
02:
03: class TextPage
04: {
05:     char[] symbols = new char[300];
06: }
07:
08: class Book
09: {
10:     String      name;
11:     TextPage    pages[] = new TextPage[100];
12:
13:     public Book ()
14:     {
15:         for (int i = 0; i < pages.length; i++)
16:             pages[i] = new TextPage();
17:     }
18: }
19:
20: class BookShelf
21: {
22:     String subject;
23:     Book[] books = new Book[100];
24:
25:     public BookShelf (String subject)
26:     {
27:         this.subject = subject;
28:         for (int i = 0; i < books.length; i++)
29:             books[i] = new Book();
30:
31:         if (subject.equals("Sports"))
32:             books[0].name = "History of Ping Pong";
33:     }
34: }
35:
36: public class Library
37: {
38:     public static void main (String args[])
39:     {
40:         String subjects[] = { "Sports", "New Age", "Religion",
```

```
41:                                "Sci-Fi", "Romance", "Do-it-yourself",
42:                                "Cooking", "Gardening", "Travel",
43:                                "Mystery", "Fantasy", "Computers",
44:                                "Business", "Young readers", "JW Books" };
45:
46:          BookShelf[] shelves = new BookShelf[25];
47:          int checkIndex = 10 + getRandomIndex(15);
48:
49:          for (int i = 0; i < shelves.length; i++)
50:          {
51:              String subject =
52:                    subjects[getRandomIndex(subjects.length)];
53:              System.out.println("Creating bookshelf: " + (i + 1) +
54:                                  ", subject: " + subject);
55:              shelves[i] = new BookShelf(subject);
56:
57:              // at a random interval check to see where the last
58:              //   "Sports" shelf was
59:              if (i == checkIndex)
61:                  System.out.println("Checking for Sports...");
62:                  for (int j = i; j >= 0; j—)
63:                  {
64:                      if (shelves[j].subject.equals("Sports"))
65:                      {
66:                          System.out.println();
67:                          System.out.println("Shelf " + (j + 1) +
68:                                          " is Sports");
69:                          System.out.println("First book is: " +
70:                                          shelves[j].books[0].name);
71:                          System.out.println();
72:                          break;
73:                      }
74:                      else
75:                          System.out.println("No match. " +
76:                                  "Subject was: " + shelves[j].subject);
77:                  }
78:              }
79:          }
80:      }
81:
82:      private static Random rnd =
83:                          new Random(System.currentTimeMillis());
84:      private static int getRandomIndex (int range)
85:      {
86:          return ((Math.abs(rnd.nextInt())) % range);
87:      }
88: }
```

If you were to run this example your output would look something like this:

```
Creating bookshelf: 1, subject: Sci-Fi
Creating bookshelf: 2, subject: Gardening
Creating bookshelf: 3, subject: Romance
```

```
Creating bookshelf: 4, subject: Travel
Creating bookshelf: 5, subject: Young readers
Creating bookshelf: 6, subject: Travel
Creating bookshelf: 7, subject: Romance
Creating bookshelf: 8, subject: Cooking
Creating bookshelf: 9, subject: New Age
Exception in thread "main" java.lang.OutOfMemoryError
        at Library.main(Compiled Code)
```

The output shows that as the tenth book shelf was being created the JVM ran out of memory. Before the advent of the *SoftReference* class you would have to think long and hard about how you would fix this problem. You could always implement a first-in first-out (FIFO) cache and check this when you wanted to check for "Sports." You would have to write the code for the cache as well as perform memory management by setting objects that are pushed out of the cache to *null* and running `System.gc()`. But now with the *SoftReference* class the solution is easy. If we add three lines of code and change the "Checking for Sports..." *for* loop in the previous example, we can convert the example to use *SoftReference* objects. Here are the modifications:

1. Place this line after line 1:

   ```
   import java.lang.ref.SoftReference;
   ```

   This adds the necessary reference (no pun intended!) that lets us use the *SoftReference* class.

2. Replace line 46 with this line:

   ```
   SoftReference[] shelves = new SoftReference[25];
   ```

   Instead of dealing with an array of *BookShelf*, we now use an array of *SoftReference* instead.

3. Replace line 55 with this line:

   ```
   shelves[i] = new SoftReference(new BookShelf(subject));
   ```

   This line is important. Here we create a *BookShelf* object but immediately encapsulate it with a *SoftReference* object. The newly created *BookShelf* from here on out will be softly reachable, so it is available for garbage collection at any time.

4. Replace lines 64–76 with these lines:

   ```
   BookShelf shelf = (BookShelf)shelves[j].get();
   if (shelf != null)
   {
       if (shelf.subject.equals("Sports"))
       {
           System.out.println();
   ```

```
                    System.out.println("Shelf " + (j + 1) +
                                    " is Sports");
                    System.out.println("First book is: " +
                                    shelf.books[0].name);
                    System.out.println();
                    break;
            }
            else
                System.out.println("No match. " +
                    "Subject was: " + shelf.subject);
        }
```

This set of lines shows the retrieval of the *BookShelf* object back into a usable form. The bolded line shows where we call `get()` to get the reference associated with the *SoftReference* object and set it equal to a *BookShelf* object. As long as the shelf variable is in scope and still holds the reference to the *BookShelf* object, the object can be used normally and will not be eligible for garbage collection. So if we wanted, we could define a higher scoped variable and rescue the *BookShelf* object from ever being reclaimed. What happens in this loop, though, is we cycle through all of the *SoftReference* objects that have already been allocated. Because the *BookShelf* objects are so memory intensive, as more objects are created, old objects get collected. For objects that have already been collected the `get()` method returns *null*. This is why the check for *null* is in the code block. The rest of the code block just substitutes the shelf variable where the *shelves[j]* variable used to be.

The output of the *Library* class with the *SoftReference* changes incorporated looks like this:

```
...previous output...
Creating bookshelf: 11, subject: Business
Creating bookshelf: 12, subject: Sports
Creating bookshelf: 13, subject: Mystery
Creating bookshelf: 14, subject: Business
Checking for Sports...
No match. Subject was: Business
No match. Subject was: Mystery

Shelf 12 is Sports
First book is: History of Ping Pong

Creating bookshelf: 15, subject: Young readers
Creating bookshelf: 16, subject: Do-it-yourself
Creating bookshelf: 17, subject: Sci-Fi
...more output...
```

For this particular run we got a hit on the "Sports" topic when we checked the cache. On other runs when there is no hit, the cache usually contains five to seven valid *BookShelf* objects.

Reference Queues

The previous example showed how to retrieve objects that were eligible for garbage collection, but when we accessed the actual object references we had to check for *null*. Because we were not sure whether the object had been collected, checking for *null* was the only way we could determine if we had a valid reference. The java.lang.ref package includes another class called a *Reference-Queue* that can be used for notification when an object is reclaimed by the garbage collector. One issue when using reference queues is that reference objects get enqueued only after their referents have been collected. When the get() method is called on the reference object it returns *null*. One way to use a reference queue to return meaningful information is to subclass the *SoftReference* class to allow storage for more application-specific information. We can modify our example to achieve this goal by doing the following:

1. Place this line after line 1:

   ```
   import java.lang.ref.ReferenceQueue;
   ```

   This adds the necessary reference for the *ReferenceQueue* class.

2. Replace line 46 with this line:

   ```
   BookShelfReference[] shelves = new BookShelfReference[25];
   ```

   Now we are using a subclass of *SoftReference* that contains application-specific information.

3. Replace line 55 with this line:

   ```
   shelves[i] = new BookShelfReference(new BookShelf(subject));
   ```

   Here we are encapsulating the new *BookShelf* object with our subclass of *SoftReference*.

4. After line 44 add these lines:

   ```
   GarbageMonitor monitor =
       new GarbageMonitor(BookShelfReference.collectedQueue);
   monitor.start();
   ```

   This will start our garbage collection monitoring thread.

5. You also need to add the *BookShelfReference* class and the *GarbageMonitor* class. These classes are defined as follows:

   ```
   01: class BookShelfReference extends SoftReference
   02: {
   03:     String subject;
   04:     static ReferenceQueue collectedQueue = new ReferenceQueue();
   ```

```
05:
06:      public BookShelfReference (BookShelf shelf)
07:      {
08:          super(shelf, collectedQueue);
09:          this.subject = shelf.subject;
10:      }
11: }
12:
13: class GarbageMonitor extends Thread
14: {
15:      ReferenceQueue queue;
16:
17:      public GarbageMonitor (ReferenceQueue queue)
18:      {
19:          this.queue = queue;
20:      }
21:
22:      public void run ()
23:      {
24:          while (true)
25:          {
26:              try
27:              {
28:                  BookShelfReference shelfRef =
29:                      (BookShelfReference) queue.remove(5000);
30:                  System.out.println("Monitor: Shelf subject '" +
31:                      shelfRef.subject + "' was collected.");
32:              }
33:              catch (Exception e)
34:              {   break;   }
35:          }
36:      }
37: }
```

The *BookShelfReference* class is a subclass of *SoftReference*. It stores the name of the shelf it encapsulates, but of more interest, it creates a static *ReferenceQueue* object. Whenever an instance of *BookShelfReference* is created it adds an entry to the static *ReferenceQueue* object. We will use the *ReferenceQueue* object to find out when the referents of the *BookShelfReference* objects get reclaimed.

The *GarbageMonitor* class is just a thread that polls a reference queue for *BookShelfReference* objects. When the thread calls remove(...) on the reference queue it returns a reference object if one is available in the queue. If one is not available it will wait five seconds and throw an exception. When the reference to the *BookShelfReference* object is returned we can check the name of the *BookShelf* that was collected.

The output of running the modified example will be similar to this:

```
Creating bookshelf: 1, subject: Business
Creating bookshelf: 2, subject: Do-it-yourself
Monitor: Shelf subject 'Business' was collected.
Creating bookshelf: 3, subject: Romance
Creating bookshelf: 4, subject: Religion
Monitor: Shelf subject 'Do-it-yourself' was collected.
Creating bookshelf: 5, subject: JW Books
Creating bookshelf: 6, subject: Business
Monitor: Shelf subject 'Romance' was collected.
...more output...
```

From looking at the output you can see the garbage collector is running at regular intervals, collecting the softly reachable objects. With our subclassed *SoftReference* object we are able to get information on what has been reclaimed by the garbage collector.

The addition of the java.lang.ref package to Java 2 has expanded the interaction a programmer can have with the garbage collector. The classes provided with the package are not the Swiss-army knife of garbage collection utilities, but they provide a level of access that will meet the needs of many programming problems. The *SoftReference* class alone is useful not only for memory-sensitive caches but for other memory-sensitive problems as well. The *ReferenceQueue* class is beneficial for getting information on objects that have been collected. At the very least, with this additional firepower you should avoid calling System.gc() every time you set a reference to *null*.

Item 12: Causing Deadlock by Calling a Synchronized Method from a Synchronized Method

Every multithreaded programmer's nightmare is to have an application "hang" for no apparent reason, especially if it does this two weeks prior to shipping (or worse yet, after the application is already in production). The most frustrating cases are the ones in which the error is not consistently reproducible, but the error occurs frequently enough so that end users would think the program is buggy and unreliable. This type of behavior can be easily produced by misusing threads within an application. I don't intend to discourage you from using threads (because they are an essential part of server programming), but instead to make you think about designing your application for thread safety up-front, not as an afterthought. The purpose of this pitfall is discuss how using the *synchronized* keyword in a multithreaded application can cause it to deadlock, therefore making the application hang.

Review of Threads, Monitors, and the "Synchronized" Keyword

Before we see an example of using the "synchronized" keyword, let me first review why it is included in the Java language. Java allows programs to be created that can run multiple *threads*. A *thread* is a unit of execution that works within the shared memory space of its *process*. A single *process* can have multiple *threads* running concurrently. For example, a server program could have one thread listening for client connections and multiple threads handling connected clients. When a connection is received a new thread is started to handle the requests for the newly connected client, while the listening thread can continue to listen for more client connections. Following this example, suppose our server is a simple e-commerce application. The main application memory stores the inventory, while the client handler threads perform the following logic:

- Check inventory for availability
- If available, deduct money from customer
- Deduct from inventory

In a multithreaded environment it is possible for one thread to be at the third step while another thread is at the second. This would create a problem if there were only one item left in inventory. If this were the case both threads would have determined that an item was available, but the first thread would actually have gotten the last item. The second thread would continue its processing and deduct money from the customer only to find out the last item had been taken. To solve this problem, these statements have to be treated as an atomic operation. This is where the "synchronized" keyword comes in. When a method is declared with the *synchronized* modifier, it restricts the execution of the method so only one thread at a time can execute it. Before we continue exploring the "synchronized" keyword, let's first look at the definition of another important Java concept: *monitors*.

A *monitor* is a construct used in Java to control access to an object. A monitor is always associated with only one object, but an object does not necessarily have an associated monitor. When a monitor is activated, it allows only one thread at a time to access its associated object. So how do you go about using monitors in your application? The answer is: use the "synchronized" keyword. Monitors are used only in conjunction with the "synchronized" keyword. When a thread makes a call on a "synchronized" method (assuming no other threads have made a call), the monitor will assign the thread a lock on the object that contains the "synchronized" method. If another thread calls the "synchronized" method while the first thread is still executing, the monitor will make the calling thread wait until the first thread is finished executing the method. When the first thread is finished, the lock on the object is released and the monitor then grants the lock to the thread that was waiting. The second thread then proceeds ahead with execution. The code that follows illustrates this concept. The code is composed of three classes: *PunchTimeCard*, *Employee*, and *Work*. Here is a description of each class:

PunchTimeCard. This class contains a single synchronized method, punch(). The method will print the number of seconds that have elapsed since the object was instantiated, and it will sleep for one second after doing so.

Employee. This class extends *Thread*. When the thread is started, all it does is call the punch() method on an instance of *PunchTimeCard* as fast as it can.

Work. This class sets up the *PunchTimeCard* object and the *Employee* objects, and then it starts the *Employee* threads.

```
01: import java.util.Date;
02:
03: class PunchTimeCard
04: {
05:     Date dt = new Date();
06:     public synchronized void punch (String name)
07:     {
08:         System.out.println(name + " punched in at: \t" +
09:           ((int)(System.currentTimeMillis() - dt.getTime()) / 1000));
10:
11:         try { Thread.currentThread().sleep (1000); }
12:         catch (InterruptedException ie) { }
13:     }
14: }
15:
16: class Employee extends Thread
17: {
18:     String          name;
19:     PunchTimeCard   ptc;
20:
21:     public Employee (String name, PunchTimeCard ptc)
22:     {
23:         this.name = name;
24:         this.ptc = ptc;
25:     }
26:
27:     public void run ()
28:     {
29:         while (true)
30:         {
31:             ptc.punch(name);
32:         }
```

```
33:      }
34: }
35:
36: public class Work
37: {
38:     public static void main (String args[])
39:     {
40:         PunchTimeCard ptc = new PunchTimeCard();
41:         Employee jerry = new Employee("Jerry", ptc);
42:         Employee sherrie = new Employee("Sherrie", ptc);
43:         jerry.start();
44:         sherrie.start();
45:     }
46: }
```

If you run this example your output will look like this:

```
Jerry punched in at:    0
Sherrie punched in at:  1
Jerry punched in at:    2
Sherrie punched in at:  3
Jerry punched in at:    4
Sherrie punched in at:  5
Jerry punched in at:    6
```

You can see that the "synchronized" keyword in punch() is causing the two threads to wait turns to access the method. If you were to remove the "synchronized" keyword in line 6 and rerun the program, the output would look like this:

```
Jerry punched in at:    0
Sherrie punched in at:  0
Jerry punched in at:    1
Sherrie punched in at:  1
Jerry punched in at:    2
Sherrie punched in at:  2
Jerry punched in at:    3
Sherrie punched in at:  3
```

Without the "synchronized" keyword in punch(), both threads can execute the method concurrently. Figure 12.1 reemphasizes what is going on when the *jerry* thread and *sherrie* thread are both trying to call punch(). In the diagram it shows what happens in both cases: when the "synchronized" keyword is used and when it is not. Let's take a look at the right side where the "synchronized" keyword is not being used. Both the *jerry* and *sherrie* threads have free access to the *ptc* object and can execute the punch() method concurrently. Now take a look at the left side where the "synchronized" keyword is being used.

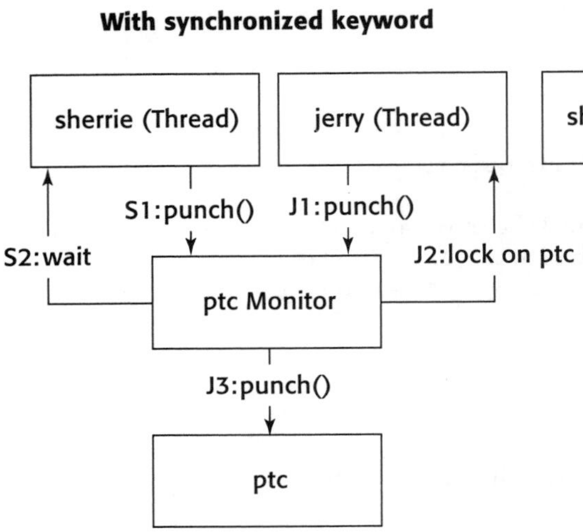

Figure 12.1   With and without synchronized.

Here is the description of the steps:

1. **J1:** In the diagram we have the thread, *jerry*, calling the punch() method first.

2. **J2:** Because *jerry* is the first thread to call the method, the monitor associated with the *ptc* object assigns the *ptc* lock to the thread *jerry*.

3. **J3:** Once the lock is granted, *jerry* can execute the punch() method on the *ptc* object.

4. **S1:** Soon after the *jerry* thread has called punch(), the *sherrie* thread calls punch().

5. **S2:** Because the *jerry* thread was still executing the method, it still maintained the lock on the *ptc* object. Therefore, the *ptc* monitor made the *sherrie* thread wait until the lock was free.

Of course, once the *jerry* thread is done executing the punch() method, the *ptc* monitor will take the lock from the *jerry* thread and give it to the *sherrie* thread; at that time the *sherrie* thread would begin to execute the punch() method.

You probably have two questions concerning the flow of events:

What happens if both threads call the punch() method at exactly the same time?

Is there any way to interrupt my thread that is stuck waiting on the "synchronized" method?

The answer to the first question is that the monitor will use an algorithm to determine which thread will be the next thread to get the lock on the object. In a general case, many threads could be waiting to call a "synchronized" method, and the algorithm would use information such as the thread priority and how long the thread has been waiting to determine which thread gets the lock next, therefore letting the thread execute the method. The answer to the second question is no, which leads us straight into our discussion of deadlocks.

Example of Deadlock Scenario

By now you should have a good enough understanding of threads, monitors, and the "synchronized" keyword to discuss how a deadlock scenario can occur. One of the ways a deadlock can occur is when two threads are waiting on each other to perform an action. This is the example I demonstrate in this item. There are many scenarios for creating deadlocks, but all of the ones I have seen fall into these categories: a thread interdependency in which two or more threads are waiting on one another (our example involves two threads), a thread that has an indefinite wait period (such as a blocking call) in which other threads depend on an object that this thread has locked, and a combination of the two. Let's move on to the example to provide some clarity and concrete-ness to the deadlock issue.

This example consists of three classes: *WiseMan, KnowledgeSeeker,* and *Sanctuary.* The premise here is that some wise men sit in a sanctuary and those seeking knowledge come and ask the wise men questions. Here is a description of what the classes do:

WiseMan. Each wise man knows how to answer a specific type of question (such as a "what" or "where" question), but for questions the wise men can't answer they will seek the answer themselves from another wise man who resides within the same sanctuary.

KnowledgeSeeker. All of the knowledge seekers are *Threads.* Each knowledge seeker deals with only one wise man, and the knowledge seeker's job is to ask the wise man the same question over and over again as fast as he can.

Sanctuary. This class creates the *WiseMan* objects and the *Knowledge-Seeker* objects, and it starts the *KnowledgeSeeker* threads. To make our deadlock scenario work, two of the knowledge seekers were assigned to the wrong wise man so that the wise men will be forced to confer with one another.

The source is fairly lengthy but the content is straightforward, so don't be discouraged by the size of the code. The bolded lines indicate the pieces of code that cause the deadlock. Here is the source for the example:

```
001: import java.util.*;
002:
003: class WiseMan
```

```
004: {
005:     String name;
006:     String questionType;
007:     Hashtable otherWiseMen = new Hashtable();
008:
009:     public WiseMan (String name, String questionType)
010:     {
011:         this.name = name;
012:         this.questionType = questionType;
013:     }
014:
015:     public synchronized String askQuestion(String s, String asker)
016:     {
017:         System.out.println("WiseMan " + name +
018:                         " takes question from " + asker);
019:         StringTokenizer st = new StringTokenizer(s);
020:         if (st.hasMoreTokens())
021:         {
022:             String thisQuestionType = st.nextToken();
023:             if (thisQuestionType.equalsIgnoreCase(questionType))
024:             {
025:                 return ("WiseMan " + name + " sayeth: " +
026:                 "The answer you are seeking lies within yourself.");
027:             }
028:             else
029:             {
030:                 WiseMan otherWiseMan =
031:                     (WiseMan) otherWiseMen.get(thisQuestionType);
032:                 if (otherWiseMan == null)
033:                     return ("Please come back another day");
034:                 else
035:                 {
036:                     System.out.println("WiseMan " + name +
037:                     " conferring with WiseMan " + otherWiseMan.name);
038:                     return ("WiseMan " + name + " sayeth: " +
039:                     otherWiseMan.askQuestion(s, "WiseMan " + name));
040:                 }
041:             }
042:         }
043:         else
044:             return ("Please repeat your question");
045:     }
046:
047:     public synchronized void addWiseMan (WiseMan wiseMan)
048:     {
049:         otherWiseMen.put(wiseMan.questionType, wiseMan);
050:     }
051: }
052:
053: class KnowledgeSeeker extends Thread
054: {
055:     String  name;
```

```
056:        WiseMan wiseMan;
057:        String  question;
058:
059:        public KnowledgeSeeker (String name, WiseMan wiseMan,
060:                                                String question)
061:        {
062:            this.name = name;
063:            this.wiseMan = wiseMan;
064:            this.question = question;
065:        }
066:
067:        public void run ()
068:        {
069:            while (true)
070:            {
071:                System.out.println("Knowledge Seeker " + name +
072:                                        " asks: " + question);
073:                String answer = wiseMan.askQuestion(question, name);
074:                System.out.println("Knowledge Seeker " + name +
075:                                        " answer: " + answer);
076:            }
077:        }
078: }
079:
080: public class Sanctuary
081: {
082:        public static void main (String args[])
083:        {
084:            WiseMan wiseManA = new WiseMan("A", "What");
085:            WiseMan wiseManB = new WiseMan("B", "Where");
086:
087:            wiseManA.addWiseMan(wiseManB);
088:            wiseManB.addWiseMan(wiseManA);
089:
090:            KnowledgeSeeker ks1 = new KnowledgeSeeker("pupil 1",
091:                        wiseManA, "What is the meaning of life?");
092:
093:            KnowledgeSeeker ks2 = new KnowledgeSeeker("pupil 2",
094:                wiseManB, "Where are the seven wonders of the world?");
095:
096:            KnowledgeSeeker ks3 = new KnowledgeSeeker("pupil 3",
097:                        wiseManA, "Where is the restroom?");
098:
099:            KnowledgeSeeker ks4 = new KnowledgeSeeker("pupil 4",
100:                        wiseManB, "What is the square root of pi?");
101:
102:            ks1.start();
103:            ks2.start();
104:            ks3.start();
105:            ks4.start();
106:        }
107: }
```

Running this example produces the following output:

```
...previous output...
01: Knowledge Seeker pupil 1 asks: What is the meaning of life?
02: WiseMan A takes question from pupil 1
03: Knowledge Seeker pupil 2 asks: Where are the seven wonders of the world?
04: Knowledge Seeker pupil 3 asks: Where is the restroom?
05: Knowledge Seeker pupil 4 asks: What is the square root of pi?
06: WiseMan B takes question from pupil 2
07: Knowledge Seeker pupil 2 answer: WiseMan B sayeth: The answer you are
    seeking lies within yourself.
08: Knowledge Seeker pupil 2 asks: Where are the seven wonders of the world?
09: WiseMan B takes question from pupil 4
10: WiseMan B conferring with WiseMan A
11: WiseMan A takes question from pupil 3
12: WiseMan A conferring with WiseMan B
13: Knowledge Seeker pupil 1 answer: WiseMan A sayeth: The answer you are
    seeking lies within yourself.
14: Knowledge Seeker pupil 1 asks: What is the meaning of life?
```

You can see in lines 10 and 12 of the output that the wise men are conferring with one another, which causes the deadlock to occur. If we analyze the output we can determine exactly what happened leading up to the deadlock. Let's take a look at Figure 12.2 and analyze the sequence of events (the figure mirrors the output starting from line 4).

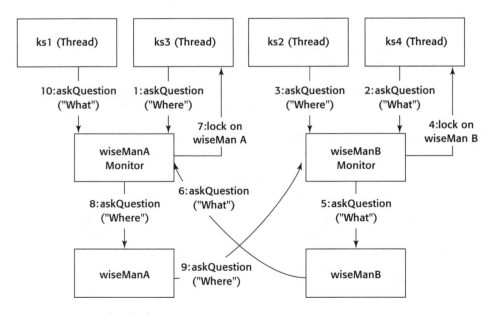

Figure 12.2 A deadlock scenario.

1. Thread *ks3* calls `askQuestion(...)` on *wiseManA* (line 4).

2. Thread *ks4* calls `askQuestion(...)` on *wiseManB* (line 5).

3. Thread *ks2* calls `askQuestion(...)` on *wiseManB* (line 8).

4. The monitor associated with *wiseManB* grants the *wiseManB* lock to thread *ks4*.

5. Thread *ks4* begins execution of method `askQuestion(...)` on *wiseManB* (line 9).

6. During execution of `askQuestion(...)` on *wiseManB*, thread *ks4* calls `askQuestion(...)` on *wiseManA* (line 10).

7. The monitor associated with *wiseManA* grants the *wiseManA* lock to thread *ks3*.

8. Thread *ks3* begins execution of method `askQuestion(...)` on *wiseManA* (line 11).

9. During execution of `askQuestion(...)` on *wiseManA*, thread *ks3* calls `askQuestion(...)` on *wiseManB* (line 12). This creates a deadlock between threads *ks3* and *ks4*. Thread *ks4* is waiting for thread *ks3* to release the lock it has on *wiseManA* so it can complete its method call. At the same time, thread *ks3* is waiting for thread *ks4* to release the lock it has on *wiseManB* so it can complete its method call. Neither thread can proceed, therefore causing a deadlock. Because thread *ks2* is waiting for the lock on *wiseManB*, it will wait forever because thread *ks4* has the lock and is deadlocked. This causes *ks2* to be sucked into the deadlock as well.

10. Thread *ks1* calls `askQuestion(...)` on *wiseManA* (line 14). Because thread *ks3* has the lock on *wiseManA* and *ks3* is deadlocked, this causes *ks1* to be sucked into the deadlock as well.

Now that you have seen a deadlock in action you are probably wondering what you can do to prevent or avoid them. The best answer is to make sure you design your application to avoid deadlocks. The example presented in this item was designed poorly on purpose just to show you how deadlocks can occur. One way to avoid the deadlock scenario is to have the wise man not confer with other wise men. Instead, the wise man could tell the knowledge seeker which wise man the seeker has to see to get the answer, without trying to find it out for the knowledge seeker. Another way would be to synchronize only when the variable *otherWiseMen* is used, instead of synchronizing the whole method.

The main key to avoiding deadlock scenarios is proper design. If you find yourself dealing with a deadlock scenario despite your design, the Java Language Specification recommends using higher-level primitives to avoid deadlock scenarios. Taking this approach is beyond the scope of this discussion, but for more information you can read some articles written by Allen Holub on threading. They are available on the JavaWorld Web site at www.javaworld .com.

Item 13: Properly Cloning an Object

Have you ever developed a multitier or Web application before in which everything works fine with one user logged on but behaves strangely with multiple users? Sometimes it appears to work correctly; other times incorrect data may be returned, data may not be saved, or the user may receive an unexpected error. A common cause for this type of behavior is the sharing of objects between different users. In particular, any object that stores state for a user's session is bound to have this problem unless you make separate copies for each user who has logged in. This is where Java *cloning* comes into play.

Cloning is the process of creating a copy of an object. Java provides a mechanism for objects to create copies of themselves by using the *java.lang.Cloneable* interface and the `Object.clone()` method. To use the mechanism inherent in Java, both of these constructs must be used as shown in the following code segment:

```
01: class CloneExample implements Cloneable
02: {
03:     int x;
04:     int y;
05:
06:     public Object clone() throws CloneNotSupportedException
07:     {
08:         return (super.clone());
09:     }
10:}
```

First, let's discuss the `Object.clone()` method. This method has two interesting characteristics. The first interesting characteristic is that the `clone()` method is *protected*, so only subclasses of *Object* can access the method. The reasoning for the *protected* declaration is so that subclasses have the choice of making the `clone()` operation more restrictive (if it were *public*, a subclass could not prevent a `clone()` operation from being performed on it). The second interesting characteristic is the that the `clone()` method is declared as *native*. Because it is *native*, its implementation lies within the JVM itself. This is where the *java.lang.Cloneable* interface comes in.

The JVM requires classes to implement the *java.lang.Cloneable* interface to explicitly declare an object as having the capability to be cloned. Once an object implements the *Cloneable* interface, calls to the `Object.clone()`

method return a shallow copy of the current object. If your object tries to call the Object.clone() method without implementing the *Cloneable* interface a *CloneNotSupportedException* will be thrown.

I just mentioned that the Object.clone() method will create only a shallow copy of the current object. What is a shallow copy anyway? And how does it differ from other types of copies?

A *shallow* copy of an object is a copy in which only the *primitive* and *reference* values are copied to the new object. This means that object members like *ints*, *floats*, and *booleans* have the same values in both the new and existing objects, but object members like *arrays*, *Hashtables*, *Vectors*, and so on are shared between the new and existing objects.

A *deep* copy of an object differs from a shallow copy because all nonprimitive object members are cloned as well. In a deep copy, if an existing object has a *Vector* object as a member, a clone operation on the existing object results in a new object being created that points to a new *Vector* object as well. In addition to shallow and deep copies, a mixture of the two can be used. One such mixture, which I will call a *mutable deep* copy, would copy only those objects that can be changed (mutable), but it would not copy objects that cannot be changed (immutable).

Let's look at an example of someone who implemented a *shallow* copy when he should have implemented a *mutable deep* copy. In the example, Farmer Bob has created the perfect sheep, and he intends to make a lot of money by cloning it and selling the clones to the neighboring farmers. His cloning logic, however, is broken so he's in for a big surprise when he makes his first sale! Let's take a look at the code:

```
01: import java.util.Hashtable;
02:
03: public class Clone1
04: {
05:     public static void main (String args[])
06:     {
07:         // Farmer Bob's perfect sheep
08:         Sheep sheep1 = new Sheep("Wooly", "Farmer Bob",
09:                         "White w/Black Patches", 123.7f);
10:
11:         // sell a copy to Farmer Rick
12:         Sheep sheep2 = (Sheep) sheep1.clone();
13:         sheep2.setOwnerName("Farmer Rick");
14:
15:         sheep2.name = "Patch";     // Farmer Rick renames sheep
16:         sheep2.setWeight(149.2f);   // feeds it day and night
17:         sheep2.setColor("Purple");  // and dyes its coat
18:
19:         // the results
```

```
20:              System.out.println("Sheep1:\n" + sheep1.toString());
21:              System.out.println("\nSheep2:\n" + sheep2.toString());
22:      }
23: }
24:
25: class Sheep implements Cloneable
26: {
27:      public  String       name;
28:      private Person        owner = new Person();
29:      private Hashtable     attributes = new Hashtable();
30:
31:      public Sheep (String name, String ownerName,
32:                        String color, float weight)
33:      {
34:          this.name = name;
35:          this.setOwnerName(ownerName);
36:          this.setColor(color);
37:          this.setWeight(weight);
38:      }
39:
40:      public String getOwnerName ()
41:      {   return (owner.name); }
42:
43:      public void setOwnerName (String ownerName)
44:      {   owner.name = ownerName;   }
45:
46:      public String getColor ()
47:      {   return ((String)attributes.get("Color"));   }
48:
49:      public void setColor (String color)
50:      {   attributes.put("Color", color);   }
51:
52:      public float getWeight ()
53:      {
54:          return (((Float) attributes.get("Weight")).floatValue());
55:      }
56:
57:      public void setWeight (float weight)
58:      {   attributes.put("Weight", new Float(weight));   }
59:
60:      public Object clone ()
61:      {
62:          try
63:          {
64:              return (super.clone());
65:          }
66:          catch (CloneNotSupportedException e)
67:          {
68:              throw new InternalError();
69:          }
```

```
70:      }
71:
72:      public String toString ()
73:      {
74:          return ("Name: " + this.name +
75:                  "\nOwner: " + this.getOwnerName() +
76:                  "\nColor: " + this.getColor() +
77:                  "\nWeight: " + this.getWeight());
78:      }
79: }
80:
81: class Person
82: {
83:      public String name;
84: }
```

The code contains three classes: *Clone1*, *Sheep*, and *Person*. *Sheep* is the primary class and contains three data members: a *String* object, a *Person* object, and a *Hashtable* object. *Clone1* contains the main() method where Farmer Bob sells a copy of his sheep to Farmer Rick, who takes several liberties with his new sheep. Running *Clone1* produces this output:

```
Sheep1:
Name: Wooly
Owner: Farmer Rick
Color: Purple
Weight: 149.2

Sheep2:
Name: Patch
Owner: Farmer Rick
Color: Purple
Weight: 149.2
```

Uh oh! Looks like Farmer Rick has now taken control of the cloning operation. Let's take a look at what happened. In the clone() method of the *Sheep* class we created a copy of the current object by calling super.clone() in line 64. Because *Sheep* extends *Object* the call to super.clone() invokes the clone() method defined in *Object*. This operation returns a new instance of the calling object's class and ensures that the values of the calling object's members are assigned to the new object's members. Seems logical enough, doesn't it? We actually cloned the *Sheep* object properly, but we made a *shallow* copy instead of a *deep* copy. We took the object references of the data members from the existing object and assigned them to the data members of the new object. We copied references instead of objects. Figure 13.1 depicts the object graphs for the *sheep1* and *sheep2* objects.

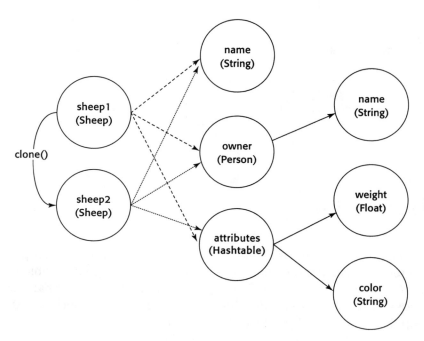

Figure 13.1   Object graph of sheep and cloned sheep.

How do we correct this problem? The way it stands now, if I change the *owner.name* or *attributes* of a sheep or any of its clones, I change them for all of the sheep. All copies of sheep share the *owner* object and the *attributes* object. In order to correct the problem, when I do a clone(), I must clone these objects as well. Here is the corrected code:

In *Sheep* this method replaces the existing clone() method:

```
01:     public Object clone ()
02:     {
03:         try
04:         {
05:             Sheep newSheep = (Sheep) super.clone();
06:             newSheep.owner = (Person) this.owner.clone();
07:             newSheep.attributes = (Hashtable) this.attributes.clone();
08:             return (newSheep);
09:         }
10:         catch (CloneNotSupportedException e)
11:         {
12:             throw new InternalError();
13:         }
14:     }
```

The *Person* class must be updated to the following:

```
01: class Person implements Cloneable
02: {
03:     public String name;
04:
05:     public Object clone()
06:     {
07:         try
08:         {
09:             return (super.clone());
10:         }
11:         catch (CloneNotSupportedException cnse)
12:         {
13:             throw new InternalError();
14:         }
15:     }
16: }
```

By cloning the *owner* and *attributes* data members we were able to solve the problem. Figure 13.2 depicts the object graphs for the *sheep1* object and properly cloned *sheep2* object. Running the new code will produce this:

```
Sheep1:
Name: Wooly
Owner: Farmer Bob
Color: White w/Black Patches
Weight: 123.7

Sheep2:
Name: Patch
Owner: Farmer Rick
Color: Purple
Weight: 149.2
```

By cloning the mutable object data members we created a *mutable deep* copy of the object. You may be wondering why we didn't clone the *name* object in either the *Sheep* or *Person* class. Because *name* is a *String* and *String* objects are immutable (they can't be changed), changing the name does not affect any other objects. When we changed the *owner.name* to "Farmer Rick," a new *String* object was created and the reference to this new object was assigned to the *name* attribute. Figure 13.2 depicts this behavior. In addition, the Hashtable.clone() method returns a shallow copy of its keys. This did not affect us in this example because one of the elements in the *Hashtable* was a *String* (and therefore immutable); the other element, a *Float* object, is also immutable. Every time one of these attributes was changed a new object was created whose reference was stored in the *Hashtable*.

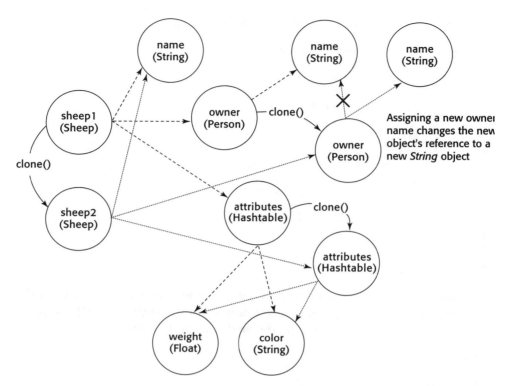

Figure 13.2   Object graph of sheep and correctly cloned sheep.

It is important to realize that you do not need to create copies of immutable objects when cloning. Because the object values themselves cannot change you would only be wasting memory. It is important, though, to make copies of mutable objects to prevent different copies of an object from sharing references to the same mutable object. The bottom line is that you have to be careful when cloning objects, so make sure that each object in your object graph is properly cloned in order to create a deep copy. Otherwise, you may be debugging "weird" behavior for weeks!

Item 14: Overriding the equals Method

On occasion, you will find it necessary to override the `equals` method so that you can compare two of your objects. As a simple example, let's say you wanted to extend the *String* class to make a case-insensitive version. You can't actually extend the *String* class because it is declared *final*. But you could use a technique called delegation. To do this, you wrap a *String* object in your own class and then implement the `equals` method, as shown here:

```
01: import java.util.Enumeration;
02: import java.util.Hashtable;
03:
04: public class CaseInsensitiveString
05: {
05:    String s;
07:
08:    public CaseInsensitiveString (String s)
09:    {
10:       this.s = s;
11:    }
12:
13:    public boolean equals (Object obj)
14:    {
15:       return (s.equalsIgnoreCase (obj.toString()));
16:    }
17:
18:    public String toString()
19:    {
20:       return (s);
21:    }
22: }
```

Your `equals` method is very simple in this case; it just needs to call *String's* `equalsIgnoreCase` method. This, however, can lead to problems. If someone tries to use your class as the key in a *hashMap*, he'll get undesirable results. Adding the main method (shown next) and executing the program will produce a *null* value.

```
01: public static void main (String[] args)
02: {
03:    Hashtable hash = new Hashtable();
04:
05:    CaseInsensitiveString cis = new CaseInsensitiveString ("abc");
06:    hash.put (cis, "value");
07:
08:    cis = new CaseInsensitiveString ("ABC");
09:    String value = (String) hash.get (cis);
10:    System.out.println (cis + " maps to " + value);
11: }
```

```
> java CaseInsensitiveString

ABC maps to null
```

This occurs because of the way the *Hashtable* class works. The documentation for this class states "To successfully store and retrieve objects from a *Hashtable*, the objects used as keys must implement the `hashCode` method and the `equals` method." That can be a little misleading because, of course, every class inherits both of these methods from the *Object* class (or another superclass that overrides them).

So even if you choose not to implement `equals` and `hashCode`, objects from any class you write could be used as keys that would successfully store and retrieve objects from a *Hashtable*. You would be treating your objects more like instantiations of the *Object* class, not of your particular class.

If you choose to implement the `equals` method, you must also override the `hashCode` method. The documentation from the `hashCode` method of the *Object* class states "If two objects are equal according to the `equals(Object)` method, then calling the `hashCode` method on each of the two objects must produce the same integer result."

In this example, the solution is simple. You need to override the `hashCode` method such that it returns the same value for any objects your class considers equal. The following implementation works. Executing your program after adding this method to your *CaseInsensitiveString* class produces the desired results.

```
1: public int hashCode()
2: {
3:     return (s.toUpperCase().hashCode());
4: }

> java CaseInsensitiveString

ABC maps to value
```

Using StringBuffer Objects as Hashmap Keys

You can avoid similar problems by understanding the way *Hashtable*s work. Now that you know the `equals` method is used to compare keys, you won't be surprised when changing the contents of an object does not change the value to which it links. In other words, you can't retrieve a *Hashtable* value unless the object you send to the `get` method *equals* the object you sent to the `put` method.

For example, if you use *StringBuffer* objects as keys into your *Hashtable*, you should not expect the same behavior you get when using *String* objects. You can't create another *StringBuffer* with the same text and use it to retrieve your *Hashtable* value. The *String* class overrides `equals`; *StringBuffer* does not. Even though you might expect the following code to output "123," it outputs *null* instead because *sb1* and *sb2* are not equal.

```
Hashtable hash = new Hashtable();
StringBuffer sb1 = new StringBuffer ("abc");
hash.put (sb1, "123");
```

```
StringBuffer sb2 = new StringBuffer ("abc");
System.out.println (hash.get (sb2)); // prints null!
```

Because using *StringBuffers* is more efficient than using *Strings* in many cases, you might be tempted to use them as keys in a *Hashtable*. If you want to minimize the number of objects created, you might even try something like this:

```
01: import java.util.Enumeration;
02: import java.util.Hashtable;
03:
04: public class StringBufferHash
05: {
06:     public static void main (String[] args)
07:     {
08:         Hashtable hash = new Hashtable();
09:         Enumeration enum;
10:         StringBuffer sb = new StringBuffer();
11:
12:         // map command line arguments to their values
13:         for (int i = 0; i < args.length - 1; i += 2)
14:         {
15:             sb.replace (0, sb.length(), args[i]);
16:             hash.put (sb, args[i+1]);
17:         }
18:
19:         enum = hash.keys();
20:         while (enum.hasMoreElements())
21:         {
22:             sb = (StringBuffer) enum.nextElement();
23:             System.out.println
24:                 (sb + " set to " + hash.get (sb));
25:         }
26:     }
27: }
```

Then, you might invoke the class like this:

```
java StringBufferHash -a aVal -b bVal -c cVal -b newB
```

You might hope to get output like this:

```
-a set to aVal
-b set to newB
-c set to cVal
```

Because *StringBuffer* does not override `equals`, you'll end up with only one key in your *Hashtable*. So the output will really be just one line, which is certainly not what you wanted:

```
-b set to bVal
```

Item 15: Avoid Using a Constructor for Implementing clone()

Item 13 detailed the differences between creating *shallow* and *deep* copies, and it provided information on the usage of `Object.clone()`. Item 15 demonstrates why you should avoid using a constructor in your implementations of `clone()`. Let's first provide a reasonable explanation of why you would want to use a constructor instead of using `Object.clone()`. Two reasons come to mind immediately:

- The object you want to clone contains no primitives, and all members are mutable so you want to create a deep copy. Using `Object.clone()` will not benefit you because all it does is copy primitives and reference values.

- It is more convenient to use your own cloning implementation because it's a pain to deal with the *Cloneable* interface and the *CloneNotSupported Exception.*

Given these two reasons there is one good reason why you want to avoid using a constructor when implementing `clone()`: It restricts subclasses from reusing the `clone()` method of the superclass.

Let's look at an example of how using a constructor interferes with the ability of a subclass to use the superclasses' `clone()` method. The source that follows shows two classes, *Mammal* and *Dog*, where *Dog* is a subclass of *Mammal*. If you look at the implementation of the `clone()` method in *Mammal* you see that it uses the *Mammal()* constructor to create a copy of itself. This works fine for classes that want to `clone()` *Mammal*, but it causes problems for subclasses that want to reuse the `clone()` functionality provided by *Mammal*. The *Dog* class tries to simplify its cloning implementation by calling `super.clone()` to handle the class members of the *Mammal* class, and then it adds its own statements to copy class members specific to *Dog*.

```
01: import java.util.*;
02:
03: class Mammal
04: {
05:     public Hashtable attributes = new Hashtable();
06:
07:     public Mammal (String name)
08:     {
09:         attributes.put("Name", name);
10:     }
11:
12:     public Object clone ()
13:     {
14:         Mammal newMammal = new Mammal((String)attributes.get("Name"));
15:         newMammal.attributes = (Hashtable)attributes.clone();
16:         return (newMammal);
```

```
17:        }
18:
19:        public String toString ()
20:        {
21:            return ("Name: " + attributes.get("Name"));
22:        }
23: }
24:
25: class Dog extends Mammal
26: {
27:        Vector tricks;
28:
29:        public Dog (String name, String breed, Vector tricks)
30:        {
31:            super (name);
32:            this.attributes.put("Breed", breed);
33:            this.tricks = tricks;
34:        }
35:
36:        public Object clone ()
37:        {
38:            Dog newDog = (Dog) super.clone();
39:            newDog.tricks = (Vector) tricks.clone();
40:            return (newDog);
41:        }
42:
43:        public String toString ()
44:        {
45:            String s = super.toString() + "\nBreed: " +
46:                       this.attributes.get("Breed") +
47:                       "\nTricks:";
48:            for (int i = 0; i < tricks.size(); i++)
49:                s = s + "\n" + tricks.elementAt(i);
50:            return (s);
51:        }
52: }
53:
54: public class CloneDog
55: {
56:        public static void main (String args[])
57:        {
58:            Vector tricks = new Vector();
59:            tricks.addElement("Roll over");
60:            tricks.addElement("Play dead");
61:
62:            Dog rover = new Dog("Rover", "Beagle", tricks);
63:            Dog roverClone = (Dog) rover.clone();
64:
65:            System.out.println(rover.toString());
66:            System.out.println("\nClone: \n" + roverClone.toString());
67:        }
68: }
```

When the `super.clone()` method is called in line 38, this runtime error occurs:

```
Exception in thread "main" java.lang.ClassCastException: Mammal
        at Dog.clone(CloneDog.java:38)
        at CloneDog.main(CloneDog.java:63)
```

Because the `clone()` method in *Mammal* used a *Mammal* constructor for creating the new object, calling `super.clone()` from the *Dog* implementation returned an object whose class was *Mammal*, therefore throwing the *ClassCastException*. Because the `clone()` method of *Mammal* will never return an object of type *Dog*, the *Dog* class must fully implement the `clone()` method itself, even to the extent of copying the superclasses' members. The new `clone()` method in *Dog* looks like this:

```
public Object clone ()
{
    Dog newDog = new Dog();
    newDog.attributes = (Hashtable)attributes.clone();
    newDog.tricks = (Vector)tricks.clone();
    return (newDog);
}
```

In addition, a no-argument constructor had to be added to both the *Dog* and *Mammal* classes to get this to work. Running the code with the new `clone()` method in place produces the desired output, which is shown here:

```
Name: Rover
Breed: Beagle
Tricks:
Roll over
Play dead

Clone:
Name: Rover
Breed: Beagle
Tricks:
Roll over
Play dead
```

The solution class *Dog* took was to use brute force. If the *Mammal* class had 50 to 100 class members, then *Dog* would have to write 50 to 100 clone statements just to copy the class members provided by *Mammal*. And what if some or all of these members are private? The only solution then is to pray that *Mammal* provides access via methods to all of its private members—even then *Dog* still has to write 50 to 100 assignment statements. There must be a better way.

The solution to this problem is for the `clone()` implementation in *Mammal* to use `super.clone()`. Doing this invokes the protected `clone()` method in the *Object* class. The implementation of `clone()` in class *Object* creates a *shallow* copy of the object that invoked the `clone()` method. So objects that call this method always get back an object that has the same class as the calling object, and whose class members contain the same values as the calling object's class members. The values of the class members from the calling object are assigned to the class members of the new object. For primitive types values are copied, and for reference types the reference is copied. This means that if you have an object for a class member, both the original and cloned version of the object uses the same object class member. Therefore, the operation performed by the `Object.clone()` method is a *shallow* copy. For a discussion of *shallow* versus *deep* copies see Item 13.[1]

The following code shows the changes made to the *Mammal* implementation to use `Object.clone()`.

Change line 3 to:

```
class Mammal implements Cloneable
```

Change the Mammal `clone()` method (lines 12–17) to:

```
public Object clone ()
{
    try
    {
        Mammal newMammal = (Mammal) super.clone();
        newMammal.attributes = (Hashtable)attributes.clone();
        return (newMammal);
    }
    catch (CloneNotSupportedException cnse)
    {
        throw new InternalError();
    }
}
```

The implementation has been changed to call the `super.clone()` method. Because this is the `clone()` method in class *Object*, the *CloneNotSupportedException* must be caught. Now the implementation of `clone()` in *Dog* (lines 36–41) can successfully call `super.clone()`. Calling this, in turn, calls the `Mammal.clone()` method that, in turn, calls the `Object.clone()` method. The `Object.clone()` method creates a *shallow* copy of the *Dog*

---

[1]In addition, Item 13 also talks about the basics of cloning including the use of the *Cloneable* interface and why the `clone()` method in class *Object* is protected.

object. Note that the `Dog.clone()` implementation clones the *tricks* class member to create a *deep* copy of the *Dog* object.

Note that in our implementation of *Mammal* `clone()` we chose to catch the *CloneNotSupportedException* instead of declaring it in the throws clause of the method declaration. This exception should not be thrown because the *Mammal* class implements the *Cloneable* interface.

As a general rule of thumb, you should always call `super.clone()` when you implement the `clone()` method for your class. Just like any rule, though, there are a few exceptions:

- If you have a subclass that implements *Cloneable*, and if the superclass provides a `clone()` method accessible by the subclass, and if you do not have the source code or any documentation for the superclasses' `clone()` method, it may not make sense to call `super.clone()`.

- If your object requires a *deep* copy and you need to create many copies in a performance-sensitive environment, it may not make sense to call `super.clone()`.

In the first scenario you have to experiment with the cloning behavior provided by the superclass object to see if it returns an object with the same class type as your subclass. If so, you still may need to make sure that all of the assignments are being done and determine whether they are shallow or deep assignments. If it turns out you cannot call `super.clone()` because of a bad cloning implementation in a superclass, you can hope that the superclass provides enough exposed class members or methods to enable you to do the cloning yourself. Note in your `clone()` implementation that even though you cannot call `super.clone()`, you can still ensure that any object that calls your method always gets an object back that has the same class type. This can be accomplished with the following line, in which you replace the word *Dog* with the name of your subclass:

```
Dog copy = (Dog) this.getClass().newInstance()
```

In the second scenario, the performance of clone depends highly on the JVM used and the options with which it is invoked. If it is determined that the `Object.clone()` method in your JVM is slow, and if your objects require a *deep* copy, you should consider using the class constructor instead of calling `super.clone()`. This will eliminate doing the assignment twice—once for the initial assignment done by `Object.clone()` and a second time for the assignment made to implement the *deep* copy.

This item listed the benefits of not using a constructor when implementing `clone()`. The benefits are reuse and simplification of cloning logic. Based on the information listed here, I hope you start using `super.clone()` in 99.9 percent of your objects that need to implement cloning.

Item 16: Method Dispatching with Reflection, Interfaces, and Anonymous Classes

Many C and C++ programmers have used function pointers to implement callbacks and method dispatch tables. Those programmers come to Java missing the power and flexibility provided by function pointers. The standard answer given to these programmers is to switch to using Java interfaces. With JDK 1.1, a second option was available via the Java reflection API. The java.lang.reflect package included a *Method* object that could be stored in an array or passed into a method just like function pointers. Which way is the best way? Are function pointers an evil artifact of C++? In this item we study two common cases that require the flexibility provided by C++ function pointers: runtime method dispatching and the command pattern. We examine multiple solutions for these two cases and close with general rules to analyze your problem domain and choose the best method.

Method dispatching separates a response from its stimulus by allowing you to dynamically choose the appropriate response at runtime based on the current context. In C++, the response is chosen from an array of structures, each structure holding a function pointer, function arguments, and possibly contextual state data. In Java, we can either use a static array or dynamically load new classes (thus methods) at runtime. The program MethodDispatch1 that follows uses reflection to implement method dispatching. In the main method (lines 30–50) we see the initialization of four static arrays: an array of object references that contain the methods to dispatch, an array of Class variables that define the argument types to be passed into our dispatch methods, an array of Method objects that are analogous (in an OOP sense) to function pointers, and an array of Object arrays that represent data to be passed to the dispatch methods. Lines 43 and 44 iterate through the methods in the arrays and dispatch to (or invoke) each method by calling the static `dispatch()` method.

```
01: /* MethodDispatch1.java */
02:
03: import java.lang.reflect.*;
04:
05: class Foo1
06: {
07:     void doIt(int i)
08:     {
09:         System.out.println("Called Foo1.doIt() with arg: " + i);
10:     }
11: }
12:
13: class Foo2
14: {
```

```
15:        void doIt(int i)
16:        {
17:            System.out.println("Called Foo2.doIt() with arg: " + i);
18:        }
19: }
20:
21: public class MethodDispatch1
22: {
23:     public static void dispatch(Object o, Method m,
24:                     Object [] args) throws InvocationTargetException,
25:                                         IllegalAccessException
26:     {
27:         m.invoke(o, args);
28:     }
29:
30:     public static void main(String args[])
31:     {
32:         try
33:         {
34:             Foo1 f1;
35:             Foo2 f2;
36:             Object [] objs = { f1 = new Foo1(), f2 = new Foo2() };
37:             Class [] carg = { int.class };
38:             Method [] meths = { f1.getClass().getDeclaredMethod("doIt",
39:                                 carg),
40:                                 f2.getClass().getDeclaredMethod("doIt",
41:                                 carg) };
42:             Object [] [] margs = { { new Integer(10) }, { new Integer(20) }};
43:             for (int i=0; i < objs.length; i++)
44:                 dispatch(objs[i], meths[i], margs[i]);
45:         } catch (Throwable t)
46:             {
47:                 t.printStackTrace();
48:             }
49:     }
50: }
```

Here is a run of the previous code:

```
E:\synergysolutions\EffectiveJava>java MethodDispatch1
Called Foo1.doIt() with arg: 10
Called Foo2.doIt() with arg: 20
```

Although method dispatching via reflection works, you are not able to guarantee the program validity at compile time. The reflection classes, by definition, refer to any method (or any class or any object, respectively), and thus compile time type checking is impossible. Java's answer to the problem predates reflection. The Java "interface" keyword offers dynamic method dispatching and compile-time type checking. An interface is an abstraction that describes a set of actions that any object may implement, thereby taking on a role. MethodDispatch2 uses an interface to provide the same functionality as MethodDispatch1, yet is guaranteed to be type safe at compile time. The key line is 30, which initializes an array of interface references instead of an array of objects (as in MethodDispatch1). An object in that array must implement the interface *Nike*, or the program will not compile. If you attempted to add object references that did not implement the interface the error message reported from the Sun javac compiler would be this:

```
Incompatible type for array. Explicit cast needed to convert Foo3 to Nike.
```

The interface *Nike* has one method called doIt(int i) that all objects in the array explicitly implement.

```java
01: /* MethodDispatch2.java */
02:
03: interface Nike
04: {
05:     void doIt(int i);
06: }
07:
08: class Foo1 implements Nike
09: {
10:     public void doIt(int i)
11:     {
12:         System.out.println("Called Foo1.dooIt() with arg: " + i);
13:     }
14: }
15:
16: class Foo2 implements Nike
17: {
18:     public void doIt(int i)
19:     {
20:         System.out.println("Called Foo2.dooIt() with arg: " + i);
21:     }
22: }
23:
24: public class MethodDispatch2
25: {
26:     public static void main(String args[])
27:     {
28:         Foo1 f1;
29:         Foo2 f2;
30:         Nike [] objs = { new Foo1(), new Foo2() };
31:         int [] margs = { 10, 20};
32:         for (int i=0; i < objs.length; i++)
33:             objs[i].doIt(margs[i]);
34:     }
35: }
36:
```

Here is the output for MethodDispatch2:

```
E:\synergysolutions\EffectiveJava>java MethodDispatch2
Called Foo1.dooIt() with arg: 10
Called Foo2.dooIt() with arg: 20
```

Notice that MethodDispatch2 and MethodDispatch1 produce the same output. While Java interfaces provide the same functionality as using reflection, they have their limits. The next program, MethodDispatch3, demonstrates the superior flexibility of reflection in regard to method dispatching. Interfaces lock you into a predefined set of methods (with fixed signatures), but reflection has no such restriction. Of course, it is this very restriction that provides the ability to check method signatures at compile time. Thus, we face a trade-off.

In the program MethodDispatch3 we have two objects that would not fit a single interface specification; however; via reflection we can dynamically dispatch to any method available in those objects.

```
01: /* MethodDispatch3.java */
02:
03: import java.lang.reflect.*;
04:
05: class Foo1
06: {
07:     void doIt(int i)
08:     {
09:         System.out.println("Called Foo1.doIt() with arg: " + i);
10:     }
11: }
12:
13: class Foo2
14: {
15:     void doIt(int i)
16:     {
17:         System.out.println("Called Foo2.doIt() with arg: " + i);
18:     }
19:
20:     void doItAgain(int i, int j)
21:     {
22:         System.out.println("Called Foo2.doItAgain(" + i + ","
23:                                                 + j + ")");
24:     }
25: }
26:
27: public class MethodDispatch3
28: {
29:     public static void dispatch(Object o, Method m,
30:                     Object [] args) throws InvocationTargetException,
31:                                             IllegalAccessException
32:     {
```

```
33:            m.invoke(o, args);
34:        }
35:
36:    public static void main(String args[])
37:    {
38:        try
39:        {
40:            Foo1 f1;
41:            Foo2 f2;
42:            Object [] objs = { f1 = new Foo1(), f2 = new Foo2() };
43:            Class [] carg = { int.class };
44:            Class [] carg2 = { int.class, int.class };
45:            Method [] meths = { f1.getClass().getDeclaredMethod("doIt",carg),
46:                                f2.getClass().getDeclaredMethod("doItAgain",
47:                                carg2) };
48:            Object [][] margs = { { new Integer(10) }, { new Integer(20),
49:                                new Integer(30)}};
50:            for (int i=0; i < objs.length; i++)
51:                dispatch(objs[i], meths[i], margs[i]);
52:        } catch (Throwable t)
53:        {
54:            t.printStackTrace();
55:        }
56:    }
57: }
58:
```

Here is a run of MethodDispatch3:

```
E:\synergysolutions\EffectiveJava>java MethodDispatch3
Called Foo1.doIt() with arg: 10
Called Foo2.doItAgain(20,30)
```

Even though reflection provides the same flexibility as function pointers, it comes at the expense of type safety. On the other hand, interfaces offer a specification-constrained plug-and-play capability with compile-time type checking. Therefore, with very few exceptions, it is best to design your programs to use interfaces.

The *Command* pattern is an abstraction whereby you encapsulate a request in an object in order to decouple the object that invokes the operation from the one that knows how to perform it. The *Command* object is an object-oriented replacement for callbacks. A callback is a function that's registered with a procedural subsystem to be called later. The most common use of callbacks is in a graphical user interface to associate a user-initiated operation like a menu selection with an action to perform. In C++, such callbacks are implemented using function pointers. One question to resolve in the implementation of *Command* objects is how to parameterize them—in other words, how to best specialize the command with an application-specific implementation. At one extreme, our *Command* object can merely delegate the request to a receiver (a form of method dispatching); on the other, our *Command* object can handle the request entirely itself. So, to implement the *Command* pattern we have multiple implementation options like procedural delegation, specialization via inheritance, and reflection. In the remainder of this item we examine the *Command* pattern as a specialized case of method dispatching; however, there are other considerations in using the *Command* pattern that are outside the scope of this book (like composite commands, supporting undo and redo, and complex commands). For analysis of these concepts refer to a text on *Design* patterns.

The CommandPattern1 application demonstrates the separation of the graphical user interface from the application using a single *Command* object. The specialization of this command object (lines 17–40) is done using a constant to dispatch to various methods in the application with a procedural switch statement. The *Command* object implements the *ActionListener* interface, which allows it to be registered with any MenuItem or Button in the graphical user interface. The *ActionListener* interface specifies only a single method called `actionPerformed()`.

```
01: /* CommandPattern1.java */
02:
03: import java.lang.reflect.*;
04: import java.awt.*;
05: import java.awt.event.*;
06: import javax.swing.*;
07:
08: class App
09: {
10:     public void binarySearch()
11:     { System.out.println("App1.binarySearch()"); }
12:
13:     public void mergeSort()
14:     { System.out.println("App1.mergeSort()"); }
15: }
16:
17: class Command implements ActionListener
18: {
19:     static final int SEARCH = 0;
20:     static final int SORT = 1;
21:
22:     App app;
23:     int cmdIndex;
24:
25:     public Command(App app, int cmdIndex)
26:     { this.app = app; this.cmdIndex = cmdIndex; }
27:
28:     public void actionPerformed(ActionEvent evt)
29:     {
30:         switch (cmdIndex)
31:         {
```

```
32:                 case SEARCH:
33:                     app.binarySearch();
34:                     break;
35:                 case SORT:
36:                     app.mergeSort();
37:                     break;
38:             }
39:         }
40: }
41:
42: class AppGui extends JFrame
43: {
44:     public AppGui(App app)
45:     {
46:         super("Command Pattern 1");
47:         getContentPane().setLayout(new FlowLayout());
48:         JButton searchButton = new JButton("Search");
49:         Command searchCommand = new Command(app,Command.SEARCH);
50:         searchButton.addActionListener(searchCommand);
51:         JButton sortButton = new JButton("Sort");
52:         Command sortCommand = new Command(app,Command.SORT);
53:         sortButton.addActionListener(sortCommand);
54:         getContentPane().add(searchButton);
55:         getContentPane().add(sortButton);
56:         addWindowListener(new WindowAdapter()
57:                     { public void windowClosing(WindowEvent we)
58:                             { System.exit(0); } } );
59:         pack();
60:         setLocation(100,100);
61:         setVisible(true);
62:     }
63: }
64:
65: public class CommandPattern1
66: {
67:     public static void main(String args[])
68:     {
69:         App app = new App();
70:         AppGui gui = new AppGui(app);
71:     }
72: }
```

A run of the preceding code produces the simple two-button graphical user interface shown in Figure 16.1. Clicking the button dispatches to the appropriate handler method.

The key problem with MethodDispatch1 is the use of the procedural method for specialization (the switch statement). Due to the switch statement the program is not guaranteed to be accurate at compile-time. Instead, we can specialize in an object-oriented manner using subclasses (inheritance). Java makes

Figure 16.1   Command Pattern GUI.

simple specialization easy with anonymous classes. CommandPattern2 uses
anonymous classes in this manner. Lines 34 and 40 create a concrete subclass
of the *Abstract Command* class using an anonymous class. Because the only
purpose of these classes is to be registered with the graphical user interface
component we do not need to save a reference to them. Also, because the
implementation of the actionPerformed method is simply method dispatching, this class is ideally suited for an anonymous implementation.

```
01: /* CommandPattern2.java */
02:
03: import java.lang.reflect.*;
04: import java.awt.*;
05: import java.awt.event.*;
06: import javax.swing.*;
07:
08: class App
09: {
10:     public void binarySearch()
11:     { System.out.println("App1.binarySearch()"); }
12:
13:     public void mergeSort()
14:     { System.out.println("App1.mergeSort()"); }
15: }
16:
17: abstract class Command implements ActionListener
18: {
19:     App app;
20:
21:     public Command(App app)
22:     { this.app = app; }
23:
24:     public abstract void actionPerformed(ActionEvent evt);
25: }
26:
27: class AppGui extends JFrame
28: {
29:     public AppGui(App app1)
30:     {
31:         super("Command Pattern 1");
32:         getContentPane().setLayout(new FlowLayout());
```

```
33:            JButton searchButton = new JButton("Search");
34:            searchButton.addActionListener(new Command(app1)
35:                    {
36:                        public void actionPerformed(ActionEvent evt)
37:                        { app.binarySearch(); }
38:                    });
39:            JButton sortButton = new JButton("Sort");
40:            sortButton.addActionListener(new Command(app1)
41:                    {
42:                        public void actionPerformed(ActionEvent evt)
43:                        { app.mergeSort(); }
44:                    });
45:            getContentPane().add(searchButton);
46:            getContentPane().add(sortButton);
47:            addWindowListener(new WindowAdapter()
48:                            { public void windowClosing(WindowEvent we)
49:                                { System.exit(0); } } );
50:            pack();
51:            setLocation(100,100);
52:            setVisible(true);
53:        }
54: }
55:
56: public class CommandPattern2
57: {
58:     public static void main(String args[])
59:     {
60:         App app = new App();
61:         AppGui gui = new AppGui(app);
62:     }
63: }
```

The CommandPattern2 application also produces the GUI in Figure 16.1. Because our *Command* object merely performs method dispatching we can specialize instantiations using a *Method* object in the same manner as we register function pointers. CommandPattern3 uses reflection to specialize the *Command* object instances prior to registering them.

```
01: /* CommandPattern3.java */
02:
03: import java.lang.reflect.*;
04: import java.awt.*;
05: import java.awt.event.*;
06: import javax.swing.*;
07:
08: class App
09: {
10:     public void binarySearch()
11:     { System.out.println("App1.binarySearch()"); }
12:
```

```
13:     public void mergeSort()
14:     { System.out.println("App1.mergeSort()"); }
15: }
16:
17: class Command implements ActionListener
18: {
19:     Object o;
20:     Method m;
21:     Object [] args;
22:
23:     public Command(Object o, Method m, Object [] args)
24:     { this.o = o; this.m = m; this.args = args; }
25:
26:     public void actionPerformed(ActionEvent evt)
27:     {
28:         try
29:         {
30:             m.invoke(o, args);
31:         } catch (Exception e)
32:           { e.printStackTrace(); }
33:     }
34: }
35:
36: class AppGui extends JFrame
37: {
38:     public AppGui(App app1) throws NoSuchMethodException
39:     {
40:         super("Command Pattern 1");
41:         getContentPane().setLayout(new FlowLayout());
42:         JButton searchButton = new JButton("Search");
43:         Method m = app1.getClass().getMethod("binarySearch", null);
44:         Command searchCommand = new Command(app1, m, null);
45:         searchButton.addActionListener(searchCommand);
46:         JButton sortButton = new JButton("Sort");
47:         Method m2 = app1.getClass().getMethod("mergeSort", null);
48:         Command sortCommand = new Command(app1, m2, null);
49:         sortButton.addActionListener(sortCommand);
50:         getContentPane().add(searchButton);
51:         getContentPane().add(sortButton);
52:         addWindowListener(new WindowAdapter()
53:             { public void windowClosing(WindowEvent we)
54:                 { System.exit(0); } } );
55:         pack();
56:         setLocation(100,100);
57:         setVisible(true);
58:     }
59: }
60:
61: public class CommandPattern3
62: {
63:     public static void main(String args[])
```

```
64:                          throws NoSuchMethodException
65:    {
66:          App app = new App();
67:          AppGui gui = new AppGui(app);
68:    }
69: }
```

Again, CommandPattern3 produces the same GUI as the previous applications (see Figure 16.1). Unfortunately, as in our MethodDispatch programs, the program cannot be guaranteed to be type-safe at compile time. For short class specialization it is best to use anonymous classes. For more complex specialization of a *Command* use explicit subclasses. As you can see, in our analysis, type safety, compile-time checking, and simplicity win out over flexibility.

Item 17: Handling Exceptions and OutOfMemoryError

If you're like many Java developers, Java is not the first programming language you learned. But like most developers, you probably found the Java syntax to be comfortingly familiar. Exception handling is likely to be one of the few exceptions to that. Other languages (such as Ada) provide similar mechanisms, but many developers are not used to programming with exceptions. Although exceptions are easy to use, the techniques require a bit of experience. New developers often either avoid exceptions altogether or use them inappropriately. In this section we discuss some of the proper and improper uses of exceptions.

The key to exceptions is that they provide a more well-defined interface between a method and its callers. This helps ensure that error conditions are handled appropriately. Functions in traditional programming languages typically express errors by returning a special code. This puts the onus on the developer to check for that code, without providing much help. If the developer fails to check, the program will still compile fine. With Java, the developer uses exceptions to explicitly define the errors that can occur within a method. In fact, any code calling that method that does not address the potential errors will fail to compile.

Because many programmers are unfamiliar with exceptions, here's a quote from Chapter 11 of the JLS to introduce some of the terminology:

> Java specifies that an exception will be thrown when semantic constraints are violated and will cause a non-local transfer of control from the point where the exception occurred to a point that can be specified by the programmer. An exception is said to be thrown from the point where it occurred and is said to be caught at the point to which control is transferred.

Exception Syntax

This syntax of exception handling is quite straightforward. As a developer you have two options: you handle the error, or you pass it on to the calling method so that it can handle the problem. Passing it on is simple: You just need to declare that the method is capable of throwing that particular exception. To handle it directly, you simply wrap any code capable of throwing an exception in a *try* block and then use a *catch* block to react if the error does occur. When you catch an exception, you can try to recover from it and continue processing, or you can just report it so the problem can be addressed.

```
try {
    ...
}
catch (SomeException e1) {
    ...
}
catch (AnotherException e2) {
    ...
}
finally {
    ...
}
```

The *finally* block is optional, and it allows you to have code that will always be run, whether or not an error occurs.

Exception Hierarchy

All exceptions in Java are descendents of the *Throwable* class. The exception hierarchy is presented in Figure 17.1. You need to be familiar with two subclasses of *Throwable* because they behave quite differently. The *RuntimeException* classes constitute a special case: They do not have to be declared or caught. All other *Exception* objects require a conscious effort on your part. You can either catch them or explicitly declare that you might throw them. In some cases you may want to do both.

Why do some exceptions require catching and not others? Instances of the *Error* class (a subclass of *Throwable*) represent abnormal conditions that should not occur, such as errors in the JVM. Recovering from them is usually not feasible, so there's not much point in catching them. Instances of the *RuntimeException* class "are exempted from compile-time checking because, in the judgment of the designers of Java, having to declare such exceptions would not aid significantly in establishing the correctness of Java programs. . . . Requiring such exception classes to be declared would simply be an irritation to Java programmers."

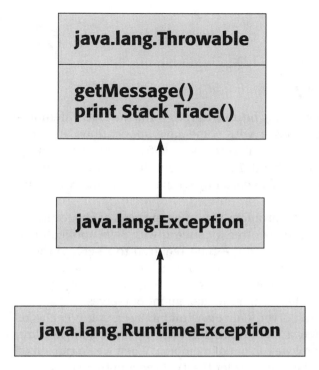

Figure 17.1   The Exception hierarchy.

For example, having to wrap every array access with a *try/catch* or adding *throws IndexOutOfBoundsException* to every method that accesses an array would just result in clutter. You'll hope to catch those bugs before you deploy a production version of your software.

Catching Exceptions

If you do have a chance of recovering from the error, you should catch it. Otherwise, you may just want to pass it up the stack and hope the code above you can deal with it. Even if you can't recover from the error, you may want to catch it as soon as possible. Quite often, the closer you are to the error, the more information you'll have about it. In those cases, you can either pass the exception on after displaying the information or create a new *Exception* that includes the information.

```
catch (SomeException e)
{
    System.err.println ("Some Exception occurred!");
    System.err.println (e.getMessage());
```

```
        e.printStackTrace (System.err);
        throw (e);
}
```

Running Out of Memory

One type of *Error* from which you may be able to recover is the OutOfMemory-Error. This is not an uncommon error with some Java applications. In some cases, a well-written program may be able to recover from this situation by releasing some memory. Although it's difficult to accurately predict where in the code this error might occur, you can certainly wrap the more likely culprits with a *try/catch*.

As an example, let's consider the problem of implementing a cache for some large objects. Because performance is often a concern with Java applications, many developers cache objects to avoid the time required to re-create them. Note that this type of problem is a great place to consider using *weak references*, which are automatically garbage collected for you. For the purposes of this example, though, we do all the memory management ourselves.

In this case, we write a data server. Our class maintains a static cache of objects, instantiated only when a client asks for one. We maintain the data objects for as long as we can (until we run out of memory). When we do run out of memory, we discard all of our data, and we let the JVM reclaim that space.

```
01: import java.util.*;
02:
03: public class DataServer
04: {
05:     private Hashtable data = new Hashtable();
06:
07:     public Object get (String key)
08:     {
09:         Object obj = data.get (key);
10:         if (obj == null)
11:         {
12:             System.out.print (key + " ");
13:             try
14:             {
15:                 // simulate getting lots of data
16:                 obj = new Double[1000000];
17:                 data.put (key, obj);
18:             }
19:             catch (OutOfMemoryError e)
20:             {
21:                 System.out.print ("\No Memory! ");
22:                 flushCache();
23:                 obj = get (key);    // try again
24:             }
```

```
25:        }
26:        return (obj);
27:    }
28:
29:    public void flushCache()
30:    {
31:        System.out.println ("Clearing cache");
32:        data.clear();
33:    }
34:
35:    public static void main (String[] args)
36:    {
37:        DataServer ds = new DataServer();
38:        int count = 0;
39:        while (true) // infinite loop for test
40:            ds.get ("" + count++);
41:    }
42: }
```

After creating 16 of those big data objects (an array of 1 million *Double*s), our program did run out of memory and throw an exception. We caught it, released our cache, and recursively tried again. Our client (the *main* in this case) never even knew we had a problem. Normally I wouldn't suggest using recursion as in line 23, but it kept the example brief. The syntax in line 40 is just a tricky way to get a unique String. For testing purposes, we didn't want the key to match anything in our cache.

The output from our program (after we interrupted it with control-C) looks like this:

> java DataServer

```
0  1  2  3  4  5  6  7  8  9  10 11 12 13 14 15 16
No Memory! Clearing cache
16 17 18 19 20 21 22 23 24 25 26 27 28 29 30 31 32
No Memory! Clearing cache
32 33 34 35 36 37 38 39 40 41 42 43 44 45 46 47 48
No Memory! Clearing cache
48 49 50 51 52 53 54 55 56 57 58 59 60 61 62 63 64
...
```

By the way, the JLS notes that Sun is "exploring enhancements to Java to simplify handling of out-of-memory conditions." Sun realizes this is one *RuntimeException* that many programmers can't afford to ignore.

PART
Three

Utilities and Collections

In C++ and Java, lists are implemented by a library, but we still need to know how and when to use it.

–BRIAN W. KERNIGHAN AND ROB PIKE,
THE PRACTICE OF PROGRAMMING

To effectively use any class, you must understand its design, purpose and limitations. This takes time and experience. Thus, we reveal our experience in order to save you time. In this part we will examine some of the classes in the java.util package. Here are the five items in this part:

Item 18, "Ordered Property Keys?," delves into the underlying mechanisms of the *Properties* class to create an ordered set of properties.

Item 19, "Handling Occasionally Huge Collections with Caching and Persistence," presents a detailed walk-through of a collection that combines caching and persistence to solve a real-world problem.

Item 20, "Property File or ResourceBundle?," discusses the differences between the two tools. Though property files are more common, they are not always the right tool for the job. This Item demonstrates a case when this is true.

Item 21, "Properties Object Pitfalls," is a thorough examination of issues and pitfalls in using properties to store application-specific configuration and resource information. Specifically, it discusses how to ensure that your properties work across platforms and without installation directory assumptions.

Item 22, "Using Vector as a Collection Instead of Old API," is a detailed examination of how Vector was expanded to support the Collections framework and why you should switch to the new API.

Item 18: Ordered Property Keys?

You finally got a chance to use that new digital camera you bought and the pictures of your long-awaited vacation look great! You're so impressed with yourself that you decide to invite your friends and family over for a slide show. You think about getting your pictures developed, dusting off the old slide projector, and hanging the screen up on the wall, but isn't this the technology age? Instead, you decide to use some of your Java programming skills and write your own SlideShow tool. Your friends and family will really be impressed when you show them your digital pictures on your computer using a program you wrote.

The code is all finished and the big day has arrived. Uncle Bob and the rest of the crew are gathered around your computer awaiting the big show. You start the SlideShow tool, which automatically comes up with a title page displaying the text "Our Trip to Grenada, the Island of Spice."

You begin by narrating the beginning of your trip, "This next slide is Patty and I getting on the airplane." You click the "Next" button on the SlideShow tool, but instead of seeing the picture of you and your wife getting on an airplane, you see the picture of your friends, Drew and Suzy, kicking back at the hotel. As you continue through the slides, you, and everybody else, realize that the slides are completely out of order. When Uncle Bob starts throwing tomatoes at the screen you know the show is a bust and you decide to invite everyone back after you have worked out the bugs in your program!

Embarrassed by the poor showing, you are determined to figure out what went wrong. The key concept of the SlideShow tool is the abstraction of the image paths from the code. The idea of abstracting the image paths from the code is to allow new slide shows to be created simply by creating a new property file with new image paths. This is a much better solution than hard coding the image paths, which would require modifying the source code every time you want to show new slides. Because there are other properties in the property file besides the image paths, the only thing we must do is follow a convention for determining which property is an image property and which is not. We can do this by adding the prefix "Image_" to all of the image properties. This sure seems like a good idea, but it doesn't seem to work because the slides are not displayed in the correct order. Let's double check the property file and make sure the slides are in the proper sequence. A printout of your property file looks like this:

```
imageRoot=c:\\images
title=Grenada Vacation
titlePage= Our Trip to Grenada, the Island of Spice
Image_departing=plane.jpg
Image_hotel=hotel.jpg
Image_friends=drew_suzy.jpg
Image_beach=beach.jpg
Image_return=patty_kirsten_keith.jpg
```

The image path properties in the property file are in the correct order. Because the property file looks correct, there must be a bug in the code. Let's look at the code block that creates the *ImageIcon* objects from the image properties in our property file.

```
01:    public ImageIcon[] getImages()
02:    {
03:        ImageIcon[] images = null;
04:        ArrayList al = new ArrayList();
05:        String imageRoot = properties.getProperty("imageRoot");
06:        Enumeration keys = properties.keys();
07:        While(keys.hasMoreElements())
08:        {
09:            String key = (String)keys.nextElement();
10:            if (key.startsWith("Image_"))
11:            {
12:                ImageIcon icon = new ImageIcon(imageRoot + File.separator
13:                + properties.getProperty(key));
14:                al.add(icon);
15:            }
16:        }
17:        int size = al.size();
18:        if (size > 0)
19:        {
20:            images = new ImageIcon[size];
21:            al.toArray(images);
22:        }
23:        return images;
24:    }
```

The getImages() returns an array of *ImageIcons*. This is accomplished by iterating through the keys, checking to see if each key starts with the string "Image_" (line 10). If the key begins with "Image_", an *ImageIcon* is created and added to the ArrayList of *ImageIcons* (lines 12–14). When the enumeration is complete, the ArrayList gets converted to an array of *ImageIcons* and returned.

Everything looks fine with the code. If the property file is correct and the code is correct the SlideShow tool would work. Let's double check the code and add the following debugging statement inside the "if" block beginning on line 10:

```
System.out.println("key  =   '" + key + "'");
```

This will tell us if we are getting the image paths back from the *Properties* object in the same order that they appear in our property file. After rerunning the code with the debug statement, we get the following output:

```
key = 'Image_hotel'
key = 'Image_friends'
key = 'Image_departing'
key = 'Image_return'
key = 'Image_beach'
```

Well, these image paths are certainly not in the same order as they appear in the property file. Does this mean that there is a bug in the keys() method of the *Properties* class? The short answer is no. The problem with our program is that we assume that the keys we iterate through from our *Properties* object are in the same order in which they appear in the property file. That turns out to be a bad assumption. Because the *Properties* class extends *Hashtable*, the keys are really being stored in a hash table, not in an ordered list. The *Hashtable* class inserts each key into an index, which is determined by the key's hash code and the current size of the hash table. The index is not determined by the order in which the keys are inserted. When the keys() method is called the keys are returned in the numerical order of their index. Therefore, the order in which the keys appear in the enumeration is not guaranteed to be the same order in which they were added to the hash table. That's bad news for the SlideShow tool.

Does this mean we must hard code the images in the source code to display them in the correct sequence? Fortunately, the answer is no. There certainly are other ways we can accomplish this goal. We can store the references to the image paths in flat files and read in the flat files. Because the SlideShow tool depends on other properties as well as image properties, we have to maintain an image list file, as well as a property file. Also, we certainly may run into other applications that would like the ability to iterate through the keys of a *Properties* object in the same order that they appear in the property file.

This functionality seems useful, but how can we get an ordered list of keys back from a *Properties* object? We can't. But we can create our own class that extends the *Properties* class to achieve this. Our new class needs an instance variable to store the ordered keys. We need to override the put(...) method and the remove(...) method so we can add and remove keys in our ordered list. And we will also need to add a method so the user can retrieve the ordered list.

Let's call our new class *EnhancedProperties* (see Item 21 for other convenience methods that can be added to this class). *EnhancedProperties* will look something like this:

```
01:    public class EnhancedProperties extends Properties
02:    {
03:         //constructors ƒ
04:
05:         ArrayList orderedKeys = new ArrayList();
05:
06:         public synchronized Object put(Object key, Object value)
07:         {
08:              Object object = super.put(key, value);
09:              orderedKeys.add(key);
10:              return object;
11:         }
12:
13:         public synchronized Object remove (Object key)
14:         {
15:              Object object = super.remove(key);
16:              orderedKeys.remove(key);
17:              return object;
18:         }
19:
20:         public synchronized Iterator getOrderedKeys()
21:         {
22:              return orderedKeys.iterator();
23:         }
24:    }
```

The *orderedKeys* instance variable on line 5 is the container that holds the ordered list of keys. The put (...) method beginning on line 6 first calls super.put (...), which caused the key to be inserted into the *Hashtable* as it normally would if we were using the *Properties* class. The call on line 9 to *orderedKeys.add(key)* will add the key to the ordered list. Each time the put (...) method is called the key will get added to the *Hashtable* and then will get added to the ordered list in the proper sequence. The remove (...) method beginning on line 13 works the same way as the put (...) method does. When the remove (...) method is called, the key is first removed from the *Hashtable* and then removed from the ordered list. The interface to the ordered list is the getOrderedKeys () method on line 20, which returns an Iterator of the ordered keys.

This relatively simple class now allows us to store the image paths in a property file and iterate through them in the order in which they appear in the property file. The original getImages () method that created an *ImageIcon* array from the "Image_" keys in the property file has to change only slightly. Lines 6–9 change to the following:

```
06:          Iterator orderedKeys = properties.getOrderedKeys();
07:          While(keys.hasNext())
08:          {
09:                  String key = (String)keys.next();
```

The only other change to the original code is replacing the *Properties* object that is created when the property file is read to an *EnhancedProperties* object. After making the changes and rerunning the code, we get the following output from the debugging statements:

```
key = 'Image_departing'
key = 'Image_hotel'
key = 'Image_friends'
key = 'Image_beach'
key = 'Image_return'
```

The image paths are now in the proper sequence. Now that you have learned that the *Properties* object extends *Hashtable*, and that the keys of a *Hashtable* do not get inserted into in an index that corresponds to the order in which they are entered, you are ready to invite Uncle Bob back for a more successful slide show.

Item 19: Handling Occasionally Huge Collections with Caching and Persistence

While testing your Java program that displays query results from a legacy database, you are frustrated to learn that everything works perfectly 9 out of 10 times. Occasionally, your program fails to display any results and the console reports an OutOfMemory error. You are storing the query results in a java.util. Vector that you are confident is the fastest and most convenient way to do so for such short-lived data as a query result. How can you get both speed (when processing the most common case) and reliability (for the occasionally huge result set)? The answer is a data structure that combines a Least Recently Used (LRU) cache with persistent storage. This discussion presents a *PersistentCacheVector* class that does this.

Figure 19.1 displays the structure of the *PersistentCacheVector*, highlighting the fact that this object is composed of four major subcomponents: a proxy *Vector* filled with "stub" entries, a hash table of cache entries, a Least Recently Used (LRU) list, and an *ObjectFile* of serialized objects.

The goals for the architecture in Figure 19.1 are these:

- Be as simple to use as the familiar java.util.Vector.

- Allow the collection to grow huge (greater than 50,000 entries, for example) without throwing an OutOfMemoryError.

PersistentCacheVector

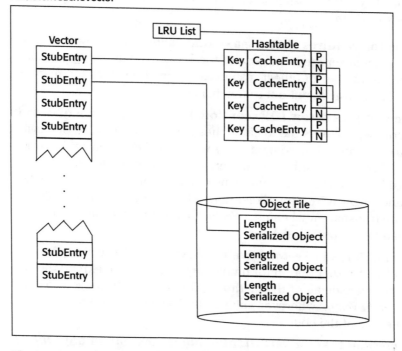

Figure 19.1   The PersistentCacheVector architecture.

- Keep frequently accessed items in memory.
- Keep the implementation details of growing to accommodate huge collections transparent to the user.

Two source files, PersistentCacheVector.java and ObjectFile.java, implement this architecture. We first examine and discuss specific portions of these source files and then present the entire listings at the end of this item. Before we examine snippets of the code, let's examine the public API for the class *Persistent-CacheVector*. The public methods are these:

```
public PersistentCacheVector(int iCacheSize);
public final void add(Serializable o) throws IOException;
public final Object get(int idx) throws IndexOutofBoundsException,
                                        IOException;
public final Object remove(int index) throws IndexOutOfBoundsException,
                                             IOException;
public final void copyTo(Object oArray []) throws IOException;
public final void close();
public final void finalize();
public final int size();
```

There are four key differences between the *PersistentCacheVector* methods and the methods in *Vector*:

The constructor requires that a maximum cache size be set. Unlike a vector, where you set the initial size of the *Vector*, the integer passed in is the maximum number of object instances that will be stored in memory. All other objects will be put out to the disk.

Some of the methods throw IOException due to the storage of data in files. Of course, it is possible to catch these exceptions instead of passing them on to the caller. For compatibility with the *Vector* class it is best to catch these inside the method; however, a disk error would then produce unpredictable results for the *Vector*. One other option is to catch the IOExceptions and throw a RuntimeException, which is not checked. This also provides the transparency behind a *Vector* façade but does not require the caller to handle the potential error.

Some of the methods in *Vector* have been left out. These are left to you as an exercise. Another option for mimicking a *Vector* is to extend the *Vector* class and override all of the methods. This option allows you to use a *PersistentCacheVector* wherever you used a *Vector* but would drastically increase the size of the code.

The `add()` method takes a *Serializable* object instead of any *Object*. Although a *Serializable* object is required to allow persistence, this does add a constraint not present when using a *Vector*. Instead of passing in a *Serializable* object we could just pass an *Object* reference and test it in the method using reflection. In my opinion, it is better to break compatibility with the *Vector* methods to ensure type safety.

The implementation of the API involves managing the data structures in Figure 19.1: the proxy *Vector* of *StubEntry* objects, the *Hashtable* of *CacheEntry* objects, the LRU list, and the *ObjectFile*. We examine each of these in detail.

The *StubEntry* inner class is the key to the illusion presented to the user. The user expects a simple *Vector* and will be given access to a *Vector* to store the objects; however, instead of storing objects it will store a proxy *StubEntry* instance that points to where the object truly resides. The object will either be in the cache or on disk (in the *ObjectFile*). The *StubEntry* has only two data elements: a flag to tell if the object is stored in the cache and an index into the RandomAccessFile (used in *ObjectFile*) if the object is serialized on disk.

```
40:    class StubEntry
41:    {
42:        /** flag that indicates if entry is in the cache or on disk. */
43:        boolean inCache;
44:        /** If entry on disk, this is where it was stored. */
45:        long filePointer = -1;
46:    }
```

The *CacheEntry* inner class is used to store the user's object in memory. The class also stores the key in the *Hashtable* where this element will be stored, and it references to the previous and next entry in the LRU list. Each *CacheEntry* object is put into the *Hashtable* using a simple key that is also stored in the *CacheEntry* instance. The fact that the key must be an object makes this slightly less efficient because the key into the *Hashtable* is simply the index of the *StubEntry* in the array. The fact that we are actually using a sparse array over the entire key space gives us a perfect, no-collision hash every time. Another option to explore that may be slightly more efficient is to store the key as an *Integer* object in the *StubEntry*. Such a scheme reduces the number of keys generated on the fly. The addition of next and previous references in the *CacheEntry* makes each instance pull double duty as a member of both the *Hashtable* cache and the LRU doubly linked list.

```
51:     class CacheEntry
52:     {
53:         /** Key that maps to the element. We use an Integer object
54:             that corresponds to the index in the Array. */
55:         Integer key;
56:         /** Object to store in cache. */
57:         Object o;
58:         /** References that support a doubly linked list. */
59:         CacheEntry prev, next;
60:     }
```

The LRU doubly linked list is accessed via two references in the *Persistent-CacheVector* class. One reference is to the head of the list (firstCacheEntry) and one to the tail (lastCacheEntry). The doubly linked list is an ordinary linked list for the purpose of tracking which entry in the cache is the least recently used entry. This is done by convention: Every time an item is accessed it is moved to the front of the list; thus, by default the last item in the list is the least recently used. Most of the code and complexity of *PersistentCacheVector* is due to the maintenance of the doubly linked list. What follows is a code snippet that adds a *CacheEntry* instance (called ce) to the LRU list. The logic is as follows: If the list is not empty, add the new item to the front of the list by setting its next pointer to the previous first entry, then set the previous first entry's previous pointer to the new entry, and finally reset the list Head pointer to the new entry. If the list is empty, simply set the head and tail pointer to the new entry.

```
108:         // add Cache Entry to LRU list
109:         if (lastCacheEntry != null)
110:         {
111:             // add to front of list
112:             ce.next = firstCacheEntry;
113:             firstCacheEntry.prev = ce;
114:             firstCacheEntry = ce;
115:         }
```

```
116:          else
117:          {
118:            // empty list
119:            firstCacheEntry = lastCacheEntry = ce;
120:          }
```

The *ObjectFile* is a simple class to store serialized objects linearly in a RandomAccessFile. A serialized object is stored as an array of bytes. No supporting data is necessary to write an array of bytes to a RandomAccessFile; however, to read an array of bytes from a RandomAccessFile you need to know how many bytes to read. So, the format of the *ObjectFile* is an integer followed by an array of bytes for each object stored. The integer represents the number of bytes that follow. The *ObjectFile* class contains the RandomAccessFile and implements methods to read and write objects in the aforementioned format.

```
07: public class ObjectFile
08: {
09:     RandomAccessFile dataFile;
10:     String sFileName;
11:
12:     public ObjectFile(String sName) throws IOException
13:     {
14:         sFileName = sName;
15:         dataFile = new RandomAccessFile(sName, "rw");
16:     }
```

For testing purposes, *PersistentCacheArray* has a `main()` method. All of the methods in the *PersistentCacheVector* were tested. Here is the output of those tests in the `main()` method:

```
E:\synergysolutions\EffectiveJava\jwiley\effective>java
jwiley.effective.PersistentCacheVector
adding 300 objects...
Size: 300
Testing get...
0,1,2,3,4,5,
Now the element at index 5 is : 6
Size is: 299
296,297,298,299,
1,2,3,4,5,Testing remove...
Size: 299
Removing 10
Size: 289
First 10.
2,4,6,8,10,12,14,16,18,20,
```

Here is a complete listing of the PersistentCacheVector.java:

```
001: /* PersistentCacheVector.java */
002: package jwiley.effective;
003:
004: import java.io.*;
005: import java.util.*;
006:
007: /**
008:  *  A replacement for a Vector that uses an LRU cache and persists all
009:  *   entries greater than the cache size.
010:  */
011: public class PersistentCacheVector implements Cloneable, Serializable
012: {
013:    /** count of the number of these objects created. */
014:    static long lCount;
015:    /** Maximum size the cache is allowed to grow to. */
016:    int iMaxCacheSize;
017:    /** Current cache size. */
018:    int iCacheSize;
019:    /** The cache. */
020:    Hashtable cache = new Hashtable();
021:    /** The Vector mirror. This will store only a
022:        VectorEntry object for each entry inserted. */
023:    Vector rows = new Vector();
024:    /** ObjectFile that stores the persisted objects.
025:        @see ObjectFile
026:    */
027:    ObjectFile of;
028:    /** Name of file where persistent objects are stored. */
029:    String sTmpName;
030:    /** First entry in the Least Recently Used (LRU) linked list.  The first
031:     entry represents the most recently accessed cache element. */
032:    CacheEntry firstCacheEntry;
033:    /** Last entry in the Least Recently Used (LRU) linked list. The last
034:     entry represents the least recently accessed cache element. */
035:    CacheEntry lastCacheEntry;
036:
037:    /**
038:     * An inner class that represents a minimal entry in the Array.
039:     */
040:    class StubEntry
041:    {
042:       /** flag that indicates if entry is in the cache or on disk. */
043:       boolean inCache;
044:       /** If entry on disk, this is where it was stored. */
045:       long filePointer = -1;
046:    }
047:
048:    /**
049:     * An inner class that represents an entry in the cache.
050:     */
051:    class CacheEntry
```

```
052:    {
053:        /** Key that maps to the element. We use an Integer object
054:            that corresponds to the index in the Array. */
055:        Integer key;
056:        /** Object to store in cache. */
057:        Object o;
058:        /** References that support a doubly linked list. */
059:        CacheEntry prev, next;
060:    }
061:
062:    /**
063:     * Constructor that sets the cache size.  File is not opened unless
064:     * array grows greater than cache size.
065:     * @param iCacheSize Maximum size the cache should be allowed to grow to.
066:     */
067:    public PersistentCacheVector(int iCacheSize)
068:    {
069:        this.iMaxCacheSize = iCacheSize;
070:    }
071:
072:    private final void openTempFile() throws IOException
073:    {
074:        boolean bInValid = true;
075:
076:        while (bInValid)
077:        {
078:            sTmpName = "tmp" + (System.currentTimeMillis())
079:                            + (++lCount) + ".obf";
080:            File f = new File(sTmpName);
081:            if (!f.exists())
082:                bInValid = false;
083:        }
084:
085:        of = new ObjectFile(sTmpName);
086:    }
087:
088:    /**
089:     * Method to add an object to this Vector. We add the
090:     * object to either the cache or disk.
091:     * @param o The object to add to the array.
092:     */
093:    public final void add(Serializable o) throws IOException
094:    {
095:        StubEntry e = new StubEntry();
096:
097:        rows.add(e);
098:
099:        if (iCacheSize < iMaxCacheSize)
100:        {
101:            e.inCache = true;
102:            CacheEntry ce = new CacheEntry();
103:            ce.o = o;
104:            ce.key = new Integer(rows.size() - 1);
105:            cache.put(ce.key, ce);
```

```
106:            iCacheSize++;
107:
108:            // add Cache Entry to LRU list
109:            if (lastCacheEntry != null)
110:            {
111:                // add to front of list
112:                ce.next = firstCacheEntry;
113:                firstCacheEntry.prev = ce;
114:                firstCacheEntry = ce;
115:            }
116:            else
117:            {
118:                // empty list
119:                firstCacheEntry = lastCacheEntry = ce;
120:            }
121:        }
122:        else
123:        {
124:          if (of == null)
125:              openTempFile();
126:
127:          e.filePointer = of.writeObject(o);
128:        }
129:    }
130:
131:    /**
132:     * Vector method to access an element at a specific index.
133:     * We retrieve the object from either the cache or from the object file.
134:     * @param idx The array index of the element to retrieve.
135:     * @returns The Object originally stored.
136:     */
137:    public final Object get(int idx) throws IndexOutOfBoundsException,
138:                                        IOException
139:    {
140:        if (idx < 0 || idx >= rows.size())
141:            throw new IndexOutOfBoundsException("Index: " + idx
142:                                        + " out of bounds.");
143:
144:        StubEntry e = (StubEntry) rows.get(idx);
145:
146:        Object o=null;
147:
148:        if (e.inCache)
149:        {
150:            // get it
151:            CacheEntry ce = null;
152:            ce = (CacheEntry) cache.get(new Integer(idx));
153:
154:            if (ce == null)
155:                throw new IOException("Element at idx " + idx + " is NULL!");
156:
157:            if ((ce != null && ce.o == null))
158:                throw new IOException("Cache Element's object at idx "
159:                                        + idx + " NOT in cache!");
```

```
160:
161:          o = ce.o;
162:
163:      if (ce != firstCacheEntry)
164:      {
165:          // remove it from its current place in list
166:          if (ce.next != null)
167:             ce.next.prev = ce.prev;
168:          else // this is the last one in the cache
169:              lastCacheEntry = ce.prev;
170:
171:          ce.prev.next = ce.next;
172:
173:          // move it to front of list
174:          ce.next = firstCacheEntry;
175:          ce.prev = null;
176:          firstCacheEntry.prev = ce;
177:          firstCacheEntry = ce;
178:      }
179:  }
180:  else
181:  {
182:      // this will now be in the cache
183:      e.inCache = true;
184:
185:      // retrieve and put in cache
186:      try
187:      {
188:          o = of.readObject(e.filePointer);
189:      } catch (ClassNotFoundException cnfe)
190:        { throw new IOException(cnfe.getMessage()); }
191:
192:      //*** Check if cache is FULL!
193:      if (iCacheSize == iMaxCacheSize)
194:      {
195:          // REMOVE LRU (tail of list).
196:          CacheEntry leastUsed = lastCacheEntry;
197:          if (leastUsed.prev != null)
198:          {
199:              leastUsed.prev.next = null;
200:              lastCacheEntry = leastUsed.prev;
201:              lastCacheEntry.next = null;
202:          }
203:          else
204:          {
205:              // removing the only entry
206:              firstCacheEntry = lastCacheEntry = null;
207:          }
208:
209:          // add retrieved object to cache
210:          CacheEntry ce = new CacheEntry();
211:          ce.o = o;
212:          ce.key = new Integer(idx);
213:          cache.put(ce.key, ce);
```

```
214:
215:                    // add Cache Entry to LRU list
216:                    if (lastCacheEntry != null)
217:                    {
218:                        // add to front of list
219:                        ce.next = firstCacheEntry;
220:                        firstCacheEntry.prev = ce;
221:                        firstCacheEntry = ce;
222:                    }
223:                    else
224:                    {
225:                        // empty list
226:                        firstCacheEntry = lastCacheEntry = ce;
227:                    }
228:
229:                    // get StubEntry for one to remove
230:                    StubEntry outStubEntry = (StubEntry)
231:                        rows.get(leastUsed.key.intValue());
232:
233:                    // get Object out of cache
234:                    CacheEntry outCacheEntry = (CacheEntry)
235:                        cache.remove(leastUsed.key);
236:                    if (outCacheEntry == null)
237:                        throw new RuntimeException("Cache Entry at "
238:                                    + leastUsed.key + " is Null!");
239:
240:                    if (outCacheEntry != null && outCacheEntry.o == null)
241:                        throw new RuntimeException("Cache object at "
242:                                    + leastUsed.key + " is Null!");
243:
244:                    Object outObject = outCacheEntry.o;
245:
246:                    outStubEntry.inCache = false;
247:
248:                    if (outStubEntry.filePointer == -1)
249:                    {
250:                        // had gone right to cache
251:                        outStubEntry.filePointer =
252:                                of.writeObject((Serializable)outObject);
253:                    }
254:                    else
255:                    {
256:                        // already in the file - size changed?
257:                        int iCurrentSize =
258:                            of.getObjectLength(outStubEntry.filePointer);
259:
260:                        ByteArrayOutputStream baos = new ByteArrayOutputStream();
261:                        ObjectOutputStream oos = new ObjectOutputStream(baos);
262:                        oos.writeObject((Serializable) outObject);
263:                        oos.flush();
264:                        int datalen = baos.size();
265:
266:                        if (datalen <= iCurrentSize)
267:                            of.rewriteObject(outStubEntry.filePointer,
```

```
268:                                           baos.toByteArray());
269:                     else
270:                         outStubEntry.filePointer =
271:                                       of.writeObject((Serializable)outObject);
272:
273:                     baos = null;
274:                     oos = null;
275:                     outObject = null;
276:                 }
277:             }
278:         else
279:             {
280:                 CacheEntry ce = new CacheEntry();
281:                 ce.o = o;
282:                 ce.key = new Integer(idx);
283:                 cache.put(ce.key, ce);
284:                 iCacheSize++;
285:
286:                 // add Cache Entry to LRU list
287:                 if (lastCacheEntry != null)
288:                 {
289:                     // add to front of list
290:                     ce.next = firstCacheEntry;
291:                     firstCacheEntry.prev = ce;
292:                     firstCacheEntry = ce;
293:                 }
294:                 else
295:                 {
296:                     // empty list
297:                     firstCacheEntry = lastCacheEntry = ce;
298:                 }
299:             }
300:
301:         }
302:
303:         return o;
304:     }
305:     // *** Methods removed for brevityf
306: }
```

Here is a complete listing of ObjectFile.java:

```
01: /* ObjectFile.java */
02: package jwiley.effective;
03:
04: import java.io.*;
05: import java.util.*;
06:
07: public class ObjectFile
08: {
09:     RandomAccessFile dataFile;
10:     String sFileName;
11:
```

```
12:     public ObjectFile(String sName) throws IOException
13:     {
14:         sFileName = sName;
15:         dataFile = new RandomAccessFile(sName, "rw");
16:     }
17:
18:     // returns file position object was written to.
19:     public synchronized long writeObject(Serializable obj) throws IOException
20:     {
21:         ByteArrayOutputStream baos = new ByteArrayOutputStream();
22:         ObjectOutputStream oos = new ObjectOutputStream(baos);
23:         oos.writeObject(obj);
24:         oos.flush();
25:
26:         int datalen = baos.size();
27:
28:         // append record
29:         long pos = dataFile.length();
30:         dataFile.seek(pos);
31:
32:         // write the length of the output
33:         dataFile.writeInt(datalen);
34:         dataFile.write(baos.toByteArray());
35:
36:         baos = null; oos = null;
37:
38:         return pos;
39:     }
40:
41:
42:     // get the current object length - restore or move?
43:     public synchronized int getObjectLength(long lPos) throws IOException
44:     {
45:         dataFile.seek(lPos);
46:         return dataFile.readInt();
47:     }
48:
49:     public synchronized Object readObject(long lPos)
50:                     throws IOException,ClassNotFoundException
51:     {
52:         dataFile.seek(lPos);
53:         int datalen = dataFile.readInt();
54:         if (datalen > dataFile.length())
55:             throw new IOException("Data file is corrupted. datalen: "
56:                                     + datalen);
57:         byte [] data = new byte[datalen];
58:         dataFile.readFully(data);
59:
60:         ByteArrayInputStream bais = new ByteArrayInputStream(data);
61:         ObjectInputStream ois = new ObjectInputStream(bais);
62:         Object o = ois.readObject();
63:
64:         bais = null;
65:         ois = null;
```

```
66:        data = null;
67:
68:        return o;
69:    }
70:
71:    public long length() throws IOException
72:    {
73:        return dataFile.length();
74:    }
75:
76:    public void close() throws IOException
77:    {
78:        dataFile.close();
79:    }
80:    // Methods removed for brevityf
81: } // end of ObjectFile class
```

In this item we have examined the combination of a least recently used (LRU) cache and a class that persists objects (*ObjectFile*) into an effective strategy for handling occasionally huge collections. The effect of this combination is a more reliable program that handles the common case efficiently and the extreme case gracefully. Building reliable programs, though not necessarily impressive for demos, is the hallmark of the seasoned professional.

Item 20: Property File or ResourceBundle?

Imagine that you are working for a hot new startup company called LOA. Your company is the latest to challenge America Online for a piece of the Internet pie. You just heard that Sun Microsystems has agreed to prompt the users of its new 100 percent pure Java operating system for your online services. The program manager just let you know that your system will be marketed internationally and that you will have to update the software to support several languages. The software currently supports only English. The program manager wants to know how long it will take you to make the necessary modifications. Ignoring your answer, he says, "The end of the week would be fine."

Because you are responsible for only the startup screen, you figure you may be able to be done in time. The current startup screen gets its message from a property file. You figure you can get a linguist to help you create the same message in each different language and store the versions in separate property files. The system would have a cut of code for each different language that reads the correct property file. Unfortunately, the program manager tells you that there will only be one cut of code, which must handle all languages. The next thought you have is to read in a system property that stores the language information. Once you know which language you are dealing with you can read in the appropriate property file for that specific language. Over lunch, you discuss your plan with one of the senior Java programmers. He commends you on a fine idea, and then he lets you in on the fact that Sun has already thought of that idea. He tells you to research the *ResourceBundle* class.

The *ResourceBundle* class differs from the *Properties* class in a few ways. The *ResourceBundle* class and subclasses *ListResourceBundle* and *PropertyResource-Bundle* are designed to work with the *Locale* class to handle locale-sensitive data. The *Properties* class does not care what the locale is. The *Properties* class is simply meant to store String key/value pairs. If your system has no requirements to work with more than one locale, you want to use the *Properties* class for storing String key/value pairs. You also want to use the *Properties* class for storing String values that are not locale sensitive. Use the *ResourceBundle* classes for locale-sensitive data. Keep locale-sensitive data and nonlocale-sensitive data separate. Another difference between the *Properties* class and the *ResourceBundle* classes is that the *ListResourceBundle* class is designed to store a String key and an Object value. That means you can store any object, not just a *String* object. The *Properties* class lets you store only String values.

The first step to internationalizing the startup screen is to determine the locale-sensitive data. So, what is local-sensitive data? Let's look at the *Locale* class to help us get a better grasp on locale-sensitive data. The *Locale* class needs to know not only the current language but also the current country. Many countries speak the same language but have different currency or specify numbers or dates in different formats. The *Locale* class also takes a third variable called the *variant*. The *variant* variable can be used to specify any difference you want. The *variant* variable is an extra variable that the programmer can use however he or she wants in order to further differentiate locales. The locale-specific information on our startup screen will simply be the text that is displayed. We need to represent the message on the startup screen, as well as the text on the buttons, in the appropriate language.

In order to internationalize the text on the startup screen, we need to create a resource bundle of property files. The term "resource bundle" simply means a group of files that support locale-sensitive data in many different languages. You can create as many resource bundles as you want. For our purposes, we will create one resource bundle containing the main message of the startup screen and one resource bundle containing the text for each button on the startup screen. Because our data is all text, the resource bundle will be backed up by a property file for each supported language. The main idea of this approach is to separate the locale-specific text from the code so that a linguist could edit the property files without getting involved with the code. Resource bundles can be backed up with property files or classes.

You can retrieve a *ResourceBundle* by calling the `ResourceBundle.get-Bundle(...)` method. You can pass in a *Locale* object specifying the locale of the resource you would like to load, or you can use the default *Locale*. In order for the *ResourceBundle* class to find the property file or class corresponding to a specific *Locale*, you must follow a specific convention for naming your property files or your classes. The javadoc pages for the *ResourceBundle* class do a good job of explaining the convention used for locating a locale-specific resource. The following is the naming convention as well as the sequence the code will go through to find a specific resource:

```
baseclass + "_" + language1 + "_" + country1 + "_" + variant1
baseclass + "_" + language1 + "_" + country1 + "_" + variant1 + ".properties"
baseclass + "_" + language1 + "_" + country1
baseclass + "_" + language1 + "_" + country1 + ".properties"
baseclass + "_" + language1
baseclass + "_" + language1 + ".properties"
baseclass + "_" + language2 + "_" + country2 + "_" + variant2
baseclass + "_" + language2 + "_" + country2 + "_" + variant2 + ".properties"
baseclass + "_" + language2 + "_" + country2
baseclass + "_" + language2 + "_" + country2 + ".properties"
baseclass + "_" + language2
baseclass + "_" + language2 + ".properties"
baseclass
baseclass + ".properties"
```

Let's say we pass a *Locale* with a language code of de (German) and a country code of CH (Switzerland) to the `getBundle(...)` method. The default *Locale* has a language code of en (English) and a country code of US (United States). Let's call our baseclass "StartupMessage." To determine the sequence that our code will follow to find our resource, substitute "StartupMessage" for baseclass, "de" for language1, "CH" for county1, "en" for language2 and "US" for country2. Our code will try to find our resource in the following order: StartupMessage_de_CH, StartupMessage_de_CH.properties, StartupMessage_de, StartupMessage_de.properties, StartupMessage_en_US, StartupMessage_en_US.properties, StartupMessage_en, StartupMessage_en.properties, Startup Message, StartupMessage.properties.

It is recommended that you start creating your resource bundle with a baseclass resource and then add resources for specific locales on top of that. This way you will always have a baseclass in case there is no resource for the passed-in *Locale* or for the default *Locale*. We start by creating our baseclass property file. This property file is named *StartupMessage*.properties and looks like this:

```
StartupScreen.message = Welcome to LOA: Please press OK to install our
software. Otherwise, press CANCEL to exit.
```

We will also create the resource for the English language and the U.S. country code *Locale*. This file is named StartupMessage_en_US.properties and contains the same information as the default file. Because the information in the two files is the same, why do we need the baseclass? Let's say the *Locale* that gets passed in to the `getBundle(...)` method is set for Chinese and the default *Locale* is set for Japanese. Because we do not have a property file for Chinese or Japanese, the code goes through its sequence to find the proper resource and eventually finds the baseclass resource. If we did not have a baseclass, the code would throw a MissingResourceException.

Now we need to create our default resource for the buttons on the startup screen. Let's call this file StartupButton.properties. This file contains the following information:

```
StartupButton.ok=OK
StartupButton.cancel=CANCEL
```

Once again, we create a resource for the English language and the U.S. country code containing the same information. This file is called StartupButton_en_US.properties.

Now that we have our locale-sensitive data separated from the code, let's take a look at how the code reads in the resources.

This code segment reads in the StartupMessage resource for the default *Locale*:

```
01: ResourceBundle startupMessageBundle;
02: startupMessageBundle = ResourceBundle.getBundle("StartupMessage");
03: String message = startupMessageBundle.getString("StartupScreen.message");
```

This code segment reads in the StartupButton resource for the default *Locale*:

```
01: ResourceBundle startupButtonBundle;
02: startupButtonBundle = ResourceBundle.getBundle("StartupButton");
03: String okButton = startupButtonBundle.getString("StartupButton.ok");
```

If the default *Locale* is set for the language en (English) and the county code is set for US (United States) then the StartupMessage_en_US.properties and the StartupButton_en_US.properties files are loaded. The nice thing about this approach is that the code does not have to change to support other locales. We simply get the linguists to edit new property files and name the property files according to the proper convention. Now the system needs only one cut of code to support several languages.

The task of internationalizing your code is a huge one. The focus of this item is to point out the differences between the *Properties* class and the *Resource-Bundle* classes, and to give you a basic idea of how to use the *ResourceBundle* classes. This is just a start. Here are some other classes that Java provides to help in internationalizing your code: *DateFormat, NumberFormat,* and *MessageFormat*.

Item 21: Properties Object Pitfalls

If you're familiar with the Java programming language you probably have used the *Properties* object already. You may have even thought that the *Properties* object would be the cure-all that would allow you to remove hard-coded values from your source code. If you are unfamiliar with the *Properties* class, note that it allows you to retrieve key/value pairs from a property file. Property files are simply text files that follow a key=value format. The main idea of a property file is to allow for the modification of a *String* variable without having to modify and recompile the source code. The *Properties* class gives the programmer the basic tools necessary for reading in a property file, as well as getting or setting a given value. A property file is a convenient way to store system configuration information or user preferences outside the code. Property files, along with the supporting *Properties* class, solve some of the problems of abstracting textual information from the code. This solution, however, also presents some problems of its own.

Let's say that we want to store system properties in a property file, such as to which DBMS our system is going to connect. By storing this information in a property file, we can connect our system to different database management systems without having to modify the source code. We can create a property file that contains the following DBMS information:

```
Default.DbName=Postgres
Default.url=//localhost:5432/bcs
Default.UserName=postgres
Default.Password=postgres
```

If we save this property file to c:\myApp\properties\System.properties, we can use the following code to read it in.

```
01:    try
02:    {
03:        FileInputStream fis = new FileInputStream("c:\\myApp\\properties
                                        \\System.properties");
04:        Properties props = new Properties();
05:        props.load(fis);
06:        String dbName = props.getProperty("Default.DbName");
07:    }
08:    catch(FileNotFoundException fnfe){} //handle exception
09:    catch(IOException ioe) {} // handle exception
```

This code segment creates a *Properties* object containing the key/value pairs in the System.properties file. By changing the values of the DBMS properties we could connect our system to a different DBMS without modifying any code. This sounds great, so what's the problem? The good aspect of this code segment is that it successfully allows us to abstract the DBMS information from the code. The problem with the code is that we have hard-coded the property file path. Suppose a user installed our system on the D drive instead of the C drive. The FileInputStream constructor on line 3 would throw a FileNotFoundException because the System.properties file would not exist at c:\myApp\properties\System.properties. So, if we don't hard-code our property file path, how do we find our System.properties?

The alternative to hard coding the property path is using the `getResource-AsStream(...)` method of the *Class* class. The `getResourceAsStream(...)` method searches the class path for a given resource. This allows the code to find the System.properties file anywhere on the disk, as long as we set our class path properly. By default, the `getResourceAsStream(String resource)` method searches the class path for the resource in one of two ways. If the resource string that gets passed in to the method begins with a '/', then the resource string is unchanged. If the resource string does not begin with a '/', then the resource string is appended to the package name, with all '.' characters converted to '/' characters. Let's suppose that class *SysProperties* is in package com.mycompany.myapp. In class *SysProperties*, the *Properties* object can be loaded like this:

```
01:    try
02:    {
03:        InputStream is = SysProperties.class.getResourceAsStream
04:        ("/System.properties");
05:        Properties prop = new Properties();
06:        if (is != null)
07:        {
08:            prop.load(is);
09:            String dbName = props.getProperty("Default.DbName");
10:        }
11:    }
12:        catch(IOException ioe) {} // handle exception
```

In this case, the `getResourceAsStream(...)` method searches each path of the class path for the System.properties file. If the argument to the `getResourceAsStream(...)` method on line 5 is changed from "/System.properties" to "System.properties," the `getResourceAsStream(...)` method searches each path of the class path for "com/mycompany/myapp/System.properties." Either way works just fine. If you want to keep all of your property files together, choose the first approach. If you want your property file in the same place as the class that uses it, choose the second approach. The important issue is that the user no longer has to have System.properties in the hard-coded c:\myApp\properties directory. We could also create a jar file that contained the classes and the property files.

Now that we have the DBMS information stored in the System.properties file, let's add a toolbar to our application. Suppose we want to store the image paths for each tool on the toolbar in the System.properties file. Storing the image paths in the property file allows us to change an image tied to a tool in the toolbar, without modifying any code. The additions to the property file look like this:

```
Save.image=c:\\myApp\\images\\save.gif
New.image=c:\\myApp\\images\\new.gif
```

The *Save.Image* and the *New.Image* properties contain the absolute file paths to the appropriate image that belongs to that tool on the toolbar. Modifying the property file in order to change images for a tool on the toolbar certainly is nicer than having to change the source code. We have the same problem, though, that we had when we hard-coded the property file path. If the user does not install MyApp in c:\myApp, the code is not able to find the save.gif or the new.gif file. Instead of using an absolute path to state where the save.gif file is located, we need to use a relative path. The path is relative to where the user installs our system. We then need to create an *Application.root* variable, which stores the directory in which the user installed MyApp. Many of the install programs, such as InstallShield, support the ability to retrieve the directory in which the user installs the application. Once the user selects the install directory, we can set the *Application.root* variable appropriately. This allows us to store system resource paths relative to the install directory. If the user installed MyApp in d:\apps\myApp our property file would look like this:

```
Application.root=d:\\apps\\myApp
Save.image=\\images\\save.gif
New.image=\\images\\new.gif
```

The source code must now retrieve the image value and append it to the *Application.root* value. The source code to get the full Save.image path looks like this:

```
01:    StringBuffer temp = new StringBuffer();
02:    temp.append(prop.getProperty("Application.root");
03:    temp.append(prop.getProperty("Save.Image");
04:    String saveImagePath = temp.toString();
05:    // code to create ImageIcon from the saveImagePath
```

Using this approach the user can install MyApp anywhere, and we are still able to find the resources the application needs.

Can you think of any other problems you might have with the system installation? Suppose the user installs your system in the /pkgs/progams directory on a Unix machine. Your system would dynamically set the *Application.root* property to /pkgs/programs. In order to load the image for the save action on the toolbar, the system would append "\\images\\save.gif" to /pkgs/programs. The full path would look like this: "/pkgs/programs\\images\\save.gif". We have just mixed the Unix path format with the Windows path format. So much for write once, run anywhere! To solve this problem, we can write a convenience method to convert the path format from one system to another. We can get the "os.name" system property to determine what type of system we are running on. If we are running on a Unix machine we can change "\\" to "/". Our Save.Image path would then look like this: "/pkgs/programs/images/save.gif".

Now that we are ready to "write once, run anywhere," we must make sure that all of the system developers use the `getResourceAsStream(...)` approach for loading the *Properties* object. So far, we have seen two examples of different ways to load a *Properties* object. The *Properties* object has been loaded using the *FileInputStream* class and the `getResourceAsStream(...)` method. There are many more ways to load the *Properties* object; if you have more than one programmer working on your system, you can bet that some of them will load the *Properties* objects differently than others. This inconsistency makes the system more unpredictable and more difficult to maintain. One way to avoid this problem is to create a class that is responsible for taking in a property file name and returning a *Properties* object. Let's call this class *PropertyLoader*. This will be the one way to load a *Properties* object (assuming that all the developers use it).

```
01:  public class PropertyLoader
02:  {
03:        //can't instantiate outside this class
04:        private PropertyLoader() {}
05:        public static Properties load(String propName)
06:        {
07:            try
08:            {
09:                InputStream is =
10:                PropertyLoader.class.getResourceAsStream(propName);
11:                if (is != null)
12:                {
13:                    Properties props = new Properties();
14:                    props.load(is);
15:                    return props;
16:                }
17:            }
18:            catch (IOException ioe){} // handle exception
19:            return null;
20:        }
21:  }
```

The *PropertyLoader* class contains a static `load(...)` method on line 5. The *PropertyLoader* class can be coded to catch the IOException itself, as shown in the previous example, or it can be coded to throw the IOException and force the callers to handle it instead. Either way, this common interface allows the programmer to get a loaded *Properties* object via the class path and not a hard-coded file path. The call to load a *Properties* object simply looks like this:

```
Properties props = PropertyLoader.load("/myApp.properties");
```

The only problem we have with the *PropertyLoader* is that it limits us to the *Properties* class. The *Properties* class gives us some nice methods. It would be nice, though, to have a handful of other convenience methods as well. For example, there may be times when you need to convert a property value from a *String* to an *int* or a *boolean*. The *Integer* and *Boolean* classes provide a method to convert a *System.prop* value to an *int* or *boolean*, respectively, but they do not provide a method to convert a *String* value from any property file, only from the System.prop file. Another nice convenience method is a `getPath-Property(...)` method that would handle the system's format conversion automatically. Instead of forcing the caller of the *PropertyLoader* to implement these convenience methods, we can create an *EnhancedProperties* class that extends *Properties* and adds all of these convenience methods A simple *EnhancedProperties* class may look like this:

```
01:  public class EnhancedProperties extends Properties
02:  {
03:      public EnhancedProperties()
04:      {
05:         super();
06:      }
07:      public EnhancedProperties(Properties defaults)
08:      {
09:         super(defaults);
10:      }
11:      public EnhancedProperties(InputStream is)   throws IOException
12:      {
13:         load(is);
14:      }
15:      public boolean propertyToBoolean(String key)
16:      {
17:         // code to convert a String value to a boolean value.
18:      }
19:      public int propertyToInt(String key)
20:      {
21:         // code to convert a String value to an int value.
22:      }
23:      public String getPathProperty(String key)
24:      {
25:         // code to convert the returned path value to the appropriate
26:         system path value.
27:      }
28:  }
```

Now we just have to change the *PropertyLoader* class to return an *EnhancedProperties* object instead of a *Properties* object. Modifying the *PropertyLoader* class to return an *EnhancedProperties* object looks like this:

```
return  new EnhancedProperties(is);
```

Because we added a convenience constructor on line 11, which took an InputStream, we can combine lines 12, 13, and 14 of the *PropertyLoader* to the line just shown. We have added only a few convenience methods to the

EnhancedProperties class; however, I am sure you can think of many more convenience methods.

Item 22: Using Vector as a Collection Instead of Old API

Old habits die hard. You have been resisting the change to the new Collections API—I can feel it. After all, it's hard to teach an old dog new tricks, especially you initial Java die-hards who cut your teeth on Java version 1.0. If you have not embraced the new Collections API, now is your chance to learn. This item will not scare you away by bombarding you with *Collections, Sets, Lists, Maps, Comparators*, and so forth. Instead, this item will take the low road—showing you an example of using *Vector* with the old API and then showing you the same example with the new Collections API. This will get your foot in the door and begin the familiarization process so that you can weed through the 25+ collection-oriented classes to pick the one that suits your needs. (No more feeling embarrassed about not knowing what an *iterator* is.)

Before we get into the examples, let's briefly define what the Collections API is. The Collections API is a framework for representing and manipulating collections, in which a collection is defined as a grouping of objects. Several types of groupings exist in the Collections API—there are standard collections, lists, maps, and sets. Each one of these categories is represented by an interface, an abstract class, and one or more concrete implementations. To round out the Collections API, entities exist that fulfill these concepts: iteration through collections, comparison within a collection, and general utilities such as searching and sorting.

This first code listing demonstrates some of the commonly used methods in the *Vector* class. It adds, removes, inserts, and fetches from the *Vector* as well as copying the *Vector* to an array of objects, using an *Enumeration* to view the elements and calling a method to remove all of the elements.

```
01: import java.util.*;
02:
03: public class OldVectorAPI
04: {
05:     public static void main (String args[])
06:     {
07:         Vector v = new Vector();
08:         v.addElement("M. Elaine");
09:         v.addElement("D. Allison");
10:         v.addElement("J. Eric");
11:         v.addElement("A. Jewell");
12:         v.addElement("N. Anh");
13:
```

```
14:            v.removeElementAt(4);
15:            v.removeElement("D. Allison");
16:            v.insertElementAt("C. Thomas", 1);
17:
18:            print(v);
19:            printElements(v.elements());
20:
21:            Object[] middleNames = new Object[v.size()];
22:            v.copyInto(middleNames);
23:            v.removeAllElements();
24:        }
25:
26:        public static void print (Vector v)
27:        {
28:            int numItems = v.size();
29:            for (int i = 0; i < numItems; i++)
30:                System.out.println(v.elementAt(i));
31:        }
32:
33:        public static void printElements (Enumeration e)
34:        {
35:            while (e.hasMoreElements())
36:                System.out.println(e.nextElement());
37:        }
38: }
```

Updating the code to use the new Collections API is very simple. Table 22.1 lists the mappings between the old and new APIs for our example.

When the *Vector* class was updated to support the Collections API it was made to implement the *List* interface. In our example, we can ensure that we

Table 22.1 Comparing the Old Vector API with the New Collection API

OLD API	NEW API
void **addElement**(Object)	boolean **add**(Object)
void **copyInto**(Object[])	Object[] **toArray**()
Object **elementAt**(int)	Object **get**(int)
Enumeration **elements**()	Iterator **iterator**()
void **insertElementAt**(Object, int)	void **add**(index, Object)
void **removeAllElements**()	void **clear**()
boolean **removeElement**(Object)	boolean **remove**(Object)
void **removeElementAt**(int)	void **remove**(int)
int **size**()	int **size**()

are using the standard Collections API by creating a new *Vector* and assign it to a *List* variable. This will ensure that *Vector*-specific methods cannot be called (without explicit casting). The new example produces the same result using the new API:

```
01: import java.util.*;
02:
03: public class NewVectorAPI
04: {
05:     public static void main (String args[])
06:     {
07:         List v = new Vector();
08:         v.add("M. Elaine");
09:         v.add("D. Allison");
10:         v.add("J. Eric");
11:         v.add("A. Jewell");
12:         v.add("N. Anh");
13:
14:         v.remove(4);
15:         v.remove("D. Allison");
16:         v.add(1, "C. Thomas");
17:
18:         print(v);
19:         printElements(v.iterator());
20:
21:         Object[] middleNames = v.toArray();
22:         v.clear();
23:     }
24:
25:     public static void print (List v)
26:     {
27:         int numItems = v.size();
28:         for (int i = 0; i < numItems; i++)
29:             System.out.println(v.get(i));
30:     }
31:
32:     public static void printElements (Iterator it)
33:     {
34:         while (it.hasNext())
35:             System.out.println(it.next());
36:     }
37: }
```

Besides the straightforward mappings shown in Table 22.1 another difference needs to be pointed out. The Collections API relies on the concept of an *iterator* to traverse the elements in a collection. Depending on the type of collection you are dealing with, the available iterator(s) can have different levels of functionality. The *Vector* class implements the *List* interface, which in turn specifies two types of iterators. The first is the *Iterator* class, which must be implemented by all collections. The second is the *ListIterator*, which provides much more functionality than the *Iterator* interface.

When you compare lines 35 and 36 in the first code listing with lines 34 and 35 in the second, you see that the methods used between the *Enumeration* class and the *Iterator* class are very similar. The `Enumeration.has-MoreElements()` method corresponds to the `Iterator.hasNext()` method, and the `Enumeration.nextElement()` method corresponds to the `Iterator.next()` method. The *Iterator* class has one more method, `remove()`, which makes it slightly more powerful than an *Enumeration*. The *Iterator* class is the least common denominator for accessing elements throughout all collections.

The *ListIterator* class provides much more functionality: It allows for list modification (add, update, delete) as well as bidirectional navigation. It is up to the programmer to decide which is better for performing operations against *Lists*—the *ListIterator* or the methods exposed through the *List* interface itself.

One of the main points about the majority of classes in the Collections API is that they are not thread safe. This is true for *Vector*'s new sibling, *ArrayList* (another implementation of *List*). During *Vector*'s upgrade to support the Collections API, it remained thread safe (*synchronized*), so now programmers can pick and choose whether they want to use the nonthread-safe version (*ArrayList*) or the thread-safe version (*Vector*).

Using the new *Vector* API versus the old *Vector* API will not buy you any performance gains, but it leaves the door open for flexibility. If it turns out that for some reason *Vector* is much slower than another Collections implementation, you can swap out implementations without having to rewrite code that depends on the old *Vector* API. By using the Collections API now you benefit in code maintainability and open the door for using many of the other Collections API classes. Jump on the bandwagon!

PART

Four

Input/Output

The general goals of I/O software are easy to state. The basic idea is to organize the software as a series of layers, with the lower ones concerned with hiding the peculiarities of the hardware from the upper ones, and the upper ones concerned with presenting a nice, clean, regular interface to the users.

—ANDREW S. TANENBAUM, *OPERATING SYSTEMS, DESIGN AND IMPLEMENTATION*

The Java IO facilities are an interesting mix of backward compatibility, convenience, and evolution. The *RandomAccessFile* class is nearly identical to the C standard library functions fseek( ), fread( ), and fwrite( ). The IO package has evolved to fully support internationalization (Readers and Writers) and serialization of objects. This makes the IO package divisible both horizontally (into layers) and vertically (into functional categories). Thus overall, the IO package has enough abstraction and complexity to cause confusion and error. The items in this part are as follows:

> **Item 23, "Serialization,"** delves into the details of Serialization in order to override the default behavior.

> **Item 24, "Unicode, UTF, and Streams,"** provides both an overview of the entire IO package and the solution to a specific problem. It also explains and demonstrates the subtle differences between a character set and character encoding.

Item 25, "Sending Serialized Objects over Sockets," demonstrates a subtle IO pitfall due to side effects from constructors.

Item 26, "Try, Catch . . . Finally?," examines a simple pitfall that is easily solved with proper exception handling.

Item 27, "Flushing Image Resources," examines an overlooked aspect of Java image processing that is essential in certain circumstances. This highlights the idea that effectiveness lies in understanding the entire API and not just the well-trodden path.

Item 23: Serialization

If you have ever serialized an *ImageIcon* object or an object that contained an *ImageIcon,* you may have noticed that the serialized object is rather substantial in size. A quick look at the source code reveals why. The *ImageIcon* class contains a transient *Image* object that gets serialized in the writeObject method. The readObject method reads the *ObjectInputStream* and re-creates the *Image* object.

The writeObject method converts the *Image* object into a height, a width, and an array of pixels. It then writes the height integer, the width integer, and the array of pixels to the *ObjectOutputStream.*

The array of pixels is what makes the serialized *ImageIcon* object so large. Let's create a quick class that serializes an *ImageIcon* object to see how large it is.

```
01:  public class SerializeIcon
02:  {
03:      public static void main(String[] args)
04:      {
05:          ImageIcon ii = new ImageIcon
06:          ("c:\\java\\demo\\jfc\\Stylepad\\resources\\hatter.gif");
07:          try
08:          {
09:              FileOutputStream fos = new FileOutputStream
10:              ("c:\\temp\\image.serial");
11:              ObjectOutputStream oos = new ObjectOutputStream(fos);
12:              oos.writeObject(ii);
13:          }
14:          catch (Exception e) {//handle exception ƒ. }
15:  }
16:  }
```

The *SerializeIcon* class creates an *ImageIcon* object of the hatter.gif file from Java's Stylepad demo. The *ImageIcon* object is serialized to the image. serial file in the c:\temp directory. The hatter.gif file is 17.3kb. After running *SerializeIcon* the image.serial file is 236.6kb. A 236.6kb file may not seem too bad, but suppose we are writing a rich text editor and support image insertion. If we insert several images and save our document, the serialized object can quickly reach a megabyte or more. In order to avoid this problem, let's create a *SmallImageIcon* class that extends *ImageIcon* and overrides the `writeObject(...)` and `readObject(...)` methods. In the `writeObject(...)` method we can find some shareware classes that converts *Image* objects to something smaller and serialize our smaller object. In the `readObject(...)` method we read our smaller object from the stream and convert back to an *Image* object. Our overridden `writeObject(...)` method looks something like this:

```
01:   private void writeObject(ObjectOutputStream s)
02:   {
      .  // code that converts our Image to a smaller serializable object
      .
03:       s.writeObject(smallerObject);
04:   }
```

Our overridden `readObject(...)` looks something like this:

```
01:   private void readObject(ObjectInputStream s)
02:   {
03:     s.readObject(smallerObject);
      .
      . // code that converts from the smallerObject back to the Image
      . // object
04:   }
```

Essentially, what we are doing by overriding the `writeObject(...)` and `readObject(...)` methods is keeping the parts of the *ImageIcon* class that we like and changing the parts that we do not like. Right? Well, sort of. Although this is how overriding a method works, this approach will not help us solve our serialization problem. Let's take a closer look at what happens when we call the `writeObject(...)` method of the *ObjectOutputStream* class to find out why our *SmallImageIcon* class does not work.

What Really Happens When We Serialize an Object?

The javadocs for the `writeObject(...)` method of the *ObjectOutputStream* class states: "... The class of the object, the signature of the class and the values of the non-transient and non-static fields of the class and all of its supertypes are written ..." Did you catch the "and all of its supertypes" part? When you think about it, it does make sense. An object is made up of all of its members plus all of the members of its superclasses. Therefore, in order to serialize an object we must serialize the object itself as well as all of its superclasses. The *ObjectOutputStream*'s writeObject(...) method pushes the class to be serialized onto a stack followed by all of its superclasses. Each class then gets popped off the stack and serialized. If the current class being serialized does not have a readObject(...) and writeObject(...) method, then the defaultReadObject(...) and defaultWriteObject(...) methods are called. The defaultWriteObject(...) method serializes the signature of the class, and the values of the nontransient and nonstatic fields are written. Because serialization is recursive, if we serialized our *SmallImageIcon* class we would also be serializing the *ImageIcon* class. This happens because *Small-ImageIcon* extends *ImageIcon*.

Let's take a closer look at what would happen if we serialized the *SmallImageIcon* class. Because superclasses get popped off the stack before subclasses the *ImageIcon* class would get serialized first. The *ImageIcon* class implements the readObject(...) and writeObject(...) methods. This means that they get called instead of the defaultReadObject(...) and defaultWriteObject(...) methods. If you look at the source code for the *ImageIcon* class you see that the *Image* member is transient. This means that it will not be serialized by default. The writeObject(...) method first calls *OutputObjectStream*'s defaultWriteObject(), which does the same thing as if *ImageIcon* did not implement the writeObject(...) method. This may seem a bit strange, but the *ImageIcon* class wants to serialize all of its nontransient and nonstatic members by using the default method but handle serializing the *Image* member by itself. After the defaultWriteObect() method is called, the *ImageIcon* class converts the *Image* member into a height, a width, and an array of pixels. It then serializes the height, the width, and the array of pixels. After the *Image-Icon* class has been serialized, the *SmallImageIcon* class gets serialized next. Once again, the writeObject(...) method is called. In this case, we convert the *transient Image* object to a *smallerObject* and serialize the *smallerObject*. Our goal was to decrease the size of the serialized *ImageIcon* object by over-riding the writeObject(...) and readObject(...) methods. Not only did we not make the serialized object smaller, we made it bigger. Because object seri-alization is recursive we have actually increased the size of our serialized object by serializing the *Image* member twice.

Fortunately, there is another way to "override" the serialization behavior of the *ImageIcon* class.

The Externalizable Interface

The *Externalizable* interface is a tag interface that extends the *Serializable* interface. The purpose of the *Externalizable* interface is to give the program-mer total control over how to serialize an object. This is both good and bad. It's good because now we can serialize the *ImageIcon* object however we like. It's bad because we can no longer take advantage of any of the default serialization.

We can control how to serialize an *ImageIcon* by creating a *SmallImageIcon* class that extends *ImageIcon* and implements *Externalizable*. Instead of using the `writeObject(...)` and `readObject(...)` methods we now use the `writeExternal(...)` and `readExternal(...)` methods. Our *SmallImageIcon* class looks something like this:

```
01:    public class SmallImageIcon extends ImageIcon implements Externalizable
02:    {
03:         public SmallImageIcon(String fileName)
04:         {
05:              super(fileName);
06:         }
                  .
             .    //The rest of the ImageIcon constructors ....
                  .
07:         public void readExternal(ObjectInput oi)
08:         {
09:            try
10:            {
11:                 setImageObserver((Image)oi.readObject());
12:                 setDescription((String)oi.readObject());
13:                 smallImage = ((SmallImage)oi.readObject());
14:                 // code to convert smallImage to Image
15:                 setImage(image);
16:            }
17:              catch(ClassNotFoundException cnfe) { //handle exception ... }
18:         }
19:         public void writeExternal(ObjectOutput oo)
20:         {
21:              out.writeObject(getImageObserver());
22:              out.writeObject(getDescription());
                  // code to convert image to smallImage
24:              out.writeObject(smallImage);
25:         }
26:    }
```

As you can see by the `readExternal(...)` and `writeExternal(...)` methods, we had to serialize all of the nontransient and nonstatic variables ourselves. Because we are implementing the *Externalizable* interface we do not have access to the default serialization methods. On the bright side, we have succeeded in creating a smaller serialized *ImageIcon* object. We are essentially doing the same thing as the *ImageIcon* class. We are serializing the nonstatic and nontransient members, and we are controlling the way the transient *Image* member gets serialized.

The key issue to remember is that Java objects by default are serialized from the superclass down to the subclass. You cannot override the serialization of a superclass by overriding the `readObject(...)` and `writeObject(...)` methods. You can, however, take complete control of the serialization of a class by implementing the *Externalizable* interface. When a class implements the

Externalizable interface, that class does not have access to the default serialization methods. It is also important to note that when a class implements the *Externalizable* interface, that class is responsible for working out how its superclass members get serialized. The serialization process is no longer recursive.

Item 24: Unicode, UTF, and Streams

Your boss just came in with the usual good news and bad news. The good news: Your Web site has just set a new company record for the most hits in a single day. The bad news: Your company wants to attract more international customers, and your boss needs a version of your applet in Spanish by next week. She tells you the translation has already been done, and she gives you a file that contains all the phrases you need in something called UTF format. *No problema*, you think; Java makes this easy, right? Yes, as long as you have a good understanding of some fairly tricky topics.

One of the nicest things about Java, or more accurately the JVM, is that it acts as a layer that protects you from the intricacies of operating system-specific behavior. Your code is portable from one system to another, without regard to the OS version, the OS, or even the hardware platform. But sometimes your programs must interact with the OS more directly, if only to persist state beyond the life of the JVM session.

One area in which this occurs is using the java.io classes. Anytime you read and write files, you're interfacing more closely with the native OS. When this happens, seemingly simple translations of Java *String* objects to and from files can lead to complex, confusing problems.

If your program never uses any characters outside of the normal ASCII set, you probably haven't encountered these problems. But more and more often, programmers are being asked to "internationalize" their applications. Perhaps, as in our example, you need to have a multilingual version of your applet. Java provides strong support that enables you to do this.

Because the subject of internationalization is complex enough for its own book, we focus on just a few issues as they relate to I/O. These issues are complex enough; in fact, we need to provide some background information on character encoding and streams before we go any further.

Unicode

You're probably already aware that Java uses a format called Unicode to encode characters. This explains the two bytes required for each character, instead of the one byte that languages like C require. What is Unicode? To quote the Unicode Consortium, "the Unicode Worldwide Character Standard is a character coding system designed to support the interchange, processing, and display of the written texts of the diverse languages of the modern world."

Currently, some 50,000 distinct characters are supported—a bit more complex than the 127 ASCII characters you're used to. If you're interested in the details, check out www.unicode.org.

UTF

In some ways, the Unicode Character Standard (UCS) is computer friendly. The first 127 characters equate to the ASCII standard, and, in fact, the first 256 characters match the ISO 8859-1 standard. Each character is represented by two bytes, which simplifies some types of processing. But there are some drawbacks. Storing two bytes for each character can waste bandwidth, especially if most of your data could be encoded with simple ASCII. More importantly, some sequences of bytes already have special meaning to the OS, and therefore UCS is not "file system safe."

These problems are addressed by a standard called UTF, which stands for UCS Transformation Format (though some sources incorrectly expand the acronym as universal text format or universal transfer format). There are different types of UTF, but essentially they provide a file system safe (and more efficient) representation of Unicode characters. For example, UTF-8 uses one byte to represent normal 7-bit ASCII characters, two bytes for 8-bit (and many other Unicode) characters, and three bytes for most of the others.

With that knowledge under your belt, you write a quick test program that reads and displays the phrases from the UTF file your boss gave you. Note that to simplify the example, line 16 simply reads a single line from the file; normally you would read each line in a *while* loop.

```
01: import java.awt.*;
02: import java.io.*;
03: import javax.swing.*;
04:
05: public class ReadUTF
06: {
07:   public static void main (String[] args)
08:   {
09:     try
10:     {
11:         File f = new File ("phrases.utf");
12:         FileReader r = new FileReader (f);
13:         BufferedReader in = new BufferedReader (r);
14:
15:         // read one line as an example
16:         String line = in.readLine();
17:         in.close();
18:
19:         JTextField text = new JTextField (lin);
20:         JDialog dialog = new JDialog
21:             ((Frame)null, "Read UTF", false);
22:         dialog.getContentPane().add (text);
```

```
23:          dialog.pack();
24:          dialog.show();
25:       }
26:    catch (IOException e)
27:       {
28:       System.out.println (e.getMessage());
29:       }
30:    }
31: }
```

Unfortunately, when the window pops up, it's not quite what you'd hoped for. As Figure 24.1 shows, your first international text is still encoded. Obviously, you have to do something special to decode the UTF into Java's internal Unicode representation.

Character decoding is done when the bytes are converted to characters. Because this happens behind the scenes, you need to understand how streams work to control the behavior.

Streams

In Java, streams are objects that allow you to move data from one form to another. For example, you can use a stream to read data from a thread or to write data to a file. The use is straightforward:

open a stream (this is done when the stream is instantiated)

read (or write) the data (usually in a while loop)

close the stream

The JDK provides quite a few stream classes, which can be somewhat confusing. Using streams is easy, but knowing which stream to use requires you to be familiar with most of them. Here are a few tricks to help you determine what the numerous stream classes do. Streams can be categorized in several ways, and understanding these categories can make it much easier to select the appropriate class for your purposes.

Input or Output

The most obvious attribute is whether the stream is designed to read or write data. Streams flow in one direction. Input streams provide `read` methods that pull data from a source, and output streams provide `write` methods that push

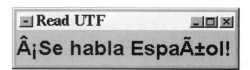

Figure 24.1   Incorrect ReadUTF display.

data to a destination. One stream object never does both, but the classes almost always come in pairs—one that reads and one that writes. JDK (java.io) class name will contain the word Input (or Reader) for input streams and Output (or Writer) for output streams.

A couple of classes seem to violate this one-way-only rule. The *Pushback-Reader* and *PushbackInputStream* provide a peek-ahead capability by allowing you to push data back into the stream. Subsequent read operations retrieve the data that was already read. This is implemented using an internal buffer, and it does not actually write the data back to the source. These classes greatly simplify the implementation of some parsing operations.

Bytes or Characters

Some streams deal with raw data in the form of bytes; others deal with characters. Byte streams are generally used to read and write binary data such as images. Character streams are used to read formatted data such as encoded text and numbers. The latter is often line-oriented data, and the character stream classes usually provide methods that read or write a whole line of data at a time. In some contexts, the term *stream* is used to refer primarily to byte streams, and *reader* or *writer* is used for character streams.

When possible, you should usually use character streams instead of byte streams. Character streams don't depend on a particular encoding format because they use Unicode. Also, they are typically more efficient than byte streams.

As the column headers in Figure 24.2 indicate, all input byte streams are descendants of the abstract *InputStream* class, and input character streams descend from the abstract *Reader* class. Likewise, output streams inherit from

Data Sinks		Input		Output	
		Byte	**Character**	**Byte**	**Character**
		InputStream	*Reader*	*OutputStream*	*Writer*
Memory		ByteArrayInputStream StringBufferInputStream	CharArrayReader StringReader	ByteArrayOutputStream	CharArrayWriter StringWriter
Pipe		PipedInputStream	PipedReader	PipedOutputStream	PipedWriter
File		FileInputStream	FileReader	FileOutputStream	FileWriter
Filters		*FilterInputStream**	*FilterReader* InputStreamReader	*FilterOutputStream**	*FilterWriter* OutputStreamWriter
		BufferedInputStream PushbackInputStream SequenceInputStream LineNumberInputStream	BufferedReader PushbackReader LineNumberReader	BufferedOutputStream	BufferedWriter
	Stream	DataInputStream CheckedInputStream DigestInputStream InflaterInputStream ProgressMonitorInputStream		DataOutputStream CheckedOutputStream DigestOutputStream DigestOutputStream	
				PrintStream	PrintWriter
		ObjectInputStream		ObjectOutputStream	

Figure 24.2 Stream classes.

OutputStream (for bytes) or *Writer* (for characters). In the figure, an italic font is used to indicate abstract classes. The lightly shaded background highlights the data sink streams.

FilterInputStream and *FilterOutputStream* are not declared abstract, but they do no processing on their own. They are essentially adapter classes for their descendents, and they make it easier for you to write custom filters.

Low Level or High Level

Some stream classes are low level and provide fine control over how the data is read or written; others provide a high-level, but friendlier interface. This distinction is more of a continuum than a simple dichotomy, and it is not reflected in the figure. As a guideline, if you find yourself having to work hard to read or write your data, see if there's another class that provides more sophisticated methods.

Data Sink or Filter

Streams can also be categorized by data source or destination type. Some read from (or write to) a data store directly, such as a file, a pipe, or an array in memory. These stores are called *data sinks*, a generic term that can refer to a source or destination. Data sink classes are used to convert data from an external format to a stream or from a stream to an external format.

Others stream classes are designed to read from and write to streams. These are called processing streams, or filters, because their purpose typically is to process the data. For example, the *Inflater* and *Deflater* streams are used to compress and uncompress data.

The simple way to tell the difference is to look at the constructors. Data sinks will always accept a nonstream object, and filters will always accept a stream (either *InputStream, OutputStream, Reader,* or *Writer*). Figure 24.2 indicates which classes are data sinks and which are filters.

Note that *pipe* streams are rather unique. Although their constructors do take streams, they're not filters, and they don't behave the same way. Input filters require input streams, and output filters require output streams. Pipes, on the other hand, reverse this: a *PipedInputStream* requires a *PipedOutputStream*, and vice versa. They are really data sink streams that happen to use other streams as their source or destination.

Chaining

Streams become more interesting, and much more powerful, when you use the output from one stream as the input for another stream. This is called *chaining*. Filters can usually be plugged into a process very easily because both their input and output are usually the same type, either *InputStream* or *Reader*. For example, a *BufferedReader* object is a *Reader*, and it requires a *Reader* when constructed.

There are two very useful exceptions to the homogeneous input/output rule. The *InputStreamReader* and *OutputStreamWriter* classes are used as a bridge between byte streams and character streams. They are character stream objects (*Reader* or *Writer*) that take byte streams (*InputStream* or *Output-Stream*) when constructed. These classes will be the key to solving our multi-lingual applet problem.

Adding a filter to your code is usually as easy as adding a single line and perhaps changing a variable name. We could remove line 13 from our program, and our code could almost work without any other changes. So why use filters? It depends on the filter, of course. In this case, the *BufferedReader* provides a `readLine()` method, which is easier than calling the `read()` method that *FileReader* pro-vides. Also, *BufferedReader* (like all the *Buffered* stream classes) allows the data to be processed in batches, and therefore it can be much more efficient.

Configurable Encoding

FileReader and *FileWriter* read and write 16-bit Unicode characters. Most native file systems use 8-bit bytes. Clearly, the characters must be encoded as they are read or written. These classes check a system property called *file.encoding* to determine what type of encoding to use. As usual, you can check this value by calling `System.getProperty` (*"file.encoding"*). When we did so, we found our system was set to "8859_1", which is the ISO 8859-1 standard, not UTF.

You're now well on your way to solving the character encoding problem. To use a different encoding format, you could change the *file.encoding* property. Or, more simply, you can use the *InputStreamReader*, which accepts an encod-ing format. You can insert a UTF *InputStreamReader* into your stream, between your *File* (line 11) and your *BufferedReader* (line 13). Because the *InputStreamReader* is a byte stream, you'll need to use the byte version of the file stream (*FileInputStream*) instead of the character version (*FileReader*). You can replace line 12 with the following:

```
12:    // FileReader r = new FileReader (f);
13:    FileInputStream is = new FileInputStream (f);
14:    InputStreamReader r =
15:        new InputStreamReader (is, "UTF8");
```

Running the program now produces the desired result, shown in Figure 24.3.

Figure 24.3   Correct ReadUTF display.

Item 25: Sending Serialized Objects over Sockets

In a complex set of interdependent APIs like the standard Java package (java.*), there are times when knowing the correct API calls is not enough. On occasion, it is necessary to study the documentation and maybe even examine the source code to understand how to properly use a complex object's API. Sending serialized objects over sockets demonstrates this principle well. The requirements for sending a serialized object are these:

Instantiate an `ObjectInputStream()`. This stream is layered on top of the socket's input stream, which is retrieved via a call to *getInput-Stream()*.

Instantiate an `ObjectOutputStream()`. This stream is layered on top of the socket's output stream, which is retrieved via a call to `getOutput-Stream()`.

Call `writeObject()` or `readObject()`. These streams are used to, respectively, send or receive objects.

The program ObjectSender1.java follows the previous steps to send an *Integer* object over a *Socket*.

```
01: /* ObjectSender1.java */
02: import java.io.*;
03: import java.net.*;
04:
05: public class ObjectSender1
06: {
07:     Socket s;
08:     ObjectInputStream ois;
09:     ObjectOutputStream oos;
10:
11:     public ObjectSender1(String host, int port) throws IOException
12:     {
13:         s = new Socket(host, port);
14:         ois = new ObjectInputStream(s.getInputStream());
15:         oos = new ObjectOutputStream(s.getOutputStream());
16:     }
17:
18:     public void sendObject(Object o) throws IOException
19:     {
20:         oos.writeObject(o);
21:     }
22:
23:     public static void main(String args[])
24:     {
```

```
25:          if (args.length < 2)
26:          {
27:            System.out.println("USAGE: java ObjectSender1 host port");
28:            System.exit(1);
29:          }
30:
31:          try
32:          {
33:              ObjectSender1 os1 = new ObjectSender1(args[0],
34:                              Integer.parseInt(args[1]));
35:              os1.sendObject(new Integer(3000));
36:              Thread.sleep(2000); // hang around a little
37:          } catch (Exception e)
38:            {
39:              e.printStackTrace();
40:            }
41:      }
42: }
```

The program ObjectReceiver1.java also follows the steps to receive an *Object* from the ObjectSender1 program. *ObjectReceiver* first instantiates a *Server-Socket* and accepts() a *Socket* connection from ObjectSender1.

```
01: /* ObjectReceiver1.java */
02: import java.io.*;
03: import java.net.*;
04:
05: public class ObjectReceiver1
06: {
07:      ServerSocket ss;
08:
09:      public ObjectReceiver1(int port) throws IOException
10:      {
11:          ss = new ServerSocket(port);
12:      }
13:
14:      public void listen() throws IOException, ClassNotFoundException
15:      {
16:          Socket s = ss.accept();
17:          ObjectInputStream ois = new ObjectInputStream(s.getInputStream());
18:          ObjectOutputStream oos = new ObjectOutputStream(s.getOutputStream());
19:          Object o = ois.readObject();
20:          System.out.println("Object: " + o);
21:      }
22:
23:      public static void main(String args[])
24:      {
25:          if (args.length < 1)
26:          {
27:              System.out.println("USAGE: java ObjectReceiver1 port");
28:              System.exit(1);
```

```
29:          }
30:
31:          try
32:          {
33:              ObjectReceiver1 or1 =
34:                  new ObjectReceiver1(Integer.parseInt(args[0]));
35:              or1.listen();
36:          } catch (Exception e)
37:            {
38:              e.printStackTrace();
39:            }
40:      }
41: }
```

Both ObjectSender1.java and ObjectReciever1.java compile just fine; however, when executed, they both immediately hang forever without sending a single object. A careful examination of the documentation reveals that instantiating the *ObjectInputStream* and *ObjectOutputStream* has side effects. This is unusual—you don't expect constructors to have side effects. *ObjectOutputStream* writes a stream header containing a magic number and version number that *ObjectInputStream* reads and verifies. *ObjectInputStream* blocks until it can read that file. Another peculiarity of this particular case is that instantiating an *ObjectInputStream* on top of a *FileInputStream* always succeeds immediately because it reads the header from the file instead of waiting for the *ObjectOutputStream* on the other side of the socket to write it. Knowing this, it is obvious why the two programs are hanging: They both instantiate `Object-InputStream()` first, which means that both sides of the socket are attempting to read a header that will never be sent. The result is blocking forever. The program ObjectReceiver2.java has the stream instantiations reversed, and thus it is able to successfully read the header and receive serialized objects.

```
01: /* ObjectReceiver2.java */
02: import java.io.*;
03: import java.net.*;
04:
05: public class ObjectReceiver2
06: {
07:     ServerSocket ss;
08:
09:     public ObjectReceiver2(int port) throws IOException
10:     {
11:         ss = new ServerSocket(port);
12:     }
13:
14:     public void listen() throws IOException, ClassNotFoundException
15:     {
16:         Socket s = ss.accept();
17:         ObjectOutputStream oos = new ObjectOutputStream(s.getOutputStream());
```

```
18:        ObjectInputStream ois = new ObjectInputStream(s.getInputStream());
19:        Object o = ois.readObject();
20:        System.out.println("Object: " + o);
21:    }
22:
23:    public static void main(String args[])
24:    {
25:        if (args.length < 1)
26:        {
27:            System.out.println("USAGE: java ObjectReceiver2 port");
28:            System.exit(1);
29:        }
30:
31:        try
32:        {
33:            ObjectReceiver2 or2 =
34:                new ObjectReceiver2(Integer.parseInt(args[0]));
35:            or2.listen();
36:        } catch (Exception e)
37:        {
38:            e.printStackTrace();
39:        }
40:    }
41: }
```

In general, a casual understanding of an API is often not enough. The Java packages are too extensive, robust, and interdependent for that to be effective. Luckily, the effort expended learning the Java APIs offers the benefit of "write once, run anywhere."

Item 26: Try, Catch . . . Finally?

Java programmers quickly become familiar with try and catch statements when using objects like URL and FileWriter—the Java compiler does not give them a choice. A program to create a new instance of FileWriter will not compile until either the FileWriter instantiation is placed inside a try block and the IOException is caught or the method prototype is modified to throw an IOException. Unfortunately, the Java compiler does not force the programmer to become familiar with the related finally statement. Why do we need it? Look at the code example that follows, and it may become apparent:

```
// This method does not guarantee that the FileWriter will be closed.
01:  public void printInfo()
02: {
03:    FileWriter fw = null;
04:    try
05:    {
```

```
06:          fw = new FileWriter("/export/home/kbohn/info");
07:          fw.write("some info");
08:          fw.close();
09:      }
10:      catch (IOException ioe)
11:      {
12:              // Handle the IOException …
13:      }
14:  }
```

At first glance, this code looks as if it will work just fine. A *FileWriter* object fw is created, some text is written, and the *FileWriter* object is closed. If the code inside a try block executes normally then the execution of the code does not enter any of the catch statements and continues normally.

But what if an *IOException* gets thrown by the *FileWriter*'s write method? If the try block does not complete normally, the execution of the program gets transferred to the nearest catch block for that type of exception. The code in the try block after the line in which the exception gets thrown does not get executed.

For example, if the code inside the try block causes exception type E to be thrown, the program looks for an immediate catch statement that handles a type E exception. This would be a catch block that declares the same class name parameter or parent class as exception type E. If an acceptable catch block is found, then the program's execution is transferred to that catch statement. The value of the exception is assigned to the parameter of the catch statement. If an acceptable catch block is not found after the try statement, then the exception gets thrown up the ladder in the same manner until an appropriate catch block is found. If no acceptable catch block is found, the program's thread will terminate after calling the uncaughtException method of the current thread's parent *ThreadGroup*.

In the previous code, if the call fw.write() on line 7 throws an IOException, the execution of the program gets transferred to the catch(IOException ioe) block on line 10. Therefore, the fw.close() call on line 8 never gets executed.

Does that simply mean a call to fw.close() needs to be added inside the catch(IOException ioe) block to make the program work whether an exception is thrown or not? It is true that adding a call in the code to fw.close() in the catch(IOException ioe) block guarantees that the *FileWriter* gets closed, whether or not an IOException gets thrown. But consider the code found in the code that follows, in which there are several catch statements after the try. An fw.close() call needs to be added to every catch statement. This makes the code harder to read and harder to maintain.

```
01: validateUnit(String unitId)
02:  {
03:  FileWriter fw = null;
```

```
04:  Try
05:  {
06:        fw = new FileWriter("/export/home/kbohn/unitLog");
07:        // getUnitName throws InvalidUnitException
08:        fw.write("Unit Name: " + getUnitName(unitId));
09:        // getUnitPrice throws InvalidPriceException
10:        fw.write("Unit Price: " + getUnitPrice(unitId));
11:        // getUnitQuantity throws QuantityUnavailableException
12:        fw.write("Unit quantity: " + getUnitQuantity(unitId));
13:        fw.close();
14:  }
15:  catch (InvalidUnitException iue)
16:  {
17:        // Handle the InvalidUnitException …
18:        if (fw != null)
19:        {
20:            try
21.            {
22:                  fw.close();
23:            }
24:            catch(IOException ioe)
25:            {
26:                  // Handle the IOException …
27:            }
26:        }
29:  }
30:  catch (InvalidPriceException ipe)
31:  {
32:        // Handle the InvalidPriceException …
33:        if (fw != null)
34:        {
35:            try
36:            {
37:                  fw.close();
38:            }
39:            catch(IOException ioe)
40:            {
41:                  // Handle the IOException …
42:            }
43:        }
44:  }
45:  catch (QuantityUnavailableException que)
46:  {
47:        // Handle the QuantityUnavailableException
48:        if (fw != null)
49:        {
50:            try
51:            {
52:                  fw.close();
53:            }
54:            catch(IOException ioe)
```

```
55:           {
56:                 // Handle the IOException …
57:           }
58:      }
59: }
60: catch (IOException ioe)
61: {
62:
63:      if (fw != null)
64:      {
65:          try
66:          {
67:               fw.close();
68:          }
69:          catch(IOException ioe)
70:          {
71:                 // Handle the IOException …
72:          }
73:      }
74: }
```

Simply adding the `fw.close()` call to all the catch statements is not an adequate solution because if another programmer modifies the `printInfo` method to throw new exceptions rather than catch them, then the burden is on the caller of `printInfo` to call the *FileWriter*'s `close` method. The Java compiler will certainly let the caller of `printInfo()` know that the new exceptions need to be caught or thrown, but the compiler will not remind the programmer that he or she needs to call the *FileWriter*'s `close` method.

The correct way to close the *FileWriter* is to add a finally block to the try and catch statements. The finally block gets executed if the try block executes normally or if the execution of the program gets transferred to one of the catch statements because an exception is thrown. A try-finally or a try-catch-finally block works the same way as the try-catch block with one important difference. The finally statement will be executed for each try block up the call ladder until an acceptable catch block is found. Placing the call to the `fw.close()` method in a finally block ensures that the call will be made and presents cleaner, more readable, and more maintainable code. The following code shows the correct way to handle the `fw.close()` call:

```
01: public void validateUnit(String unitId)
02: {
03:      FileWriter fw = null;
04:      Try
05:      {
06:          fw = new FileWriter("/export/home/kbohn/unitLog");
07:          // getUnitName throws InvalidUnitException
08:          fw.write("Unit Name: " + getUnitName(unitId));
09:          // getUnitPrice throws InvalidPriceException
```

```
10:                fw.write("Unit Price: " + getUnitPrice(unitId));
11:                // getUnitQuantity throws QuantityUnavailableException
12:                fw.write("Unit quantity: " + getUnitQuantity(unitId));
13:        }
14:        catch (InvalidUnitException iue)
15:        {
16:                // Handle the InvalidUnitException …
17:        }
18:        catch (InvalidPriceException ipe)
19:        {
20:                // Handle the InvalidPriceException …
21:        }
22:        catch (QuantityUnavailableException que)
23:        {
24:                // Handle the QuantityUnavailableException …
25:        }
26:        catch (IOException ioe)
27:        {
        // Handle the IOException …
28:        }
29:        finally
30:        {
31:                if (fw != null)
32:                {
33:                        try
34:                        {
35:                                fw.close();
36:                        }
37:                        catch(IOException ioe)
38:                        {
39:                                // Handle the IOException …
40:                        }
41:                }
42:        }
43: }
```

Using the finally statement in this example saved 31 lines of code compared to the previous block of code, and it used only one `fw.close()` call. Remember that the finally statement gets called if the try block executes normally or abnormally, so get in the habit of using the finally statement after all try blocks that require some cleanup.

Item 27: Flushing Image Resources

You've been asked to provide a GUI for a new video camera security system, VidGuard. The API to this system allows you to request an image. This request causes VidGuard to capture a frame from the live video feed and save that data as a JPEG image file. Your software requests and displays the image every 30 seconds or whenever the operator clicks a button to ask for it.

Java provides many classes that make handling image data quite easy. Luckily for you, built-in support is provided for JPEG and GIF formats. All you need to do is convert the file into an *Image* object and display it. The thumbnail design for your first approach might look something like this:

```
initialize:
    create the GUI
    add a button listener (let operator request update)
    start a timer that invokes update every 30 seconds

update:
    request a snapshot
    load the image file
    update the display to show the new image
```

After reading the online Java tutorial and scanning the documentation, you decide the *ImageIcon* class provided in the Swing extensions is the easiest way to do what you want. *ImageIcon* constructors take a filename or URL and return a displayable image. This approach is simple and elegant, but it is not quite sufficient.

When you run your program, it seems to work fine at first. The image capture works, and the image is displayed and updated every 30 seconds and when the operator clicks on the image button. You may not notice for hours, but the image never actually changes unless the program is restarted.

A few trace statements show that your code is requesting a new image properly, both when the *Timer* fires and when the operator clicks. Although you'd like to blame the VidGuard software, you can use another image-viewing program to confirm that the VidGuard file is being updated correctly. You can even delete the file, and your program still shows the old image! It looks like the JVM is ignoring your request to create a new image. You decide to write a quick program to test your theory:

```
01: import java.awt.*;
02: import java.awt.event.*;
03: import java.io.*;
04: import javax.swing.*;
05:
06: public class ImageFile
07: {
08:     public static void add (JPanel pnl, String name)
09:     {
10:         System.out.println ("Loading " + name);
11:         ImageIcon icon = new ImageIcon (name);
12:         JButton button = new JButton (icon);
13:         pnl.add (button);
14:     }
15:
```

```
16:    public static void main (String[] args)
17:    {
18:        JPanel panel = new JPanel();
19:
20:        ImageFile.add (panel, "left.gif");
21:        ImageFile.add (panel, "right.gif");
22:
23:        // swap image files to simulate an update
24:        File f1 = new File ("left.gif");
25:        if (f1.delete())
26:            System.out.println (f1.getName()+" rmvd");
27:        File f2 = new File ("right.gif");
28:        if (f2.renameTo (f1))
29:            System.out.println (f2.getName() +
30:                " renamed " + f1.getName());
31:
32:        ImageFile.add (panel, "left.gif");
33:
34:        JDialog dialog = new JDialog
35:            ((Frame)null, "ImageFile", false);
36:        dialog.getContentPane().add (panel);
37:        dialog.pack();
38:        dialog.show();
39:    }
40: }
```

Your program uses two GIF files, a left arrow and a right arrow. You load and display both. That works fine. Then you add some code (shown as lines 23–30) to delete the left-arrow GIF file and replace it with the right-arrow file. You then create a new image (line 32), which should contain the right-arrow image (even though the file name is now left.gif), and add it to your display. You now hope to see three arrows: left, right, right. The actual result (left, right, left) is shown in Figure 27.1.

```
> java ImageFile
Loading left.gif
Loading right.gif
left.gif rmvd
right.gif renamed to left.gif
Loading left.gif
```

Figure 27.1   Incorrect ImageFile display.

What's going on? As it turns out, the JVM caches the image data using the file name (or URL) as the key. The *ImageIcon* class uses the default `Toolkit` methods to load the image. The documentation for this class indicates that "The underlying toolkit attempts to resolve multiple requests with the same filename to the same returned Image. Since the mechanism required to facilitate this sharing of *Image* objects may continue to hold onto images that are no longer of use for an indefinite period of time . . ."

Even though this is a nice feature in the interests of efficiency, it makes your job as a developer a little more challenging. Because the time period is indefinite, you certainly can't write code that depends on the cache. But because that is the current implementation, you must write code that allows for it.

In this case, the VidGuard API allows you to specify the file name used to store the snapshot. Using a simple counter, you modify your code to change the name each time a request is made. Sure enough, the image now gets correctly updated.

But what if you have no control over the name of the data source? What if you're accessing a URL hooked to a remote live camera on some Web page? For our example, we use a URL (lines 45–46 in the code that follows) that shows an image of Times Square, updated every 15 seconds or so.

```
01: import java.awt.*;
02: import java.awt.event.*;
03: import java.net.*;
04: import javax.swing.*;
05:
06: public class LiveImage implements ActionListener
07: {
08:     JButton button;
09:     URL url;
10:     Timer timer;
11:     final int INTERVAL = 30 * 1000; // 30 seconds
12:
13:     public LiveImage (String title, String path)
14:         throws MalformedURLException
15:     {
16:         button = new JButton();
17:         button.addActionListener (this);
18:
19:         url = new URL (path);
20:         update();
21:         JDialog dialog =
22:             new JDialog ((Frame)null, title, false);
23:         dialog.getContentPane().add (button);
24:         dialog.pack();
25:         dialog.show();
26:
27:         timer = new Timer (INTERVAL, this);
28:         timer.start(); // calls actionPerformed
```

```
29:    }
30:
31:    public void update()
32:    {
33:        System.out.println ("Updating " + url);
34:        button.setIcon (new ImageIcon (url));
35:    }
36:
37:    public void actionPerformed (ActionEvent e)
38:    {
39:        update();
40:    }
41:
42:    public static void main (String[] args)
43:    {
44:        String title = "Times Square Live";
45:        String path = "http://images.earthcam.com/" +
46:            "ec_metros/newyork/newyork/lindys.jpg";
47:        try
48:        {
49:            new LiveImage (title, path);
50:        }
51:        catch (MalformedURLException e)
52:        {
53:            System.err.println (e.getMessage());
54:        }
55:    }
56: }
```

Because we have no control over the URL address, we can't change the key used to cache the image. You try to create a new *URL* object (using the same address), but that fails. We must find a way to force the JVM to discard the image cache. This is fairly easy (once you know about it). The *Image* class (which is accessible from your *ImageIcon* via the `getImage` method) provides a flush method.

As the documentation states, this method "flushes all resources being used by this *Image* object. This includes any pixel data that is being cached for rendering to the screen as well as any system resources that are being used to store data or pixels for the image. The image is reset to a state similar to when it was first created so that if it is again rendered, the image data will have to be recreated or fetched again from its source." Just what you wanted.

Adding a few lines of code at the beginning of your `update()` method (after line 33) works just fine. This has the added benefit of releasing the resources associated with the old images, so you wisely decide to update your VidGuard code as well.

```
ImageIcon icon = (ImageIcon) button.getIcon();
if (icon != null)
    icon.getImage().flush();
```

It's good to know about the flush method for other reasons, too. If you ever need to process large images, you'll probably want to avoid the *ImageIcon* class and use the lower-level interfaces instead. For example, the *MediaTracker* and *ImageConsumer* classes let you monitor the progress of the load operation that is running in another thread.

If you encounter an error while loading an image, you'll need to call flush to reset things before trying again. Loading errors can be fairly common, especially when a network is involved. Make sure you check for errors using a method like *MediaTracker*'s isErrorAny(), and always call flush if you detect a problem.

PART

Five

GUI Presentation

The source for determining whether or not a feature should be included in the product shouldn't rest solely on the technological underpinnings of that feature. The driving force behind the decision should not be that 'we have the technical capability to do this.' The primary factor should always be the goals of the user.

—ALAN COOPER, ABOUT FACE,
THE ESSENTIALS OF USER INTERFACE DESIGN

Cross platform graphical user interface frameworks are extremely difficult to create. The technical hurdles to overcome are substantial. There have been many attempts with mediocre results. In fact, many would argue that the Abstract Window Toolkit (the Java platform's first attempt at a cross-platform GUI) only achieved mediocre results. The necessity for and development of the Swing Components framework is testament to the deficiencies of the AWT. However, being built on top of the AWT means that dependencies still exist (and the corresponding added complexity due to such dependencies). So, in the end, due to the very nature of cross-platform graphical user interfaces, Java developers must master a complex API. The items in this part will help you do so. They are:

Item 28, "Providing Progress Feedback," examines one solution to the performance problem—improving the *perceived* performance.

Item 28: Providing Progress Feedback

Here's a scenario you're probably all too familiar with. You've just delivered a prototype of a new Java application to one of your customers at a beta test site. You want to make sure that your GUI is intuitive and easy to use, so you're anxiously watching as he tries the application for the first time.

He clicks the button to start your program. Nothing happens. He waits. Nothing happens. He clicks the button again, thinking he may have missed it the first time. He double-clicks it, thinking that may be how it needs to be started. You cringe, knowing he just started loading three more copies of your program into memory.

Although performance is improving with every release of the JVM, it is still a significant concern for Java developers. Anything you can do to improve the performance—or perceived performance—of your software needs to be considered. Providing appropriate feedback is often an easy and effective way to dramatically improve the perceived performance of a program.

Optimizing code to change the actual performance may be required—and we discuss some techniques that may help in Part 7, "Performance." But optimizing is something you generally want to put off until the end of the development phase. It tends to make the code more complex and therefore harder to debug.

If you're prototyping or using any kind of Rapid Application Development methodology, you probably want to avoid committing too many resources to optimization. You may just be wasting your time optimizing code that won't even end up in the final product.

The good news is that improving perceived performance is often quite easy to do, and we discuss some techniques in this section. There are some subtleties. If you subscribe to any Java developer mailing lists, you've probably seen this scenario described numerous times: "I added a ProgressBar to my application, but it never shows any progress until my application is done loading . . ." We solve that minor mystery for you in this section as well.

Using a Busy Cursor

One of simplest and most common ways to let your user know that something is going on is to use a "busy" cursor. A busy cursor is simply a cursor icon that makes it obvious to the user that the system is busy doing something. Some applications use a wristwatch icon, or a coffee cup, or a spinning globe; by default the JRE provides an hourglass.

All you need to do to change the cursor is to call the `setCursor` method on your component (usually your *JFrame* or *JDialog*) before beginning your operation. You can use the built-in *Cursor.WAIT_CURSOR* or one that's been customized for your application.

To be safe, you should capture the current cursor first, then restore it when your operation is complete. This wrapper approach allows you to safely perform nested operations that might change the cursor, too.

```
Cursor cursor = component.getCursor();
component.setCursor(new Cursor (Cursor.WAIT_CURSOR));
// do something here
component.setCursor (cursor); // restore it
```

As a convenience, you might consider providing a static method that does this for you, as illustrated in the code that follows. This technique is useful in some situations. To do it right, though, you really need to catch and throw a wrapped *Exception* so you can deal with possible errors that might occur in your invoked method:

```
01: import java.awt.*;
02: import java.awt.event.*;
03: import java.lang.reflect.*;
04: import javax.swing.*;
05:
06: public class BusyCursor
07: {
08:    public static Object invoke (Component c,
```

```
09:                                Object obj,
10:                                String meth,
11:                                Object[] arguments)
12:    {
13:       Object result = null;
14:
15:       Cursor cursor = c.getCursor();
16:       c.setCursor (new Cursor(Cursor.WAIT_CURSOR));
17:
18:       try
19:       {
20:         Class c = obj.getClass();
21:         Method m = c.getDeclaredMethod (meth, null);
22:         m.invoke (obj, arguments);
23:       }
24:       catch (Exception e) { }
25:
26:       c.setCursor (cursor);   // restore it
27:
28:       return (result);
29:    }
30:
31:    public void someSlowMethod() // just for demo
32:    {
33:       try { Thread.sleep (5000); }
34:       catch (InterruptedException e) { }
35:    }
36:
37:    public static void main (String[] args)
38:    {
39:       final BusyCursor demo = new BusyCursor();
40:
41:       final JFrame frame = new JFrame ("BusyCursor");
42:       JButton button = new JButton ("DO STUFF");
43:       button.addActionListener (new ActionListener() {
44:         public void actionPerformed (ActionEvent e) {
45:            BusyCursor.invoke
46:               (frame, demo, "someSlowMethod", null);
47:         }
48:       });
49:       frame.getContentPane().add (button);
50:       frame.pack();
51:       frame.setVisible (true);
52:    }
53: }
```

This example can be run to see how the concept works. Just click on the button, and watch the cursor change while the operation is performed. Figure 28.1 shows the results of that action. Note that this changes only the way the cursor looks. It does not disable the user's ability to click on another button, for example. But it's enough for most users to get the idea.

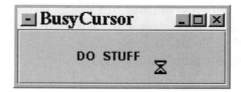

Figure 28.1 A busy cursor.

Although simple, this approach does have some drawbacks. Some applications don't have GUIs, and therefore you can't change their cursor at all. Also, some applications can take what seems like ages to start up, and so a visible interface doesn't exist until long after the user has decided something isn't working.

Personally, I prefer to use lazy loading (see Item 43) as much as possible, so that the initialization period can be minimized. Even so, there are times when an application just takes too long to start. In those cases, and for many other reasons, you may want to pop up a progress monitor of some sort.

Using a Progress Monitor

To monitor progress, you have a few options to consider. The online Swing Tutorial does a good job of explaining the *JProgressBar* and the *ProgressMonitor* classes and showing how to decide which one to use. For our purposes, we use the *ProgressMonitor* as displayed in Figure 28.2.

As evidenced in the mailing lists, lots of inexperienced developers have trouble using progress monitors. Almost always, the symptoms they describe are the same: Their progress monitor doesn't get updated until the end of the task being monitored. The solution is quite simple: Make sure you're monitoring progress in a separate thread.

In order to make that easy to do, we discuss two simple classes you can use: *Measurable* and *Monitor*. The *Monitor* class (found in the final block of code in

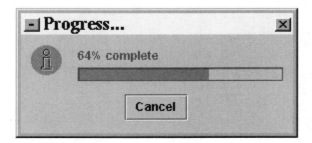

Figure 28.2 A progress monitor.

this item) provides an easy way to use a *ProgressMonitor* to provide visual feedback of a task. In order to use a single *Monitor* class with more than one task, we'll define a simple interface called *Measurable* (see the following code). Any task can be monitored if it implements this interface:

```
public interface Measurable
{
   public int getProgress();
   public String getActivity();
   public void stopTask();
}
```

The *Monitor* class will, in a separate thread, periodically ask the *Measurable* object what its current progress (line 40) and activity (line 50) are. We instantiate a *Timer* object (line 33) to cause an *actionPerformed* callback every second. This interval is arbitrary; it could obviously be a parameter in a more sophisticated implementation. You might even want to let the interval adapt depending on the progress being made.

The *Monitor* will then use the status information to update a *ProgressMonitor* (lines 50–51). It's up to the task being measured to respond in a meaningful way when asked for its current progress and activity.

Although the *ProgressMonitor* class does not require it, to keep our example simple we always use progress as a percentage value. Once our task's progress reaches 100, the *Monitor* knows it's complete and stops monitoring (lines 43–44).

One nice feature that *ProgressMonitor* provides is an interface that lets the user interrupt the task. Again, it's up to the task to react appropriately when the stopTask method is called. In our example (line 70), we simply call System.exit.

The *Monitor* class handles spawning a separate thread when you invoke the spawn() method (line 74). For a more robust approach, the *Monitor* class could extend *SwingWorker*. The *SwingWorker* class provides more control over the spawned thread, but we wanted to keep the code as simple as possible for this example.

```
01: import java.awt.*;
02: import java.awt.event.*;
03: import javax.swing.*;
04:
05: public class Monitor implements ActionListener
06: {
07:    private Measurable task;
08:    private ProgressMonitor pm;
09:    private Timer timer;
10:
11:    public Monitor (Measurable task)
```

```
12:     {
13:        this.task = task;
14:     }
15:
16:     public void spawn (final Component component)
17:     {
18:        Runnable worker = new Runnable() {
19:           public void run() {
20:              startMonitor (component);
21:           }
22:        };
23:
24:        Thread thread = new Thread (worker);
25:        thread.start();
26:     }
27:
28:     public void startMonitor (Component c)
29:     {
30:        pm = new ProgressMonitor (c,null,"",0,100);
31:        pm.setProgress (1); // force popup
32:        pm.setMillisToDecideToPopup (0);
33:        timer = new Timer (1000, this); // 1 second
34:        timer.start();
35:     }
36:
37:     // called each time the Timer fires
38:     public void actionPerformed (ActionEvent event)
39:     {
40:        int progress = task.getProgress();
41:        if ((progress >= 100) || pm.isCanceled())
42:        {
43:           pm.close();
44:           timer.stop();
45:           if (progress < 100)
46:              task.stopTask(); // interrupt
47:        }
48:        else
49:        {
50:           pm.setNote (task.getActivity());
51:           pm.setProgress (progress);
52:        }
53:     }
54:
55:     public static void main (String[] args) // demo
56:     {
57:        JFrame frame = new JFrame ("Monitor Demo");
58:        frame.setVisible (true);
59:
60:        Measurable task = new Measurable() {
61:           private int p;
62:           public int getProgress()
```

```
63:            {
64:                return (p += (int)(Math.random()*20));
65:            }
66:            public String getActivity()
67:            {
68:                return (p + "% complete");
69:            }
70:            public void stopTask() { System.exit(0); }
71:        };
72:
73:        Monitor monitor = new Monitor (task);
74:        monitor.spawn (frame);
75:        frame.setTitle ("Back in main thread");
76:    }
77: }
```

Item 29: Using repaint() Instead of validate() for Re-Layout of Components

Using the `Component.repaint()` method instead of the `Container.validate()` method does not produce the desired result when re-laying out components in a *Container*. The problem arises when you have a *Container* class (or subclass) to which you have been adding components. Normally all components are added to the *Container* class before it is displayed. When the container is displayed, the components that have been added to the container are positioned as you would expect them to be. But if a component inside the displayed container is moved, added, or deleted, the changes are not reflected in the display of the container.

Typically when a component needs to be redrawn on the screen a programmer calls the `Component.repaint()` method in order to trigger the `Component.update(...)` method. The `update(...)` method takes the *Graphics* object argument and uses it to render the component on the screen. This is the way most components are displayed (components with native peers usually rely on their native counterparts to do the rendering). We would assume that because the *Container* class is a subclass of the *Component* class, calling `repaint()` for updating the display of a container would also work. Let's see what happens when we try to add a component and move a component by calling `repaint()` to update the screen.

When you run the *TextFieldList* class, a window will be displayed with some buttons at the top and some text fields beneath it. The three buttons labeled *Dock >*, *Add Text Field*, and *Remove Text Field* perform the following functions: *Dock >* changes the location of the three buttons on the screen. On successive clicks the position of the buttons will be moved to the left, then the bottom, then the right, then the top again. *Add Text Field* adds a text field to the screen. *Remove Text Field* removes a text field from the screen.

```
001: import java.awt.*;
002: import java.awt.event.*;
003: import java.util.Vector;
004:
005: public class TextFieldList extends Frame implements ActionListener
006: {
007:     int       dockPosition = 0;
008:     int       textFieldTotal = 0;
009:     Button    dockButton = new Button("Dock >");
010:     Button    addTextFieldButton = new Button("Add Text Field");
011:     Button    removeTextFieldButton = new Button ("Remove Text Field");
012:     Panel     pButtons = new Panel();
013:     Panel     pCenter = new Panel();
014:     Vector    v = new Vector();
015:
016:     public TextFieldList (String title)
017:     {
018:         super(title);
019:
020:         setLayout(new BorderLayout());
021:         pButtons.setLayout(new FlowLayout());
022:         pCenter.setLayout(new FlowLayout());
023:
024:         pButtons.add(dockButton);
025:         pButtons.add(addTextFieldButton);
026:         pButtons.add(removeTextFieldButton);
027:
028:         dockButton.addActionListener(this);
029:         addTextFieldButton.addActionListener(this);
030:         removeTextFieldButton.addActionListener(this);
031:
032:         addTextField(pCenter);
033:         addTextField(pCenter);
034:         add("North", pButtons);
035:         add("Center", pCenter);
036:
037:         setSize(600,400);
038:         setVisible(true);
039:     }
040:
041:     private void addTextField (Panel p)
042:     {
043:         TextField tf = new TextField("Text: " + textFieldTotal, 30);
044:         v.addElement(tf);
045:         p.add(tf);
046:         textFieldTotal++;
047:     }
```

```
048:
049:        private void removeTextField (Panel p)
050:        {
051:            if (textFieldTotal > 0)
052:            {
053:                textFieldTotal—;
054:                p.remove((Component)v.elementAt(textFieldTotal));
055:                v.removeElementAt(textFieldTotal);
056:            }
057:        }
058:
059:        public void actionPerformed (ActionEvent evt)
060:        {
061:            Object source = evt.getSource();
062:
063:            if (source == addTextFieldButton)
064:            {
065:                addTextField(pCenter);
066:                pCenter.repaint();
067:            }
068:            else if (source == removeTextFieldButton)
069:            {
070:                removeTextField(pCenter);
071:                pCenter.repaint();
072:            }
073:            else if (source == dockButton)
074:            {
075:                remove(pButtons);
076:                switch (dockPosition)
077:                {
078:                    case 0:
079:                        add("West", pButtons);
080:                        break;
081:                    case 1:
082:                        add("South", pButtons);
083:                        break;
084:                    case 2:
085:                        add("East", pButtons);
086:                        break;
087:                    case 3:088:                        add("North", pButtons);
089:                        break;
090:                }
091:                if (dockPosition == 3)
092:                    dockPosition = 0;
093:                else
094:                    dockPosition++;
095:
096:                repaint();
097:            }
098:        }
```

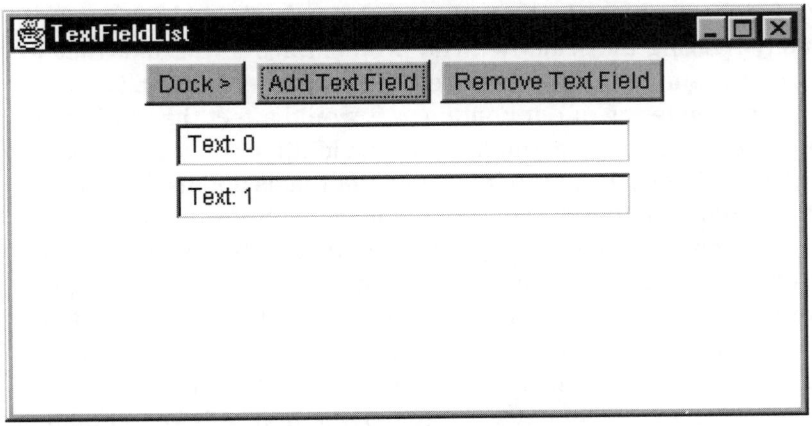

Figure 29.1   Components are not re-layed out.

```
099:
100:     public static void main (String args[])
101:     {
102:         new TextFieldList("TextFieldList");
103:     }
104: }
```

When the *TextFieldList* class is running, if you click the *Dock >* button twice and the *Add Text Button* three times, your window should look like Figure 29.1. As you can see, the screen still looks the same as when it first came up. If you resize the window manually the components that were added to the container and the button that was moved are now displayed in their proper position. After resizing your window it should look like Figure 29.2.

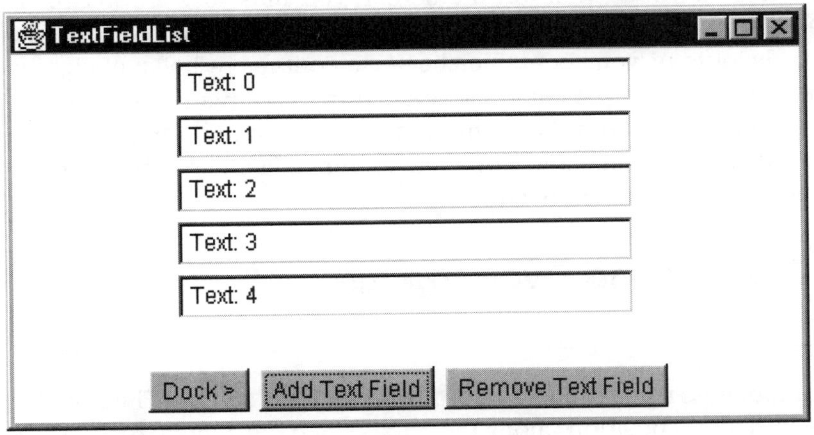

Figure 29.2   Components are re-layed out.

How do we fix the problem so that we can dynamically add components without manually resizing the window? The problem lies in the fact that we made an incorrect assumption. We assumed that calling `repaint()` would somehow affect the rendering of our container. It would affect the rendering if you put code in the `update()` method, but it would affect only the viewable part of the container, that is, the part of the container that is not displaying components. We know that containers use layout managers to position the components managed by the container, so this must be the source of the problem when adding or repositioning a component. Because the layout manager is responsible for positioning the components inside the container we must find a way to notify the layout manager to perform a re-layout. This can be accomplished using two methods available from the *Container* class: `invalidate()` and `validate()`. The `invalidate()` method tells the container that its current layout is not valid and a re-layout needs to be performed. The `validate()` method checks to see if the containers layout is invalid and, if it is, causes a re-layout of the container.

To make the *TextFieldList* class handle adds and moves dynamically, replace all calls to `repaint()` (lines 66, 71, and 96) with these two method calls:

```
invalidate()
validate()
```

When you run the modified source code you see that when you click the *Dock* > and *Add Text Field* buttons the window is updated dynamically. (Incidentally, the `remove()` method available in the *Container* class dynamically removes components from a container without a call to `repaint()` or calls to the `invalidate()` and `validate()` methods.)

The same issue exists in both the AWT and the Swing packages for add or moves of components, but not for removal of components. In Swing, to remove a *JComponent* from a *JContainer* on the screen you must use `repaint()` instead of the `validate()/invalidate()` pair. Be careful when you change the contents or layouts of your container because containers behave slightly differently from normal components. Use `validate()/invalidate()` for re-layout of containers for both AWT and Swing, `repaint()` for repainting components in AWT and Swing, and `repaint()` for re-laying out Swing containers when components are removed.

Item 30: Z-Order and Overlapping Components

Positioning components using X and Y coordinates is fairly simple. The X value represents the horizontal position (along the X axis), and the Y value represents the vertical position (along the Y axis). A Z coordinate can be used to represent a third dimension, or the depth of a component. The Z value specifies the position along the Z axis, a line from the viewer toward the screen.

The term Z-order is slightly different from a Z value. The Z-order refers to the relative position of a component along the Z axis with respect to other components. Simply put, Z-order determines which components appear to be in front of or behind which other components. Because most graphical user interfaces don't try to simulate three dimensions, the magnitude of the Z value is not usually important. The value is meaningful only as it relates to other Z values.

Layout Managers

Layout managers are used to position components within a container. Because computer screens are two-dimensional, most layout managers provide methods that accept only X and Y coordinates. With most of the layout managers provided by the JDK, a Z value is not necessary. It's not possible to specify components that overlap. Some managers, such as *GridBagLayout*, allow you to specify components at the same location. In general, though, if you use a layout manager to position components for you, you don't have to worry about the Z-order.

What if you want to position the components yourself, and you decide not to use a layout manager? This can be a common situation when dealing with graphics applications. For example, you may want to draw a pie chart and then add labels for each wedge. How can you force the labels to appear on top of the wedges?

If you handle the drawing yourself, then you simply draw the wedges first and then draw your labels. But what if you want to use components such as *JTextField* objects for your labels? When you add the components into a container (such as a *JPanel*), notice that the positioning methods (such as setBounds) allow you to specify the X and Y positions, but not the Z position.

The program that follows creates a simple bar chart and listens for mouse clicks. Different components are used for the background and the bars. Note that on line 15, we remove the default layout manager and then use the set-Bounds method to position the components (lines 29 and 39):

```
01:  import java.awt.*;
02:  import java.awt.event.*;
03:  import javax.swing.*;
04:
05:  public class BarChart extends JPanel
06:  implements ActionListener
07:  {
08:      static int barHeight = 40;
09:      int barCount;
10:
11:      public BarChart()
12:      {
```

```
13:        super();
14:        setPreferredSize (new Dimension (200, 200));
15:        setLayout (null);
16:
17:        addBackground(); // oops! must be done last
18:
19:        addBar ("March", 100, Color.red);
20:        addBar ("April", 120, Color.yellow);
21:        addBar ("May",   160, Color.green);
22:        addBar ("June",  130, Color.white);
23:    }
24:
25:    private void addBackground()
26:    {
27:        JButton background = new JButton();
28:        background.setActionCommand ("background");
29:        background.setBounds (0, 0, 200, 200);
30:        background.setOpaque (false);
31:        background.addActionListener (this);
32:        add (background);
33:    }
34:
35:    private void addBar(String lbl, int w, Color c)
36:    {
37:        JButton bar = new JButton (lbl);
38:        int y = barCount * (barHeight + 10);
39:        bar.setBounds (10, y, w, barHeight);
40:        bar.setBackground (c);
41:        bar.addActionListener (this);
42:        add (bar);
43:        barCount++;
44:    }
45:
46:    public void actionPerformed (ActionEvent e)
47:    {
48:        System.out.println
49:            ("Button = " + e.getActionCommand());
50:    }
51:
52:    public static void main (String[] args)
53:    {
54:        BarChart panel = new BarChart();
55:        JFrame frame = new JFrame ("BarChart");
56:        frame.getContentPane().setLayout
57:            (new BorderLayout());
58:        frame.getContentPane().add
59:            (panel, BorderLayout.CENTER);
60:        frame.pack();
61:        frame.show();
62:    }
63: }
```

If you run the program, everything looks fine at first, as shown in Figure 30.1. Because the "background" component is not opaque, each of the bars is visible. However, when you click somewhere, which component will get the event, the background or one of the bars? In other words, what determines the z-order of overlapping components?

The key is the order in which the components are added to the container. The *Container* class maintains an ordered list of components. Documentation in that class states "the order of the list will define the components' front-to-back stacking order within the container."

Intuitively, you might be inclined to create and add your components in the same order in which you want them drawn. First, you add your background, then your graph bars, and then your labels. That approach fails. Your background ends up covering your other components because components within a container are drawn in reverse order.

Amy Fowler (of Sun's Java Swing Team) explained this in a posting to the Advanced Java mailing list: "For 1.1, we wanted to make the stacking order be back-to-front (felt more natural compared to other toolkits), but because 1.0 defaulted to front-to-back, we were forced to spec it that way."

The documentation for the *Container* class has been updated to reflect this: "The order of the list will define the components' front-to-back stacking order within the container. If no index is specified when adding a component to a container, it will be added to the end of the list (and hence to the bottom of the stacking order)."

As a mnemonic, you might notice that components added on top in the code appear on top in the display. The previous code example shows this implemented in the wrong order. To fix it, simply move the `addBackground` call (line 17) after the *addBar* calls.

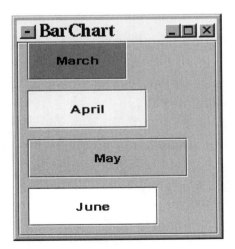

Figure 30.1   A BarChart.

You can also specify the Z-order indirectly by using one of the add methods that accepts the index argument:

```
add (component, 0);  // add on top
```

Note that the index (in this case zero) does not represent a depth, or relative Z-order, as in a *JLayeredPane* (discussed in the following subsection). The index refers to the position within the *Container*'s list. The list order, as you now know, is used to determine the components' Z-order. If you try to specify an index that is invalid (such as –5, or any number larger than the number of components within the container), the *Container* class throws an *IllegalArgumentException*.

You can't specify multiple components to be at the same depth by adding them at the same index: Only one component can occupy a given position within the list. In Sun's implementation of the JDK, the source code for the Java class libraries reveals that this list is implemented using an array. If you insert a second component at index zero, the component that was there (if any) will be pushed into the next position, and so on.

If you want to add the components in the order in which you want them drawn, then you could add them by specifying an index of zero, as shown in line 31:

```
01: import java.awt.*;
02: import javax.swing.*;
03:
04: public class ZOrder extends JPanel
05: {
06:     int h = 60;    // height
07:     int w = 100;   // width
08:     int overlap = h * 2 / 3;
09:     int buffer = 20;
10:
11:     public ZOrder()
12:     {
13:         super();
14:         setPreferredSize (new Dimension (350, 200));
15:         setLayout (null);
16:
17:         // add 3 buttons using w/o specifying index
18:         for (int i = 1; i <= 3; i++)
19:         {
20:             JButton bar = new JButton("default " + i);
21:             bar.setBounds (i*buffer, i*overlap, w, h);
22:             add (bar);
23:         }
24:
25:         // push 3 buttons onto the top of the stack
```

```
26:        for (int i = 4; i <= 6; i++)
27:        {
28:           JButton bar = new JButton ("stack " + i);
29:           bar.setBounds ((i * buffer) + 100,
30:               ((i-3) * overlap), w, h);
31:           add (bar, 0);
32:        }
33:     }
34:
35:     public static void main (String[] args)
36:     {
37:        ZOrder panel = new ZOrder();
38:        JFrame frame = new JFrame ("ZOrder");
39:        frame.getContentPane().setLayout
40:           (new BorderLayout());
41:        frame.getContentPane().add
42:           (panel, BorderLayout.CENTER);
43:        frame.pack();
44:        frame.show();
45:     }
46: }
```

The output of this program is shown in Figure 30.2. You can see how the components are ordered depending on which add method you use.

Unfortunately, some GUI development applications may not meet the newest Java specifications. For example, they may store the components in reverse order. So, your interface may look correct while in the IDE, but the components will appear in the opposite order when you actually run the program.

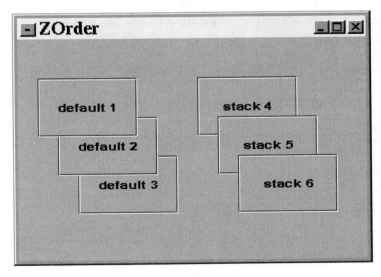

Figure 30.2   Demonstrating Z-order.

JLayeredPane

If your application is more complex than these examples, you should consider using a *JLayeredPane*. This container class implements real Z-ordering, so your components can be assigned to relative layers. Constants are defined for common layers, so that drag-away toolbars, modal dialogs, pop-up menus, and drag-and-drop components can be drawn on the appropriate layer.

The *JLayeredPane* class overrides the *Container* class's protected addImpl method. This means you can use the *Container*'s add (Component, Object) method with an *Integer* object for the constraints argument:

```
layeredPane.add (child, JLayeredPane.DEFAULT_LAYER);
```

Note that although you're sending an *Integer* object, the *constraints* argument is very different from the *int* index argument described previously. In this case, the *Integer* represents a relative Z-order. Lower values represent lower layers, which is the opposite of the list index last-in-first-out behavior. Although this discrepancy can be fairly confusing, the documentation for the *JLayeredPane* class describes this quite well.

You do need to remember that if you add more than one component to the same layer, you'll have to handle any overlap just as you would if you had only one layer. You can also move components from one layer to another (using the setLayer, moveToFront, or moveToBack methods), if you need to do something fancy.

You can examine the code example that follows, which shows our bar chart program rewritten using a *JLayeredPane*. The changes (in bold) are quite simple, but the components no longer need to be added in any particular order. Also, the intention of the code is clearer, so future changes are less likely to introduce bugs:

```
01: import java.awt.*;
02: import java.awt.event.*;
03: import javax.swing.*;
04:
05: public class BarChartLayered
06: extends JLayeredPane implements ActionListener
07: {
08:     static int barHeight = 40;
09:     int barCount;
10:
11:     public BarChartLayered()
12:     {
13:         super();
14:         setPreferredSize (new Dimension (200, 200));
15:         setLayout (null);
16:
```

```
17:          addBackground(); // order no longer matters
18:          addBar ("March", 100, Color.red);
19:          addBar ("April", 120, Color.yellow);
20:          addBar ("May",   160, Color.green);
21:          addBar ("June",  130, Color.white);
22:     }
23:
24:     private void addBackground()
25:     {
26:          JButton background = new JButton();
27:          background.setActionCommand ("background");
28:          background.setBounds (0, 0, 200, 200);
29:          background.setOpaque (false);
30:          background.addActionListener (this);
31:          int layer =
32:              JLayeredPane.DEFAULT_LAYER.intValue() - 1;
33:          add (background, new Integer (layer));
34:     }
35:
36:     private void addBar (String lbl, int w, Color c)
37:     {
38:          JButton bar = new JButton (lbl);
39:          int y = barCount * (barHeight + 10);
40:          bar.setBounds (10, y, w, barHeight);
41:          bar.setBackground (c);
42:          bar.addActionListener (this);
43:          add (bar, JLayeredPane.DEFAULT_LAYER);
44:          barCount++;
45:     }
46:
47:     public void actionPerformed (ActionEvent e)
48:     {
49:          System.out.println
50:              ("Button = " + e.getActionCommand());
51:     }
52:
53:     public static void main (String[] args)
54:     {
55:          BarChartLayered panel =
56:              new BarChartLayered();
57:          JFrame frame =
58:              new JFrame ("BarChart Layered");
59:          frame.getContentPane().setLayout
60:              (new BorderLayout());
61:          frame.getContentPane().add
62:              (panel, BorderLayout.CENTER);
63:          frame.pack();
64:          frame.show();
65:     }
66: }
```

Item 31: Solving the Validate, Revalidate, Invalidate Mystery

After 12 hours of programming, it is time to pack up and go home. If you live in the Washington, D.C. area, the hard part of your day may be just beginning. It could take you 30 minutes to get home, or depending on traffic, it could take you four hours to get home. Fortunately, several sites on the Internet post up-to-date images of the traffic at key locations on your route home. Based on the current traffic situation, you can adjust your route and avoid trouble spots. To view these Web sites, you can bring up the browser of your choice and bookmark the URLs for each image you need to see, or you can write a quick Java program that retrieves the traffic images for you and displays them in a scrollable window.

Because today was such a short day, you decide to stay a little late to begin coding your new Traffic Monitor application. The Traffic Monitor application consists of a *JFrame*, which contains a *JMenu Bar* and a *JScrollPane*. The menu bar contains the "Add" menu with an "Add Images" menu item. The scroll pane contains a panel, which holds the image for each location on your route home. When the "Add Images" menu item is selected, a thread will be spawned to retrieve each location image you would like to see. Each thread contacts the server and attempts to download the traffic image for that location. Once the image is downloaded, it is added to the panel in the scroll pane.

The code is complete, and you're eager to see the current traffic situation. You start the application, the GUI appears on the screen, and you click on the "Add Images" menu item. To your surprise, no traffic images appear in the GUI. After adding several debugging statements you determine that the threads are getting kicked off correctly, and the images are being downloaded and added to the panel. Everything seems to be working, yet nothing is displayed. That's when that little light bulb in your head starts to flicker. You realize that you have a dreaded repaint problem.

Because you know that your code works fine except for the "repaint" problem, you decide to write a small test program that simply adds a local image to the panel every time you click on the "Add Images" menu item. This avoids the delay that occurs as the program downloads the images from the traffic servers and speeds up the debugging process. The test program looks like this:

```
01:    public class Test
02:    {
03:      private int PREFERRED_WIDTH = 200;
04:      private int PREFERRED_HEIGHT = 75;
05:      private JPanel mainPanel;
06:      private JScrollPane scrollPane;
07:      private JFrame frame;
```

```
08:    public Test()
09:    {
10:        mainPanel = new JPanel(new FlowLayout(FlowLayout.LEFT));
11:        showFrame();
12:    }
13:    private void showFrame()
14:    {
15:        JMenuBar menuBar = new JMenuBar();
16:        JMenu menu = new JMenu("Add");
17:        JMenuItem item = new JMenuItem("Add Images");
18:        item.addActionListener(new AddIconListener());
19:        menu.add(item);
20:        menuBar.add(menu);
21:        scrollPane = new JScrollPane();
22:        scrollPane.getViewport().add(mainPanel);
23:        frame = new JFrame("Traffic Monitor");
24:        frame.getContentPane().add("North", menuBar);
25:        frame.getContentPane().add("Center", scrollPane);
26:        frame.setSize(PREFERRED_WIDTH, PREFERRED_HEIGHT);
27:        frame.show();
28:    }
29:    public class AddIconListener implements ActionListener
30:    {
31:        public void actionPerformed(ActionEvent ae)
32:        {
33:            try
34:            {
35:                URL url = new URL(("file:/images/SaveAs.gif");
36:                ImageIcon icon = new ImageIcon(url);
37:                JLabel label = new JLabel(icon);
38:                mainPanel.add(label);
39:            }
40:            catch(Exception e)
41:            {
42:                e.printStackTrace();
43:            }
44:        }
45:    }
46:    public static void main(String[] args)
47:    {
48:        Test test = new Test();
49:    }
50: }
```

The GUI in Figure 31.1 appears when you run the test program. But after clicking on the "Add Images" menu item, the GUI still looks the same. The icon did not appear in the panel. Here is where the fun begins. Let's find out why.

The Test class contains the following components: *JLabel, JPanel, JScrollPane,* and *JFrame.* From previous experience we know that calling

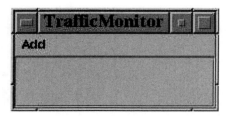

Figure 31.1 A broken traffic monitor.

repaint() or invalidate() or validate() or revalidate() will most likely solve the problem. We can call each of these methods on each of the components to figure out which one will work (except *Jframe*, which does not have the revalidate() method). It might not take that long to try each possibility until we get one to work, but it would be nice to have a more scientific understanding of the problem. If we understand the problem better, we can avoid the trial-and-error method of solving the problem and therefore solve the problem more quickly the next time we run into it. Let's start at the beginning. What exactly happens when we add *label* to the *mainPanel* in the actionPerformed method on line 38?

The *mainPanel* object sets itself as the parent of *label*. The *mainPanel* object then invalidates itself, which recursively invalidates all of its ancestors. At this point, *label* is a child of *mainPanel*, and every component from *mainPanel* up to *frame* has been marked as invalid. Because all of the components from *label* to *frame* have been marked as invalid, there is no reason to call invalidate on any of those components. Therefore, we can rule out calling invalidate as a possible fix to our bug. When the add(...) method on line 38 is finished, the program is in a state in which almost all of its components are invalid. From here, it's a good guess that we have to either revalidate or validate one or all of the invalid components to fix the problem.

If we take a quick look at the revalidate() method, we find that it will invalidate the calling component and recursively invalidate all of the calling component's ancestors. The calling component is then added to the *RepaintManager* as an invalid component. The *RepaintManager* will then call each ancestor's isValidateRoot() method until the first ancestor returns true. At this point the ancestor that returns true from its isValidateRoot() method will validate itself as well as recursively validate all of its children. By default the *JScrollPane*, *JRootPane*, and *JTextField* objects return true from their isValidateRoot() method. In this case, if we call mainPanel.revalidate(), *mainPanel* is invalidated, which recursively invalidates all of its ancestors. The *mainPanel* object is added to the *RepaintManager* as an invalid component. The *RepaintManager* finds the first ancestor to return true from its isValidateRoot() method. In this case, the *scrollPane* is the first ancestor to return true. The *RepaintManager* then calls scrollPane.validate(), which will validate all of its children as well. Now we know two good bits of information. The revalidate() method will invalidate itself and all of its ancestors, and the validate() method will validate itself and all of its children. We know the add(...) method has already invalidated all the ancestor components of *mainPanel*, and because we can call validate() to validate the components, we can remove revalidate() from our list of possible fixes.

Now let's see if the repaint() method can help. The repaint() method adds the calling component to the *RepaintManager* as a dirty region. The *RepaintManager* then repaints the dirty region. Repainting the dirty region, however, does not validate any of the invalid components. Repainting is mainly used for repainting existing components that are damaged. Calling repaint() does not force the layout manager to re-lay out the invalid components. Because repaint() will not validate any invalid components, we can now remove the repaint() method from our list of possible fixes.

The only method left to try is validate(). The validate() method will cause the layout manager to re-lay out its invalid components. Now we need to figure out on which component to call validate(). Because we know that the validate() method also validates all of the calling component's children, we could probably just call frame.validate() to fix the problem. But do we really need to validate the *frame* object? Let's try calling it from *label*, *mainPanel*, *scrollPane*, and *frame*. If we add label.validate() to the *Test* class after we call mainPanel.add(label) on line 38, we can see what happens. After running the program with this change, we find out that the display does not look any different than it did originally. Let's change label.validate() to mainPanel.validate(). After making this change, the icons finally appeared in our panel. Unfortunately, adding a bunch of icons to our display causes it to look like the one found in Figure 31.2.

Because we want the *scrollPane* to update automatically, it makes sense to call validate() on the *scrollPane* object. Let's replace mainPanel.validate() with scrollPane.validate(). After running the program with this change and adding several icons, we see that the display found in Figure 31.3 appears.

Figure 31.2 Traffic monitor without scrolling.

Figure 31.3 Traffic monitor with scrolling.

Calling `scrollPane.validate()` solved the problem so there is no need to call `frame.validate()`. Calling `scrollPane.validate()` is the most efficient way to solve our problem; however, there may be a situation in which we do not have access to the *scrollPane* object. In this case, we could call `get-Parent()` on the *mainPanel* object and walk up the ancestor chain until we find the first ancestor to return true from its `isValidateRoot()` method. We would then call `validate()` on that object. The other thing we could do is simply call `mainPanel.revalidate()`, which would essentially do the same thing. Remember, calling `mainPanel.revalidate()` invalidates *mainPanel* and all of its ancestors unless they are already invalid. The `revalidate()` method then adds the *mainPanel* to the *RepaintManager* as an invalid component. The *RepaintManager* then calls each ancestor's `isValidateRoot()` method until the first ancestor returns true. In this case, the first ancestor to return true from the `isValidateRoot()` method is the *scrollPane* object. The *RepaintManager* then calls `scrollPane.validate()`, which also validates its children. The key here is this: If you have access to the object that returns true from its `isValidateRoot()` method, then call `validate()` on that object. If you do not have access to the `isValidateRoot()` object, then call `revalidate()` on one of the children objects.

Item 32: Stacking Items Vertically

The layout managers provided in JDK 1.1 have been widely criticized as inadequate for all but simple graphical user interfaces. The exception to that criticism is the *GridBagLayout*, which is instead faulted for being too complex (see Item 33). The most common approach to overcoming the deficiencies of a single layout manager is to nest multiple panels, each with different layout managers, inside a frame. The *FlowLayout* manager increases the effectiveness of this "nested container" strategy by providing a simple way to position components in a horizontal line. A glaring omission in the original set of Java layout managers was a layout manager that behaved in the same manner as a *FlowLayout* but instead positioned items vertically. This item demonstrates two solutions to this problem: a custom layout manager and the new *BoxLayout* manager in the javax.swing package.

To illustrate the problem, consider the layout of a graphical form with a column of labels on the left and a column of text field and/or text areas on the right. Figure 32.1 presents such a form laid out with a *GridLayout*.

A quick examination of Figure 32.1 reveals the inadequacy of *GridLayout* in this situation. There is too much vertical space between components. This is

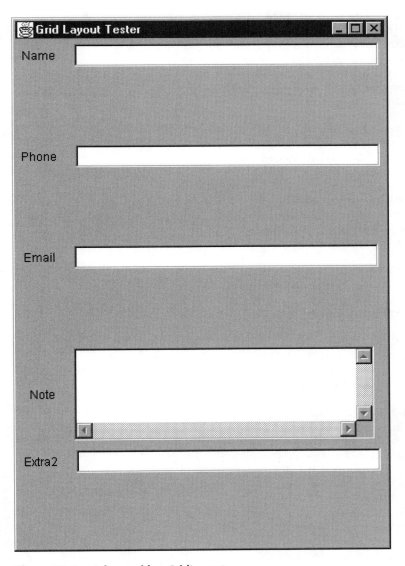

Figure 32.1 A form with a GridLayout.

due to the requirement of a *GridLayout* to have evenly spaced cells. Notice lines 18–41 in the listing for TestGridLayout.java that demonstrate the nested container strategy. The benefit of nested containers in this example is that we eliminated the horizontal space between our label and our text fields or text area:

```
01: /** TestGridLayout.java */
02: import java.awt.*;
03: import java.awt.event.*;
04:
05: public class TestGridLayout extends Frame
06: {
07:     TextField nameTextField;
08:     TextField phoneTextField;
09:     TextField emailTextField;
10:     TextArea noteTextArea;
11:     TextField extra2TextField;
12:
13:     public TestGridLayout()
14:     {
15:         super("Grid Layout Tester");
16:         setBackground(Color.lightGray);
17:
18:         Panel p1 = new Panel();
19:         p1.add(new Label("Name"));
20:         nameTextField = new TextField(40);
21:         p1.add(nameTextField);
22:
23:         Panel p2 = new Panel();
24:         p2.add(new Label("Phone"));
25:         phoneTextField = new TextField(40);
26:         p2.add(phoneTextField);
27:
28:         Panel p3 = new Panel();
29:         p3.add(new Label("Email"));
30:         emailTextField = new TextField(40);
31:         p3.add(emailTextField);
32:
33:         Panel p4 = new Panel();
34:         p4.add(new Label("Note"));
35:         noteTextArea = new TextArea(5,40);
36:         p4.add(noteTextArea);
37:
38:         Panel p5 = new Panel();
39:         p5.add(new Label("Extra2"));
40:         extra2TextField = new TextField(40);
41:         p5.add(extra2TextField);
42:
43:         Panel vPanel = new Panel();
44:         vPanel.setLayout(new GridLayout(5,1));
```

```
45:                vPanel.add(p1); vPanel.add(p2); vPanel.add(p3);
46:                vPanel.add(p4); vPanel.add(p5);
47:
48:            add("Center", vPanel);
49:            addWindowListener(new WindowAdapter()
50:                            {
51:                                public void windowClosing(WindowEvent we)
52:                                {
53:                                    System.exit(1);
54:                                }
55:                            });
56:            pack();
57:            setLocation(100,100);
58:            setVisible(true);
59:        }
60:
61:        public static void main(String args[])
62:        {
63:            new TestGridLayout();
64:        }
65: }
```

Line 44 of TestGridLayout sets up a single column to stack the panels vertically. This strategy works fine if all of the components being stacked (in this case
Panels) are the same height. Unfortunately, that is not the case. *GridLayout* is
inadequate for stacking different-sized components vertically. One way to solve
this problem is to create a custom layout manager. A *LayoutManager* is any
class that implements the *LayoutManager* interface. A layout manager specifies
a layout policy for positioning components within a container. A layout manager
asks each component how much space it needs, then arranges the components
as best as it can based on the component sizes and space available. Note: one of
the best reasons for layout managers is that when the window is resized, the layout manager can re-lay out the component automatically for the new size.

Here are the steps to implement a layout manager:

1. Create a class that implements the *LayoutManager* interface. Let's examine the *LayoutManager* interface:

```
01: package java.awt;
02: public interface LayoutManager
03: {
04:     void addLayoutComponent(String name, Component comp);
05:     void removeLayoutComponent(Component comp);
06:     Dimension preferredLayoutSize(Container parent);
07:     Dimension minimumLayoutSize(Container parent);
08:     void layoutContainer(Container parent);
09: }
```

2. The first two methods, addLayoutComponent() and removeLayout-
   Component(), are used if you need any special, component-specific,

information from the user in order to use the layout manager. The simplest example of this is the *BorderLayout*, which requires you to input the border direction for each component.

3. The next two methods are used for the layout manager to calculate the preferred and minimum size of all components in the container using this particular layout manager. In other words, the height and width of the container very much depend on your strategy for "laying out" the components.

4. The last method is by far the most important, yet it depends on the previous methods. The `layoutContainer()` method actually does the job of positioning the components in the container using the `setBounds()` method (formerly called `reshape()`).

5. Test your layout by setting your layout manager in the *Container* with the `setLayoutManager()` method.

Following is an example of a custom layout, *VerticalFlowLayout*, that stacks components one on top of another.

```
01: /** VerticalFlowLayout.java */
02: import java.awt.*;
03:
04: public class VerticalFlowLayout implements LayoutManager
05: {
06:     int iVerticalGap;
07:
08:     public VerticalFlowLayout()
09:     {
10:         iVerticalGap = 2;
11:     }
12:
13:     public VerticalFlowLayout(int vGap)
14:     {
15:         iVerticalGap = vGap;
16:     }
17:
18:     public void addLayoutComponent(String name, Component comp)
19:     {
20:         // Unnecessary we are not using the name to
21:         // differentiate components like some layout managers do.
22:     }
23:
24:     public void removeLayoutComponent(Component comp)
25:     { }
26:
27:     public Dimension preferredLayoutSize(Container parent)
28:     {
29:         return getLayoutSize(parent, false);
```

```
30:        }
31:
32:        public Dimension minimumLayoutSize(Container parent)
33:        {
34:            return getLayoutSize(parent, true);
35:        }
36:
37:        private Dimension getLayoutSize(Container parent, boolean min)
38:        {
39:            int iNumComponents = parent.getComponentCount();
40:            Dimension outDim = new Dimension(0,0);
41:            for (int i=0; i < iNumComponents; i++)
42:            {
43:                Component c = (Component) parent.getComponent(i);
44:                Dimension cDim = (min) ? c.getMinimumSize() :
45:                                            c.getPreferredSize();
46:                // width will be width of largest component
47:                outDim.width = Math.max (cDim.width, outDim.width);
48:                outDim.height += cDim.height;
49:                if (i != 0)
50:                    outDim.height += iVerticalGap;
51:            }
52:            Insets border = parent.getInsets();
53:            outDim.width += border.left + border.right;
54:            outDim.height += border.top + border.bottom;
55:            return outDim;
56:        }
57:
58:        public void layoutContainer(Container parent)
59:        {
60:            Dimension available = parent.getSize();
61:            Dimension required = preferredLayoutSize (parent);
62:            boolean useMinimum = required.height < available.height;
63:            Insets insets = parent.getInsets();
64:            final int x = insets.left;
65:            int y = insets.top;
66:            final int w = Math.max (available.width, required.width);
67:            final int excessHeight = available.height - required.height;
68:
69:            int count = parent.getComponentCount();
70:            for (int i = 0; i < count; i++)
71:            {
72:             Component comp = parent.getComponent (i);
73:             if (comp.isVisible())
74:             {
75:                int h = (useMinimum) ? comp.getMinimumSize().height :
76:                                    comp.getPreferredSize().height;
77:                if (excessHeight > 0)
78:                    h += (h * excessHeight / required.height);
79:                comp.setBounds (x, y, w, h);
80:                y += (h + iVerticalGap);
```

```
81:            }
82:          }
83:      }
84: }
```

The two key methods in the *VerticalFlowLayout* manager are the getLay-outSize() method and the layoutContainer() method. The purpose of getLayoutSize() is to calculate the required size (both minimum and preferred, based on the value of the *min boolean*) that the container will require using this layout manager. To perform this calculation, we iterate through all the components, get their preferred or minimum size, then add them based on this layout manager's policy. Lines 44–48 calculate the height and width. The width is the maximum width of the largest component in the container. The height is the sum of all the components' height including a vertical gap (spacing) between components. The layoutContainer() method actually does the job of positioning the components. The actual position of each component is performed using the setBounds() method. The setBounds() method has four parameters: X coordinate, Y coordinate, width, and height. If you wanted to determine the absolute position of components you could do so by setting the layout manager to *null* and use the setBounds() method. Lines 64 and 65 initialize our X and Y coordinates to just outside of the parent container's top and left borders (called insets). The policy for this layout manager is simple: All components are stacked vertically, which means the key requirement is to correctly modify the Y coordinate. Line 78 demonstrates an added feature in which we will stretch the component to fill extra vertical space. This is especially effective for text areas. Now we are ready to test our custom layout manager. The listing for TestVerticalLayout.java follows. Notice that the code is nearly identical to the preceding TestGridLayout.java listing.

```
01: /** TestVerticalLayout.java */
02: import java.awt.*;
03: import java.awt.event.*;
04:
05: public class TestVerticalLayout extends Frame
06: {
07:     TextField nameTextField;
08:     TextField phoneTextField;
09:     TextField emailTextField;
10:     TextArea noteTextArea;
11:     TextField extra2TextField;
12:
13:     public TestVerticalLayout()
14:     {
15:         super("Vertical Layout Tester");
16:         setBackground(Color.lightGray);
17:
```

```
18:         Panel p1 = new Panel();
19:         p1.add(new Label("Name"));
20:         nameTextField = new TextField(40);
21:         p1.add(nameTextField);
22:
23:         Panel p2 = new Panel();
24:         p2.add(new Label("Phone"));
25:         phoneTextField = new TextField(40);
26:         p2.add(phoneTextField);
27:
28:         Panel p3 = new Panel();
29:         p3.add(new Label("Email"));
30:         emailTextField = new TextField(40);
31:         p3.add(emailTextField);
32:
33:         Panel p4 = new Panel();
34:         p4.add(new Label("Note"));
35:         noteTextArea = new TextArea(5,40);
36:         p4.add(noteTextArea);
37:
38:         Panel p5 = new Panel();
39:         p5.add(new Label("Extra2"));
40:         extra2TextField = new TextField(40);
41:         p5.add(extra2TextField);
42:
43:         Panel vPanel = new Panel();
44:         vPanel.setLayout(new VerticalFlowLayout(5));
45:         vPanel.add(p1); vPanel.add(p2); vPanel.add(p3);
46:         vPanel.add(p4); vPanel.add(p5);
47:
48:         add("Center", vPanel);
49:         addWindowListener(new WindowAdapter()
50:                         {
51:                            public void windowClosing(WindowEvent we)
52:                            {
53:                                System.exit(1);
54:                            }
55:                         });
56:         pack();
57:         setLocation(100,100);
58:         setVisible(true);
59:     }
60:
61:     public static void main(String args[])
62:     {
63:         new TestVerticalLayout();
64:     }
65: }
```

Line 44 is where we set the *VerticalFlowLayout* manager. A run of *Test-VerticalLayout* produces Figure 32.2.

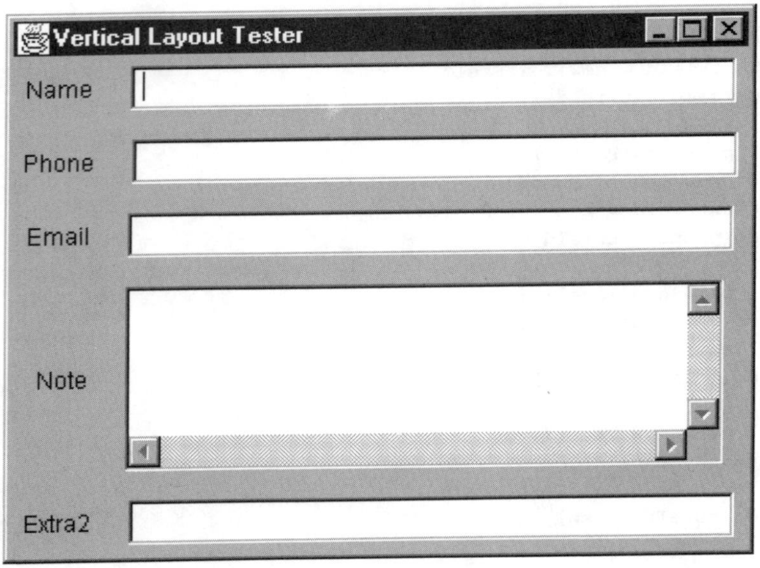

Figure 32.2   A form with a VerticalFlowLayout.

As Figure 32.2 demonstrates, the *VerticalFlowLayout* properly stacked different-sized components. With the *VerticalFlowLayout* in our set of layout managers, the nested container strategy is effective for the majority of user interfaces. Thinking along these same lines, the engineers at Sun Microsystems added a new layout with the introduction of the Java Foundation Classes called the *BoxLayout*. The *BoxLayout* is a layout manager that aligns components in either a horizontal or a vertical line. In effect, this layout combines the capabilities of both the *FlowLayout* and the *VerticalFlowLayout*. Using a *BoxLayout* to position the same form as the previous two examples produces Figure 32.3.

Along with the *BoxLayout* manager is a new container called a *Box*. The *Box* container is a convenience class to simplify using a *BoxLayout*. In fact, the source *TestBoxLayout* uses the static method in the *Box* class to create a *VerticalBox*, which is a container that uses a preconfigured *BoxLayout* manager to align components vertically.

```
01: /* TestBoxLayout.java */
02:
03: import javax.swing.*;
04: import java.awt.*;
05: import java.awt.event.*;
06:
07: public class TestBoxLayout extends Frame
08: {
09:     TextField nameTextField;
10:     TextField phoneTextField;
```

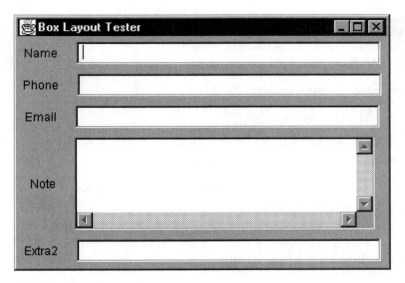

Figure 32.3   A form with a BoxLayout.

```
11:        TextField emailTextField;
12:        TextArea noteTextArea;
13:        TextField extra2TextField;
14:
15:        public TestBoxLayout()
16:        {
17:            super("Box Layout Tester");
18:            setBackground(Color.lightGray);
19:
20:            Panel p1 = new Panel();
21:            p1.add(new Label("Name"));
22:            nameTextField = new TextField(40);
23:            p1.add(nameTextField);
24:
25:            Panel p2 = new Panel();
26:            p2.add(new Label("Phone"));
27:            phoneTextField = new TextField(40);
28:            p2.add(phoneTextField);
29:
30:            Panel p3 = new Panel();
31:            p3.add(new Label("Email"));
32:            emailTextField = new TextField(40);
33:            p3.add(emailTextField);
34:
35:            Panel p4 = new Panel();
36:            p4.add(new Label("Note"));
37:            noteTextArea = new TextArea(5,40);
38:            p4.add(noteTextArea);
39:
```

```
40:              Panel p5 = new Panel();
41:              p5.add(new Label("Extra2"));
42:              extra2TextField = new TextField(40);
43:              p5.add(extra2TextField);
44:
45:           Box vBox = Box.createVerticalBox();
46:              vBox.add(p1); vBox.add(p2); vBox.add(p3);
47:              vBox.add(p4); vBox.add(p5);
48:
49:              add("Center", vBox);
50:              addWindowListener(new WindowAdapter()
51:                            {
52:                                public void windowClosing(WindowEvent we)
53:                                {
54:                                    System.exit(1);
55:                                }
56:                            });
57:              pack();
58:              setLocation(100,100);
59:              setVisible(true);
60:      }
61:
62:      public static void main(String args[])
63:      {
64:          new TestBoxLayout();
65:      }
66: }
```

In this item we have demonstrated two methods for vertically stacking items in a layout: a custom layout (*VerticalFlowLayout*) and the *BoxLayout* manager. When combined with the nested container strategy, these layout managers can be combined to properly position even complex user interfaces.

Item 33: How to Use GridBagLayout Properly

From a purely personal point of view, I must say that the *GridBagLayout* has been one of the most frustrating layout managers to use. When comparing it to the other Java layout managers, it seems out of place, as if it's too complicated to use. Other layout managers such as *BorderLayout* and *FlowLayout* are easy to grasp intellectually and easy to use. The *GridBagLayout* has a bit more meat to it than the other layout managers, although the concepts presented in the Javasoft documentation do not seem overly complicated. When you try to put these concepts into practice, however, odd things seem to happen. The description of this pitfall tries to unravel the mysteries behind this unintuitive behavior.

With a quick look at the Javasoft documentation and some reliance on my intuition, it seems to me that the *GridBagLayout* is simply a grid that gets built dynamically based on the components and their desired position. The *Grid-BagLayout* class works in conjunction with the *GridBagConstraints* class. Each component managed by an instance of *GridBagLayout* needs to have an associated instance of *GridBagConstraints*, which contains information for laying out the component. *GridBagConstraints* contains several properties, which include *gridx, gridy, gridwidth,* and *gridheight.* Using these properties to specify a component layout seems to make sense at an intuitive level. Let's look at an example:

```
01: import java.awt.*;
02:
03: public class LoginFrame
04: {
05:     public static void main (String args[])
06:     {
07:         Frame f = new Frame("Login");
08:         GridBagLayout layout = new GridBagLayout();
09:         f.setLayout(layout);
10:
11:         GridBagConstraints gbc = new GridBagConstraints();
12:         gbc.gridx = 1;
13:         gbc.gridy = 1;
14:         gbc.gridwidth = 2;
15:         gbc.gridheight = 1;
16:
17:         Label userNameLabel = new Label("User Name:");
18:         layout.setConstraints(userNameLabel, gbc);
19:         f.add(userNameLabel);
20:
21:         gbc.gridx = 3;
22:         gbc.gridy = 1;
23:         gbc.gridwidth = 4;
24:         gbc.gridheight = 1;
25:         gbc.fill = GridBagConstraints.HORIZONTAL;
26:         TextField userNameText = new TextField();
27:         layout.setConstraints(userNameText, gbc);
28:         f.add(userNameText);
29:
30:         gbc.gridx = 1;
31:         gbc.gridy = 2;
32:         gbc.gridwidth = 2;
33:         gbc.gridheight = 1;
34:         Button okButton = new Button("OK");
35:         layout.setConstraints(okButton, gbc);
36:         f.add(okButton);
37:
38:         gbc.gridx = 5;
```

```
39:            gbc.gridy = 2;
40:            gbc.gridwidth = 2;
41:            gbc.gridheight = 1;
42:            Button cancelButton = new Button("Cancel");
43:            layout.setConstraints(cancelButton, gbc);
44:            f.add(cancelButton);
45:
46:            f.setSize(300,150);
47:            f.setVisible(true);
48:        }
49: }
```

This example displays a frame that contains four AWT elements: a *Label*, a *TextField*, and two *Buttons*. The frame uses the *GridBagLayout* to lay out the components, and each component has an associated *GridBagConstraints* object that provides the layout information for the component to the *GridBagLayout*. Note that when the `setConstraints(...)` method is called on the instance of *GridBagLayout* it creates a copy of the *GridBagConstraints* object passed in. This is why this code needs to create only one instance of the *GridBagConstraints* object to use for all of the components. The intended layout I was expecting is shown in Figure 33.1. (Because there is no way to specify the overall size of the grid, I don't expect the white space to the right and bottom to actually appear.) The actual output of the code is depicted in Figure 33.2.

You can see that the components seem to clump together in the middle of the frame and that the relative sizes of the components I was hoping for seems to have been ignored. By looking at the *GridBagLayout* documentation I can see that my *weightx* and *weighty* parameters of the *GridBagConstraints* need to be set to something other than 0 to avoid this behavior. When they are set to 0, all leftover white space[1] gets added evenly to the edges. If we were to put the following two lines[2] immediately after line 15 the layout would now look like Figure 33.3.

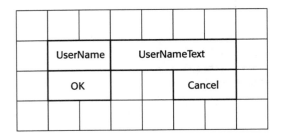

Figure 33.1   Expected component layout using GridBagLayout.

[1]The leftover white space is the amount of available space minus the sum of the component sizes.

[2]Note that since we are only using one *GridBagConstraints* object as our "template" we only need to set it at the beginning so that applies to all components.

```
gbc.weightx = 1;
gbc.weighty = 1;
```

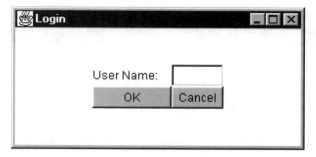

Figure 33.2   Actual component layout using GridBagLayout.

This seems to have solved the clumping problem, but the component proportions I was hoping for are still not being layed out properly. In fact, if you look at Table 33.1, you see that the *GridBagLayout* has opted to totally suppress some of the columns I was counting on for this layout. The table shows the column number (x coordinate), the weight assigned to the column, and the size of the column (in pixels). The same thing also happened for the rows in the layout.

Why is the *GridBagLayout* suppressing these columns and rows? The answer lies with the way it uses the contained components to calculate the weights and sizes. Let's see how the *GridBagLayout* calculates the column weights it needs to lay out the Login frame:

- It first looks at column components whose gridwidth = 1 (the default starting point). For those components `column_weight[gridx + gridwidth - 1] = weightx`. In our example we have no components whose gridwidth is 1, so no column weights get set.

- Next it looks at column components whose gridwidth = 2 (the next size component). For those components `column_weight[gridx + gridwidth - 1] = weightx`. Some logic is also performed for components

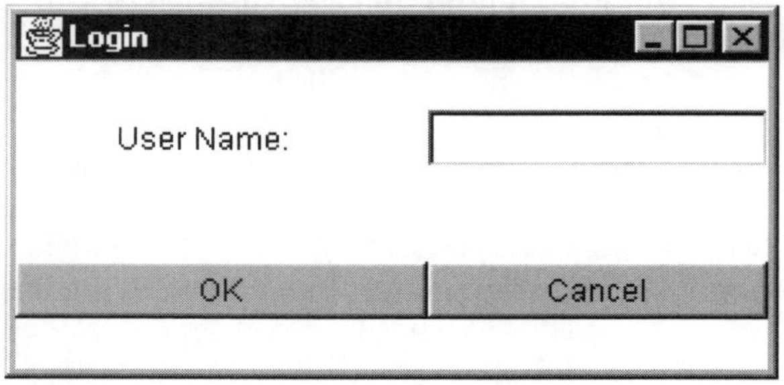

Figure 33.3   Component layout with *weight*s set using GridBagLayout.

Table 33.1 Weights and Sizes (in Pixels) of Columns in LoginFrame

COLUMN #	WEIGHT	SIZE
0	0.0	0
1	0.0	0
2	1.0	160
3	0.0	0
4	0.0	0
5	0.0	0
6	1.0	132

that exist in the same column. This logic is described this way: For all columns that a particular component encompasses, the column weights are added up. If these weights are the same or bigger than the existing component's weight, then the component's weight is ignored. Otherwise, the component's weight is distributed across the columns it spans. In our case, first the User Name label gets examined and the result is column_weight[2] = 1. Second, the OK button gets examined and because it is in the same row at the User Name label and has the same weight, its weight is ignored. Last we examine the cancel button, which results in column_weight[6] = 1.

■ Next it looks at column components of the next bigger size (this proceeds until all sizes have been examined). In our case, the next size is 4, and the same rules apply as in the previous steps. Because the User Name text field spans column 6, the weight associated with it gets discarded (because 6 already had the same weight).

Now you know how the weights are assigned, but how are those column sizes determined? Let's take a look at what the *GridBagLayout* is doing to determine column sizes.

GridBagLayout first calculates the minimum column sizes. It does this in a similar fashion to the weights described previously. The formula is:

```
column_minwidth[gridx + gridwidth - 1] =
component.getPreferredSize().width³ + ipadx + insets.left + insets.right.
```

Because the ipadx and insets are 0 in our example, the right side of the equation simplifies to just be the component's preferred width. Going through the list

---

[3]If it turns out the desired sum of the component's getPreferredSize() will not fit in the layout, it uses getMiniumSize() instead.

of our components, we first check components of size 2. The first is the User Name label, whose preferred width is 81 pixels. The next component of size 2 is the OK button, whose preferred width is 31. Because the *GridBagLayout* assigned these components to the same column, it takes the largest of the values, which is 81. Doing the same thing for the Cancel button and the User Name text field, we take the value of the preferred width of the cancel button, which is 53. Now we have column_minwidth[2] = 81 and column_minwidth[6] = 53.

The next step is to calculate the actual column widths based on the amount of space available for layout. The formula for this is:

```
column_size[index] = column_minwidth[index] + ((parent.width - (sum of all
column_minwidth[])) / (sum of all column_weight[])) * column_weight[index].
```

This formula calculates the amount of white space left over after the minimum column widths have been accounted for, and it distributes the white space proportionally, depending on the column weights. In our example, the amount of whitespace is 158 pixels (292 − 134).[4] Because the sum of weights across columns is 2.0, plugging these values back into the formula we get:

```
column_size[2] = 81 + (158 / 2) * 1 = 160 and
column_size[6] = 53 + (158 / 2) * 1 = 132
```

Now that the column sizes have been determined the *GridBagLayout* places the components in their assigned column and lays them out. During the layout process the *GridBagLayout* examines the *anchor* and *fill* properties of the associated constraints object to see how the component should be laid out within its provided area. The outcome of this laborious discussion on weight and column size calculation is that some columns can be totally suppressed (their weight and size are 0) and that the column sizes are controlled by the calculated minimum column sizes and additional white space as calculated by the column weights. Because this was not really the behavior I had expected (at least not at an intuitive level), we now have to figure out how to contend with this behavior to make the frame lay out as expected.

What we can do is use some properties of the *GridBagLayout* to override these calculations. The *GridBagLayout* supports the properties *columnWeights*, *columnWidths*, *rowWeights*, and *rowHeights* in order to override the sizes and weights calculated by the *GridBagLayout*. Each of these properties is an array that contains the new values. If we were to insert the following lines of code at line 10 we would see the frame in Figure 33.4. This is the result I had hoped for from the beginning.

---

[4]Sum of column_minwidth[] = 81 + 53 = 134. The parent.width is the amount of available area to layout in the container. We specified 300 for the width of the frame, however the size of the native window border on the left and right take up an additional 8 pixels. Therefore we have only 292 pixels left to use for the layout.

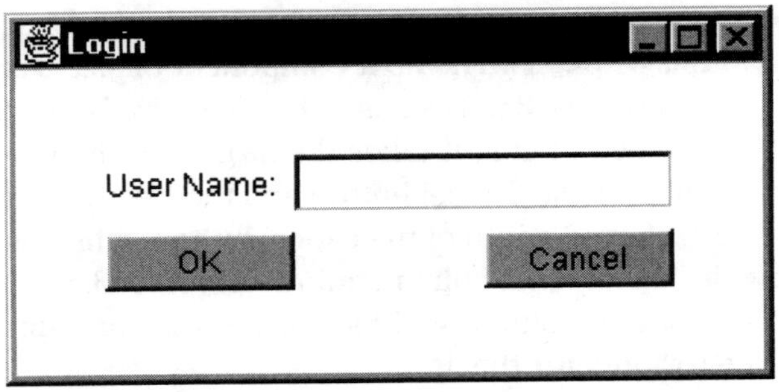

Figure 33.4   Desired layout using GridBagLayout.

```
layout.columnWeights = new double[8];
layout.columnWidths = new int[8];
for (int i = 0; i < layout.columnWeights.length; i++)
{
    layout.columnWeights[i] = 1.0;
    layout.columnWidths[i] = 100;
}

layout.rowWeights = new double[4];
layout.rowHeights = new int[4];
for (int i = 0; i < layout.rowWeights.length; i++)
{
    layout.rowWeights[i] = 1.0;
    layout.rowHeights[i] = 100;
}
```

In the example shown here I wanted to have areas of white space that I did not want to be suppressed. These areas were on the top, bottom, left, and right of the components so the layout looked centered. It is not possible to specify the exact size of white space areas like this without overriding the calculated values as I have done here. If your layout does not need areas of white space that need to be exactly calculated, you will be able to adjust the amount of white space between components based on the weights. Just to reiterate how the weights are used to distribute extra space, let's take a look at a simple example with two buttons.

```
01: import java.awt.*;
02:
03: public class WeightExample
04: {
05:     public static void main (String args[])
06:     {
07:         Frame f = new Frame("Weight Example");
08:         GridBagLayout layout = new GridBagLayout();
```

```
09:            f.setLayout(layout);
10:
11:            GridBagConstraints gbc = new GridBagConstraints();
12:            gbc.gridx = 0;
13:            gbc.gridy = 0;
14:            gbc.gridwidth = 1;
15:            gbc.gridheight = 1;
16:            gbc.weightx = 4;
17:            gbc.weighty = 1;
18:            Button b1 = new Button("Button 1");
19:            layout.setConstraints(b1, gbc);
20:            f.add(b1);
21:
22:            gbc.gridx = 1;
23:            gbc.gridy = 0;
24:            gbc.gridwidth = 1;
25:            gbc.gridheight = 1;
26:            gbc.weightx = 1;
27:            gbc.weighty = 1;
28:            Button b2 = new Button("Button 2");
29:            layout.setConstraints(b2, gbc);
30:            f.add(b2);
31:
32:            f.setSize(300,150);
33:            f.setVisible(true);
34:    }
35: }
```

In this code segment we are laying out two buttons, as shown in Figure 33.5. The first button has a weight of 4, and the second button has a weight of 1. Table 33.2 shows how size is calculated, following the procedures we discussed before for calculated weights and sizes.

Because we have a simple layout, we have two columns with equal weights of 1. Each component has a preferred size of 59 so this will be our minimum size. The actual size is computed by distributing the extra white space based on

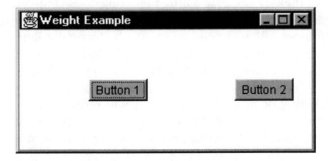

Figure 33.5 Layout with white space between components.

Table 33.2   Weights and Sizes (in Pixels) of Columns in WeightExample

COLUMN	#	WEIGHT	MINSIZE	SIZE
0	1.0	4	59	198
1	1.0	1	59	93

the weights. The size column can then be calculated (note that the decimal portion is dropped):

```
size[0] = 59 + ((292 - 118) / (4 + 1)) * 4 = 198
size[1] = 59 + (292 - 118) / (4 + 1) * 1 = 93
```

You should note that if we increase the width parameter in the constraint object associated with either component it has no effect on the layout. As seen earlier, these extra columns are suppressed.

Now that you have learned how the *GridBagLayout* actually performs its magic of calculating weights and sizes for layout, you are better prepared to use it with less trial and error. The key points to be aware of are the suppressing of columns, the distribution of white space, and the ability to override the calculated behavior by setting properties in *GridBagLayout*. The best way to go about this is to use graph paper to lay the components out, then run through the calculation exercises to see how your layout will look with *GridBagLayout*.

Item 34: Avoiding Flicker

Why does my window keep flickering when I draw on it? This is one of the most common questions asked by developers working on their first graphical application. If you've done any work at all with graphics, you have encountered this problem. Even some otherwise high-quality professional software applications exhibit this problem.

Why should you worry about flicker? Because a little flickering doesn't affect the functionality of the product, developers tend to ignore it. Correct implementation, though, results in more efficient code and a much cleaner-looking user interface. Although solving the problem is fairly easy, it does require a good understanding of the paint mechanisms in Abstract Windowing Toolkit (AWT) and Swing.

First, what is flicker? Flickering occurs when you clear and redraw something that you really don't need to. Although the drawing may happen very quickly, the human eye is pretty good at detecting change. This can result in a rather disturbing interface.

Flickering happens when the background of a window is cleared or repainted, which then requires the objects in the foreground to be redrawn. What causes all this repainting to occur? A paint request can be triggered several ways. Because AWT and Swing have some important differences in the way components are painted, we discuss them separately.

Painting in AWT

The system triggers a paint request whenever a component is made visible or resized. The application triggers a request when the state of a component changes. For example, clicking on a button can result in a different screen representation, to indicate a pressed button. There are some important differences in the way the AWT handles system- versus application-triggered paint requests.

We discuss this in more detail later in this section, but here's an overview first. When the paint request is triggered, the windowing toolkit uses a callback to invoke the `paint` method on the component. Specifically, for a *java.awt. Component*, this method to override is:

```
public void paint (Graphics g)
```

This *Graphics* object is initialized to provide the appropriate color, font, X/Y offset, and clipping rectangle for your component. You can change these as you like, but you have to use this object to render your output.

In line 35 of the following example application, the `mouseDragged` method calls `repaint`. Rather than calling `paint` directly, this is the preferred way to asynchronously request a paint operation. It provides immediate feedback as the person uses the mouse to draw on the screen. The `repaint` method can be invoked in various ways. The simple, no-argument method is appropriate in many cases. For efficiency, though, you may need to use one of the other constrained methods if your output is complex or time-consuming.

It's important to understand exactly which methods will be called when the paint request occurs. For system-triggered requests, the AWT simply causes the event dispatching thread to invoke `paint()` on the component. For application-triggered requests, the program typically calls `repaint()`, which registers a request to the AWT. The AWT then causes the event dispatching thread to invoke a method called `update()`.

These requests are handled asynchronously. If multiple requests are registered before the first one is handled, the AWT is smart enough to combine these requests into a single operation. If the region constraints are different, the request that is eventually triggered uses the union of all the regions.

By default, the `update()` method simply clears the component's background and then calls `paint()`. This clearing of the background is the most common cause of flickering, as running the program that follows demonstrates. This is a simple drawing program, which displays a multicolored striped background, and lets the user drag the mouse to draw lines on it. Each line is stored as a *Rectangle* object, which is simply a convenient way to store the end-points of the line:

```
01: import java.awt.event.*;
02: import java.awt.*;
03: import java.util.Vector;
04:
05: public class AvoidFlicker extends Panel
06: implements MouseMotionListener, MouseListener
07: {
08:     Vector lines = new Vector();
09:     int x, y;
10:
11:     public AvoidFlicker1()
12:     {
13:         addMouseMotionListener (this);
14:         addMouseListener(this);
15:     }
16:
17:     public void mouseClicked   (MouseEvent e) { }
18:     public void mouseEntered   (MouseEvent e) { }
19:     public void mouseExited    (MouseEvent e) { }
20:     public void mouseMoved     (MouseEvent e) { }
21:     public void mouseReleased  (MouseEvent e) { }
22:
23:     public void mousePressed   (MouseEvent e)
24:     {
25:         x = e.getX();
26:         y = e.getY();
27:     }
28:
29:     // add lines as the user drags the mouse
30:     public void mouseDragged (MouseEvent e)
31:     {
32:         lines.addElement
33:           (new Rectangle (x, y, e.getX(), e.getY()));
33:         x = e.getX(); y = e.getY();
35:         repaint();
36:     }
37:
38:     public void paint (Graphics g)
39:     {
40:         // paint the background (stripes of color)
41:         Dimension size = getSize();
42:         for (int y = 0; y < size.height; y += 2)
```

```
43:        {
44:            int blue = 255 - (y % 256);
45:            Color color = new Color (128, 128, blue);
46:            g.setColor (color);
47:            g.fillRect (0, y, size.width, 2);
48:        }
49:
50:        // paint the foreground (user-drawn lines)
51:        g.setColor (Color.black);
52:        int numberOfPoints = lines.size();
53:        for (int i = 0; i < numberOfPoints; i++)
54:        {
55:            Rectangle r =
56:                (Rectangle) lines.elementAt (i);
57:            g.drawLine (r.x, r.y, r.width, r.height);
58:        }
59:        super.paint (g); // always call for container
60:    }
61:
62:    public static void main (String[] args)
63:    {
64:        AvoidFlicker panel = new AvoidFlicker();
65:        Frame f = new Frame ("Avoiding Flicker");
66:        f.add ("Center", panel);
67:        f.setSize (300, 300);
68:        f.show();
69:    }
70: }
```

Because the update() method clears the background, drawing on the component causes an ugly flashing effect. How can we avoid it? Obviously, we need to stop the update() from clearing the background. That's easy; we simply override update() to look like this:

```
// override so background is not cleared
public void update (Graphics g)
{
    paint (g);
}
```

That's a pretty good start. If you add that method to the *AvoidFlicker* class and run the new version, you'll see it's much improved. The ugly flashing is gone, but if you look closely you'll still notice a flickering effect as the line is drawn. What's happening now? Each time you call paint(), the background of the component is drawn, and then the foreground lines are drawn top of it. Drawing the background essentially clears the foreground, which causes the flickering effect.

Suppose you could just change your paint() method to draw only the background the first time it's called. You might try something like this:

```
public void paint (Graphics g)
{
   if (firstTime)
   {
      firstTime = false;
      // paint the background
      ...
   }
   // paint the foreground
   ...
}
```

That won't work. The paint() method has to redraw the component completely (at least within the given clipping rectangle). Your program must assume that the area defined by the *Graphics* object's clipping rectangle needs to be redrawn. Because your window may become obscured (such as when another window is drawn on top of it), the paint() method must always redraw the background. In graphics terminology, this is often referred to as "damage"; redrawing the component repairs the damage.

The key to the correct solution is in the update() method. Unlike paint(), update() does not have to assume that the component has been damaged. This allows the update() method to draw only the things it needs to, in this case the foreground lines. This is often called incremental painting.

If we modularize our code a bit (always a good idea in any case), we can replace the paint() method with two simpler methods and then call them.

```
void paintBackground (Graphics g)
{
   ...
}

void paintForeground (Graphics g)
{
   ...
}

public void paint (Graphics g)
{
   paintBackground (g);
   paintForeground (g);
}
```

The update() method can now be smarter by just calling paintForeground():

```
public void update (Graphics g)
{
   paintForeground (g);
}
```

If you update the *AvoidFlicker* class and run it now, you'll notice the flicker is gone.

Painting in Swing

So far we've discussed the painting as it is handled in the Abstract Windowing Toolkit (AWT) classes. There are some important differences in the way Swing components work. For this example, the most significant difference is that Swing provides built-in support for double-buffering.

Each *JComponent* has a property that determines whether it is rendered using double-buffering. Support for this is implemented at the level of a containment hierarchy (basically a window), however, so the property on the container overrides all of its components. Generally, you'll want double-buffering to be on, and this is the default value for that property.

Double-buffering means that the components are actually drawn in a second (off-screen) buffer and then moved onto the screen. This results in smoother, flicker-free graphics. If fact, if we convert the original flawed program example to use Swing instead of AWT components, the flickering problem won't even occur.

Try it and see. The conversion is fairly simple; only a few lines need to change. First, add an import line:

```
import javax.swing.*;
```

Change the AWT components to be Swing components by renaming *Panel* to *JPanel* (line 5) and *Frame* to *JFrame* (line 65). Then remove line 59, the call to `super.paint(g)`.

Also unlike the AWT, Swing does not call the `update()` method when painting components. You can simply override the `paint()` method and let Swing solve the flicker problem for you. An even better implementation could take advantage of Swing's additional paint methods. Overriding `paint()` will work, but in Swing, `paint()` actually calls `paintComponent()`, `paintBorder()`, and `paintChildren()`. Usually you should just override the component's `paintComponent()` method.

Although, in general, using Swing components does avoid the flicker problem, you may need to make your painting code a little smarter. Because Swing doesn't allow you to override the `update()` method, your entire component (background and foreground in this example) gets painted each time *paint-Component*( ) is called. If your paint code is time-consuming, you may have to use the clipping region more often and repaint only the areas that need repainting. Understanding the paint/repaint/update mechanisms allows you to produce significantly better code.

Item 35: Components with Embedded HTML

Did you ever volunteer for one of those tasks that you thought would take you a couple of hours and ended up taking you a couple of weeks? Consider this task: Find all the tool tips that are too long for their GUI and modify them so they take up several lines instead of one really long line. How long do you think it will take you to complete this task? Let's say it turns out that there is only one tool tip that you have to fix. Now how long do you think it will take you? Ten minutes, maybe an hour if you decide to surf the net a bit before you check your task in?

You are confident that the only thing you have to do is place a "\n" inside the tool tip where you want it to wrap to the next line. After trying this approach, you realize it does not work. The tool tip that you modified seemed to contain an extra space instead of wrapping on to a new line. Plan A is a bust. Let's move on to plan B. But, what is plan B? How else can you get a string to wrap to the next line? Now how long do you think it will take you?

After surfing the net for a while you notice some loosely documented feature that lets you embed HTML in certain *JComponents*. You have found plan B! Not only can you force a line wrap using HTML, but you can also do things like underline, bold, change fonts, italicize, and much more. You will really impress your boss when you submit your task with marked-up tool tips. Let's create some test code to try out this functionality.

```
01:   public class TestHTML
02:   {
03:       private static final int PREFERRED_WIDTH = 200;
04:       private static final int PREFERRED_HEIGHT = 100;
05:
06:       public TestHTML()
07:       {
08:           JFrame frame     = new JFrame("Test");
09:           JToolBar toolBar = new JToolBar();
10:           // save button
11:           JButton saveButton = new JButton(loadIcon("save.gif"));
12:           saveButton.setToolTipText("Save");
13:           toolBar.add(saveButton);
14:           // bold button
15:           JButton boldButton = new JButton(loadIcon("bold.gif"));
16:           boldButton.setToolTipText("<html><b>Bold</b></html>");
17:           toolBar.add(boldButton);
18:           // underline button
19:           JButton underlineButton =
20:                   new JButton(loadIcon("underline.gif"));
21:           underlineButton.setToolTipText("<html><u>Underline
22:           </u></html>");
```

```
23:          toolBar.add(underlineButton);
24:          // line wrap button
25:          JButton lineWrapButton =
26:                  new JButton(loadIcon("linewrap.gif"));
27:          lineWrapButton.setToolTipText("<html>Toggle
28:          line<br>wrap</br></html>");
29:          toolBar.add(lineWrapButton);
30:          // exit button
31:          JButton exitButton = new JButton(loadIcon("exit.gif"));
32:          exitButton.setToolTipText("Exit");
33:          toolBar.add(exitButton);
34:          frame.getContentPane().add("North", toolBar);
35:          frame.pack();
36:          frame.setSize(PREFERRED_WIDTH, PREFERRED_HEIGHT);
37:          frame.show();
38:      }
39:
40:      public static void main(String[] args)
41:      {
42:          new TestHTML();
43:      }
44:  }
```

The test code above creates a JToolBar with a save, bold, underline, word wrap, and exit button. On line 16 we set the tool tip text for the bold button using HTML tags to indicate that we want the tool tip to be bold. The tool tip looks like the one found in Figure 35.1.

On line 21 we set the tool tip text to be underlined using the underline HTML tag. And on line 26 and 27 we set the tool tip text to line wrap using the break HTML tag. The underline and line wrap tool tips look like those found in Figures 35.2 and 35.3.

The tool tips look great, but here is the catch. This functionality exists only on certain versions of Java. Also, embedded HTML is supported only for certain

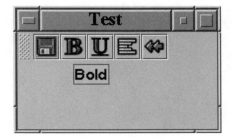

Figure 35.1   Bold tool tip.

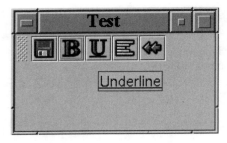

Figure 35.2   Underline tool tip.

Figure 35.3   Line wrap tool tip.

components, and only a subset of HTML tags are supported. The table found in Figure 35.4, shows the current HTML support.

Notice in the Swing 1.1.1 Beta 2 version you can also add embedded HTML to *JMenuItems*. Let's add a menu bar to our *TestHTML* class and experiment a bit. Here is the code needed to add some menu items to our frame:

```
01:   JMenuBar menuBar = new JMenuBar();
02:   JMenu menu = new JMenu("test");
03:   JMenuItem boldItem = new JMenuItem("bold");
04:   JMenuItem underlineItem = new JMenuItem("underline");
05:   boldItem.setMnemonic('b');
06:   underlineItem.setMnemonic('u');
07:   menu.add(boldItem);
08:   menu.add(underlineItem);
09:   menuBar.add(menu);
10:   frame.setJMenuBar(menuBar);
```

Adding this code to the previous class produces a screen shot of standard menu items, found in Figure 35.5.

API Version	Corresponding JFC 1.1 Release	Corresponding Java 2 Release	Status of HTML support
Swing 1.1	JFC 1.1 (with Swing 1.1)	Java 2 v 1.2, Java 2v 1.2.1	HTML supported in styled text components only.
Swing 1.1.1 Beta 1	JFC 1.1 (with Swing 1.1.1 Beta 1)	*none*	HTML support added for JButton on JLabel. Because table cells and tree nodes use labels to render strings, tables, and trees automatically support HTML as well.
Swing 1.1.1 Beta 2	JFC 1.1 (with Swing 1.1.1 Beta 2)	*none*	HTML support added for JMenuItem, JMenu, JCheckBoxMenuItem, JRadioButtonMenuItem, JTabbedPane, and JToolTip.
Swing 1.1.1 *(expected)*	JFC 1.1 (with Swing 1.1.1) *(expected)*	Java 2 v 1.2.2.2 *(expected)*	Same as Swing 1.1.1 Beta 2.

Figure 35.4 Component support for HTML.

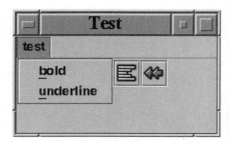

Figure 35.5   Standard menu items.

Notice that the bold menu item has an underscore beneath the "b," and the underline menu item has an underscore beneath the "u" to illustrate the keyboard mnemonics. Now let's beef up our menu items and add some HTML. We will change the bold and underline menu items to the following:

```
01:    JMenuItem boldItem =
02:            new JMenuItem("<html><b>bold</b></html>");
03:    JMenuItem underlineItem =
04:            new JMenuItem("("<html><u>underline</u></html>");
```

After adding HTML to our menu items we get the screen shot found in Figure 35.6.

Our HTML looks great, but what happened to our mnemonic underscores? Sorry, but I don't know. I hope that in newer releases of Swing this problem will be fixed. I just wanted to point out that the HTML feature is out there to use; it is cool, but there are still some problems. Continue checking Sun's Web site for more documentation regarding embedded HTML support. There is no doubt that this new feature will be enhanced and made more robust. It is also important to note that there is currently no programmatic way to tell if a given component supports embedded HTML. At the moment you should use this feature only if your code is guaranteed to be running on a Java version that supports it.

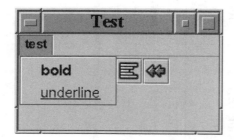

Figure 35.6   HTML menu items.

GUI Control

MVC consists of three kinds of objects. The Model is the application object, the View is its screen presentation, and the Controller defines the way the user interface reacts to user input. Before MVC, user interface designs tended to lump these objects together. MVC decouples them to increase flexibility and reuse.

–GAMMA, HELM, *JOHNSON, AND VLISSIDES, DESIGN PATTERNS: ELEMENTS OF REUSABLE OBJECT-ORIENTED SOFTWARE*

My favorite analogy for navigating through a user interface is driving a car. A good user interface should be fun to drive. It should corner well and hug the road. It should be fast and responsive. So, when you sit down in front of the GUI you just created, ask yourself "Is this GUI a Ferrari or a Model T?" This part should help you create more responsive user interfaces. The items in this part are as follows:

Item 36, "Better Data Validation," examines several techniques to improve your application's data validation. This item includes discussions on filtering, post-entry validation, and asynchronous validation.

Item 37, "Desensitizing GUI Components Based on Application State," examines multiple approaches to desensitizing components and suggests the best approach for your applications.

Item 36: Better Data Validation

Data entry is often a critical part of GUI applications. After the installation process, it's often the first experience with your product that a prospective customer will have. It's also the gate to your castle—the first chance you have to protect the integrity of your data. Invalid data can result in serious and often unexpected problems. Even seemingly minor problems with data can result in catastrophic system failures. Consider the $300 million Mars Climate Orbiter mission that crashed because one team used metric units and one did not.

Providing bad data is also one of the most common techniques hackers use to break into systems. An otherwise secure Web site can be breached simply by entering a carefully constructed invalid argument to a CGI program.

At some level, most programs have to make assumptions about the data they use. For efficiency, you just can't have every method validate all of its arguments each time an argument is invoked. Therefore, the earlier you can perform this validation, the better.

Most programmers test their code using valid data. More experienced ones know how to test the boundary conditions. Really good testers try to break their programs using data most users would never think of entering. After all, if your GUI allows a user to enter invalid data into your system, whose fault is it?

Because data validation often goes hand in hand with data entry screens, it's important to ensure that the implementation is user friendly. Ideally, it should not even be possible for the user to enter bad data into your form. At a minimum, the data must be validated before it actually gets processed. In this section, we discuss some techniques for doing both.

Tailored Components

Whenever possible, ensuring valid input means using an interface that constrains (without hampering, we hope) the user. There are numerous options: pick lists, combo boxes, sliders, palettes, and others. Good interfaces are often highly customized components, closely tied to a particular type of data. A very good interface can greatly facilitate the data-entry process. You can provide default values, history lists of previous entries, context-sensitive selections, single-key selection, and many other bells and whistles.

But sometimes forcing the user to select each value from a list of valid ones is less than ideal. It may be acceptable (even desirable) in some cases, but it has its limits. Selecting a date from a calendar pop-up is fine, but having to click each digit on a calculator interface can be irritating.

Lots of Web pages make this mistake in the interest of ensuring valid address data. Selecting the abbreviation for your state is nice if you live in Alabama, but not so great if you have to slide off three submenus to get to Virginia. As a rule of thumb, menus with five to nine items are good. Fifty is too many. Use a *ComboBox*, and let me just type the two letters.

Filtering

In some cases you simply have no choice; the data must be typed in. The idea behind filtering is to prevent the input of invalid data. As an example, let's implement a simple form that allows a user to enter a temperature. Because it will be used to control the temperature of our nuclear reactor's cooling tanks, we decide to spend the extra hour to ensure that the values will be valid.

Although a *JSlider* component might be ideal for similar situations, we might need to allow very precise temperatures. There are lot of real numbers between 0 and 1, after all. So, if we concede that the temperature must be typed in, how can we ensure that our Homer Simpson will enter only valid values? We *could* check each character to ensure that it is in the range 0 through 9, but that approach can lead to all sorts of problems.

What if you have to deal with floating-point numbers? Or negative numbers? OK, you could add '.' and '-' into your list of valid characters. But then what about Arabic numbers? The Java Unicode characters for those digits aren't in the 0 through 9 range. What about exponents? 6.0221367E23 could certainly be considered a valid number (at least by Avogadro), but it would fail your test because "E" is not a digit. How about hexadecimal numbers?

Well, we want our filter class to be reusable, but we also want it to filter out bad data. We'll compromise. We can use the *Character* class to solve some of these problems. The isDigit() method would at least deal with the internationalization issue. When you have to filter keystrokes, this is probably your best option.

Consuming Events

Now that we have an approach, how do we actually intercept the invalid characters before they can get into our form? The key to this is Java's *InputEvent* class. Input events can be intercepted. The documentation notes that "Input events are delivered to listeners before they are processed normally by the source where they originated. This allows listeners and component subclasses to 'consume' the event so that the source will not process them in their default manner."

We can implement a *KeyListener* fairly easily. All we need to do is provide a keyTyped method that either ignores the key or filters it by consuming the event. To give the user some feedback, we'll beep when an invalid key is typed. Because most of our code is general purpose, we'll use an abstract class. That way, customizing the filter requires just a few lines of code.

```
01: import java.awt.*;
02: import java.awt.event.*;
03:
04: public abstract class FilterAdapter
05: implements KeyListener
06: {
07:     static Toolkit tk = Toolkit.getDefaultToolkit();
08:     boolean audio = true;
09:
10:     public FilterAdapter (Component comp)
11:     {
12:         comp.addKeyListener (this);
13:     }
14:
15:     public void enableAudio (boolean status)
16:     {
17:         this.audio = status; // enable audio feedback
18:     }
19:
20:     public abstract boolean isKeyValid (KeyEvent e);
21:
22:     // implement KeyListener
23:     public void keyTyped (KeyEvent e)
24:     {
25:         if (e.isActionKey()) // ignore action keys
26:             return;
```

```
27:           if (isKeyValid (e))
28:              return;
29:
30:           e.consume (); // filter this keystroke
31:           if (audio)
32:              tk.beep ();
33:        }
34:     public void keyPressed  (KeyEvent e) { }
35:     public void keyReleased (KeyEvent e) { }
36: }
```

Then, to get a filter that allows only numeric data, we just need to extend *Filter* and implement the isKeyValid method. Note that if we wanted, we could modify isKeyValid to allow negative signs or other potentially numeric characters. We also have to explicitly allow the *backspace* and *delete* keys (lines 16–17). You can't actually consume these events, but if you don't allow them our *Filter* will beep whenever they're typed.

```
01: import java.awt.*;
02: import java.awt.event.*;
03:
04: public class NumericFilter extends Filter
05: {
06:     public NumericFilter (Component comp)
07:     {
08:        super (comp);
09:     }
10:
11:     public boolean isKeyValid (KeyEvent e)
12:     {
13:        char c = e.getKeyChar();
14:        return (Character.isDigit (c) ||
15:               (c == '.') || // decimal point
16:               (c == KeyEvent.VK_BACK_SPACE) ||
17:               (c == KeyEvent.VK_DELETE));
18:     }
19: }
```

To use this filter, you simply instantiate it using any *Component*. There, now we've prevented the user from entering invalid data—almost. It's still possible to enter a value like "98.6.1," and the JVM won't like that when we try and convert it into a number.

Post-Entry Validation

Sometimes it's simply not possible to filter out all bad data. For example, a user might want to enter a ZIP code. You can't use filtering to prevent a one-digit number from being entered. A ZIP code with fewer than five digits isn't valid, but it might be on its way to becoming valid.

In cases like this, you must validate the data after it's already been entered. That doesn't mean that you have to wait until the user submits the entire form. There's nothing that irks a user more than entering a lot of data, only to find out afterwards that the format she used is not the one your system allows.

One popular technique is to validate the field when it loses focus—for example, when the user presses the Tab key to move to the next field. This is especially good if your validation process is slow. If you have to perform a database search or a remote method invocation to validate the data, you don't want to do this every time the user types a key. If you do use this approach for efficiency, you want to avoid validating the data unless it has actually changed. That way, simply "tabbing" through your fields does not require revalidation that results in an unresponsive interface.

Efficiency permitting, a better method would be to validate the data any time it changes. Providing immediate feedback generally helps a user learn your system, too. Because most data-entry operations are fairly slow (in CPU terms anyway), this approach is often reasonable for many types of validation.

Design Issues

First, we need some infrastructure. You should keep several goals in mind when designing your data validation classes. You want to be able to plug in different validators with your data source. For example, you may want to validate a telephone number, a Social Security number, a credit card number, an IP address, or a date of birth. Java interfaces make this fairly easy; simply define an interface called *Validator* and have each class implement it.

The only mandatory requirement for a data validator is that it provides a method that accepts data and returns true or false to indicate the validity of that data. Our interface ensures this with the `isValid(Object)` method in line 7.

Although you can't use the static attribute in your interface, it's a good idea to provide a static method that validates a given value. We've done this in lines 31–36 of the Numeric Validator code listing. Note that we avoided duplicating any code by calling the `isValid` method. Then any program can use your validator with a single line of code:

```
if (MyValidator.accepts (data))
```

Asynchronous Validation

Because validation is often used with data entry forms, you want to add some methods to facilitate this. The validator needs to know when the data source changes. So how do we trigger this immediate validation? You might be tempted to use a *KeyEvent* as we did to filter the data. If you try to retrieve the value, you'll find it does not reflect the user's keystroke. Remember, input events are sent to the listeners before they are processed by the source. We must rely on the data source to provide an appropriate event for us.

Typical data entry components produce events in which a validator can listen for asynchronously. For this example, we take advantage of Swing's *Document* interface (lines 10–12). All *JTextComponent* objects provide access to their data model, which implements the *Document* interface. This interface allows us to listen for changes to the data.

If you want your validators to be even more reusable, you could eliminate this coupling by defining and implementing your own *ValueChanged* interface. In the interest of brevity, we won't add that level of abstraction.

```
01: import java.util.EventListener;
02: import javax.swing.event.DocumentEvent;
03: import javax.swing.event.DocumentListener;
04:
05: public interface Validator extends DocumentListener
06: {
07:    public boolean isValid (Object value);
08:    public boolean validate (Object value);
09:    // implement DocumentListener
10:    public void removeUpdate  (DocumentEvent e);
11:    public void changedUpdate (DocumentEvent e);
12:    public void insertUpdate  (DocumentEvent e);
13:    // support StatusListeners
14:    public void addStatusListener (StatusListener l);
15:    public void
16:       removeStatusListener (StatusListener l);
17: }
```

You'll also want your validator to inform interested observers whenever the *state* of the data changes. In other words, the validator should fire an event when a change in the data source results in a change in the validity. That way, a listener that cares only about whether the data is valid doesn't have to listen for changes in the data—just changes in the state. For example, you may have a Wizard GUI that needs to enable the Next or Finish button when the user has entered valid data. We take care of this by requiring our validator to implement add and remove methods for *StatusListeners* (lines 14–16). The implementation of these classes is provided in the code listing that follows.

```
01: import java.util.EventObject;
02:
03: public class StatusEvent extends EventObject
04: {
05:    private Object value;
06:    private boolean status;
07:
08:    public StatusEvent
```

```
09:        (Object source, Object value, boolean status)
10:    {
11:        super (source);
12:        this.value = value;
13:        this.status = status;
14:    }
15:
16:    public Object getValue()
17:    {
18:        return (value);
19:    }
20:
21:    public boolean getStatus()
22:    {
23:        return (status);
24:    }
25: }
```

Here is the *StatusListener* interface:

```
01: public interface StatusListener
02: {
03:    public void stateChanged (StatusEvent event);
04: }
```

Validation Adapter

Because each validator needs to handle receiving *Document* events and firing *stateChanged* events, you should provide an abstract adapter class to encapsulate all this common code. By extending *ValidationAdapter*, your validator classes have to implement only the isValid(Object) method. To avoid code duplication, note that the validate() method simply calls isValid (line 15) and then fires an event if the state has changed.

```
01: import java.util.Vector;
02: import javax.swing.event.DocumentEvent;
03: import javax.swing.text.*;
04:
05: public abstract class ValidationAdapter
06: implements Validator
07: {
08:    Vector listeners = new Vector();
09:    boolean wasValid = false;
10:
11:    public abstract boolean isValid (Object value);
12:
13:    public boolean validate (Object value)
14:    {
15:        boolean isValidNow = isValid (value);
```

```
16:          if (isValidNow != wasValid) // state changed
17:          {
18:              fireChangedEvent (value, isValidNow);
19:              wasValid = isValidNow;
20:          }
21:          return (isValidNow);
22:      }
23:
24:      // implement DocumentListener
25:      public void removeUpdate  (DocumentEvent e)
26:      {
27:          validateDocument (e.getDocument());
28:      }
29:      public void changedUpdate (DocumentEvent e)
30:      {
31:          validateDocument (e.getDocument());
32:      }
33:      public void insertUpdate  (DocumentEvent e)
34:      {
35:          validateDocument (e.getDocument());
36:      }
37:
38:      void validateDocument (Document doc)
39:      {
40:        try
41:        {
42:          validate (doc.getText (0, doc.getLength()));
43:        }
44:        catch (BadLocationException e) { }
45:      }
46:
47:      public void addStatusListener (StatusListener l)
48:      {
49:          listeners.add (l);
50:      }
51:      public void
52:          removeStatusListener (StatusListener l)
53:      {
54:          listeners.remove (l);
55:      }
56:
57:      public void fireChangedEvent (Object value,
58:                                    boolean status)
59:      {
60:          StatusEvent event =
61:            new StatusEvent (this, value, status);
62:          for (int i = listeners.size()-1; i >= 0; i—)
63:          {
64:            StatusListener sl =
65:                (StatusListener) listeners.elementAt(i);
66:            sl.stateChanged (event);
```

```
67:        }
68:    }
69: }
```

Note that with this implementation, one validator object can be used only to validate a single data source. It would not be hard (but it is beyond the scope of this example) to enhance our adapter to support multiple data sources.

Validation Techniques

For our Temperature GUI, we want to make sure the value entered is numeric. So how should the actual validation be performed? This depends on the data, of course, but here are some guidelines. In order to encourage reuse, our validators cannot make the assumption that the data has already been filtered.

Performing some complex algorithm to determine if the data is valid can be risky, especially if the format of the data is subject to change. For example, if you wanted to ensure that a text field contained a number, you *could* write a method that checked each character to ensure they were all in the range 0 through 9. But we've already seen the problems that can lead to. Besides, just because a decimal point might be valid in a numeric field doesn't mean that two decimal points would be valid.

Part of the problem is that we are not treating the data holistically. Because the data is being input one character at a time, this might lead us to process it character by character, as we had to when filtering. This tendency, though, should be avoided. Instead of checking each character, checking the entire value is often much easier.

Validation Using Exceptions

One of the easiest ways to implement validation is to exploit Java's *Exceptions*. In many cases, you can perform an operation that *assumes* the value is valid and then let the JVM throw an *Exception* if it's not. All you have to do is catch the *Exception* and return false.

For example, to validate numeric data, you could call the static `parseDouble` method (lines 19–25). This way you'll be sure your *Validator* agrees with the JVM. Just make sure you catch all possible *Exceptions*, even *RuntimeExceptions*.

Similarly, if you want to ensure that a valid file name was entered, use the *File* class. Don't try to check each character against a list of legal characters (especially when that list is different for each operating system).

```
01: public class NumericValidator
02:     extends ValidationAdapter
03: {
```

```
04:    double min = Double.MIN_VALUE;
05:    double max = Double.MAX_VALUE;
06:
07:    public void setRange (double min, double max)
08:    {
09:      this.min = min;
10:      this.max = max;
11:    }
12:
13:    public boolean isValid (Object value)
14:    {
15:      boolean valid = false;
16:
17:      if (value != null)
18:      {
19:        try
20:        {
21:          double d =
22:            Double.parseDouble (value.toString());
23:          valid = ((d >= min) && (d <= max));
24:        }
25:        catch (NumberFormatException e) { }
26:      }
27:
28:      return (valid);
29:    }
30:
31:    public static boolean accepts (Object value)
32:    {
33:      return
34:        (new NumericValidator().isValid (value));
35:    }
36: }
```

Notice how easy it is to write a validator using the *ValidationAdapter* class? We even added the ability to do range checking because that's a fairly common requirement with numeric data.

Putting it all together, we can provide a sample class that applies both filtering and validation against an otherwise normal *JTextField*. If you run it, you'll find that nonnumeric characters are indeed intercepted. Invalid or out-of-range numbers cause the field background to turn pink.

```
01: import java.awt.*;
02: import javax.swing.*;
03:
04: public class DataValidator extends JTextField
05: implements StatusListener
06: {
07:    public DataValidator()
```

```
08:    {
09:        setHorizontalAlignment (JTextField.RIGHT);
10:
11:        // filter and validate the data
12:        Filter f = new NumericFilter (this);
13:        NumericValidator v = new NumericValidator();
14:        v.setRange (0, 100);
15:        v.addStatusListener (this);
16:        getDocument().addDocumentListener (v);
17:    }
18:
19:    public void stateChanged (StatusEvent e)
20:    {
21:        if (e.getStatus())
22:            setBackground (Color.white);
23:        else
24:            setBackground (Color.pink);
25:    }
26:
27:    public static void main (String[] args)
28:    {
29:        DataValidator dv = new DataValidator();
30:        JFrame frame = new JFrame ("Validator");
31:        frame.getContentPane().setLayout
32:            (new BorderLayout());
33:        frame.getContentPane().add
34:            (dv, BorderLayout.CENTER);
35:        frame.pack();
36:        frame.show();
37:    }
38: }
```

Chained Validators

Once you develop a good, reusable set of *Validator* classes, you'll probably encounter situations in which you want to use more than one to validate a single field. For example, you may want to ensure that a credit card number is formatted correctly, but also that it's a valid card number and has a sufficiently high credit balance to cover the amount of charges.

There's no reason why you can't chain validators together. One simple way to do this is to provide an implementation of the *Validator* interface that maintains a vector of other *Validator* objects. Its isValid method could invoke the isValid method of each chained validator in turn, similar to the way the *java.io.SequenceInputStream* class works.

These validators should be tested in order so that more complex (slower) validation is done only if easier (faster) validation succeeds. After all, there's no point in checking the balance of a credit card number that's not in the proper format.

Code 36.9: SequenceValidator.java (fragment)

```
public boolean isValid (Object value)
{
  for (int i = 0; i < validators.size(); i++)
  {
     Validator v = (Validator) validators.elementAt(i);
      if (! v.isValid (value))
        return (false);
  }
  return (true);
}
```

End Notes

To prevent this section from getting even longer, we left out any special handling of *null* values. Just be aware that when you implement a validator, you'll have to decide whether *null* is a valid value. You probably want to make this configurable because it often depends on the particular situation.

Also, any discussion of text validation is incomplete without at least a brief mention of *regular expressions*. For those of you who are comfortable using them, you can find an open source implementation at www.cacas.org/java/gnu/regexp.

Item 37: Desensitizing GUI Components Based on Application State

As we discussed in the last section on data validation, a good GUI doesn't let the user do something wrong. How many times have you clicked a button, only to have the application tell you "That operation is not valid! *Beep!*" Well, if it can tell that it's not valid, why did it let you select it? This happens even on otherwise very sophisticated, professional applications.

Java does provide some help in solving this problem. Every *Component* supports a setEnabled(boolean) method, which allows you to "turn off" the component. This is often called *desensitizing*. As an added benefit, this method changes the component's appearance so that the user can tell it's no longer an option. If necessary, you can control this appearance, but usually the default is adequate.

Deciding how and when to disable your components is much less clear-cut. There are several solutions, each with some pros and cons. For small, simple applications, almost any approach will work. But as your application becomes more complex, it becomes much harder to accurately update the components. This section discusses one approach we've found to be effective, and others that have proven over time to be problematic.

The Over-Reactive Approach

Typically, a component should be enabled or disabled depending on certain conditions. For example, a "Change Font" option would be enabled only if the user has selected some text. You might be tempted to write your code like this:

```
public void selectionChanged (SelectionEvent e)
{
    boolean selected = e.getSelectedText().length > 0;
    changeFontButton.setEnabled (selected);
    changeColorButton.setEnabled (selected);
    centerTextButton.setEnabled (selected);
    deleteTextButton.setEnabled (selected);
    // lots more selection-dependent buttons
    ...
}
```

This can be an efficient way to update your buttons, but it has drawbacks. Embedding the GUI control along with your normal event handling tends to complicate your methods, and it encourages code duplication. Also, even though you get an event, it doesn't necessarily mean the application's state has changed. It's also quite common to end up with multiple copies of the same setEnabled call spread throughout your code.

The Brute-Force Approach

Another approach is to have a single method that sets the state for every component and to call that method every time the application's state changes. This does isolate the GUI control logic in one place, which is nice. Whenever you add or remove a button, you know this method will change, and you don't have to worry about missing a few setEnabled calls. Its major drawback is performance. Determining the application state and then setting the status of every button each time anything changes is not a good idea, unless your application is very small.

```
public void selectionChanged (SelectionEvent e)
{
    boolean selected = e.getSelectedText().length > 0;
    resetState();
}

public void resetState()
{
    // determine all conditions and set each component
    boolean selectedText = ...
    button1.setEnabled (selectedText);
    ...
}
```

The Abstract Approach— A State-Monitor Class

A better approach is to implement a *StateMonitor* class. This class is responsible for enabling or disabling GUI components whenever your application state changes. Your application has to inform the *StateMonitor* whenever it enters or leaves a state, but it doesn't have to worry about which buttons to change. As part of a Model-View-Controller design, this abstraction can really simplify your code and make it more reusable.

What will our *StateMonitor* need to do? First, it will need to let us set the state as changes are made in our application. Like the brute-force approach, this has the advantage of encapsulating all the enabling/disabling code in one place.

```
public void selectionChanged (SelectionEvent e)
{
    boolean selected = e.getSelectedText().length > 0;
    stateMonitor.addState ("Selection", selected);
}
```

In this case, though, we'll determine the state in the event callback and pass that information to our *StateMonitor*. It will then see if that state has changed and update any affected components accordingly. Because our *StateMonitor* knows which state the application was in, it can tell if any change is necessary.

Even though it is feasible to map out every possible state of an application (especially one this simple), we won't need to do so. Complex applications can end up having hundreds or even thousands of distinct states. Luckily, many of these states are unrelated to each other, and they can be handled independently.

For example, an Undo button is enabled if and only if an undoable operation has been performed. A Save button is enabled if and only if changes have been made to the model. A Search button is enabled whenever our model is not null. These three boolean conditions result in eight possible states (2^3).

As you can imagine, a complex application can quickly grow beyond our ability to represent it with a single state. Because these conditions are unrelated, we can represent them as just three states—as long as our *StateMonitor* can support multiple simultaneous states. With that in mind, we'll use a *Vector* to store the list of current states, instead of a simple *String* (line 7).

The *StateMonitor* will also need to let us associate our application's components with the various states we define. We'll do this using a *Hashtable* that maps each of our state objects to a vector of components that should be enabled for that state (line 9).

As states are added and removed, our monitor will need to enable and disable the registered components. We could simply disable all components and then re-enable the ones associated with our active states. But to be more efficient, we'll let our monitor keep track of how many active states are affecting each component. We'll use another *Hashtable* for this, which will map each component to an *Integer* object (line 11).

This technique is similar to the way some garbage collection algorithms work. A counter is incremented for each reference to an object, and the object's memory is reclaimed only when the count is zero. Our *StateMonitor* will disable a component only when the number of associated active states becomes 0. And it will enable the component only when that number becomes 1. In other words, we won't reenable a component that is already enabled. This is implemented in lines 51–54.

```java
01: import java.awt.*;
02: import java.util.*;
03:
04: public class StateMonitor
05: {
06:   // currently active states
07:   Vector states = new Vector();
08:   // maps states to components
09:   Hashtable active = new Hashtable();
10:   // maps components to activity count
11:   Hashtable components = new Hashtable();
12:
13:   public void activate (Component c, Object state)
14:   {
15:     Vector v = (Vector) active.get (state);
16:     if (v == null)
17:       v = new Vector();
18:     if (! v.contains (c))
19:       v.add (c);
20:     active.put (state, v);
21:   }
22:
23:   public void addState (Object state)
24:   {
25:     if (! states.contains (state))
26:     {
27:       states.add (state);
28:       update (state, 1);
29:     }
30:   }
31:
32:   public void removeState (Object state)
33:   {
34:     if (states.contains (state))
35:     {
36:       states.remove (state);
37:       update (state, -1);
```

```
38:       }
39:    }
40:
41:    void update (Object state, int delta)
42:    {
43:      Vector v = (Vector) active.get (state);
44:      for (int i = 0; i < v.size(); i++)
45:      {
46:        int newCount = delta;
47:        Component c = (Component) v.get(i);
48:        Integer count = (Integer) components.get (c);
49:        if (count != null)
50:            newCount += count.intValue();
51:        if (newCount == 0)
52:            c.setEnabled (false);
53:        else if (newCount == 1)
54:            c.setEnabled (true);
55:        components.put (c, new Integer (newCount));
56:      }
57:    }
58: }
```

List Viewer

As an example that uses the *StateMonitor*, let's design a reusable *ListViewer* component. We want to provide four buttons to navigate through our list: *Previous*, *Next*, *First*, and *Last*.

The buttons should be enabled only when they are appropriate. This depends on how many elements we have in our list and which element we are currently viewing. For example, if we're already viewing the last element, the Next and Last buttons should be disabled.

After a bit of analysis, we determine that our application needs to support four different states:

- Zero or one element (no buttons enabled)
- Positioned on first element (only next and last enabled)
- Positioned on last element (only previous and first enabled)
- Positioned anywhere but first or last (all buttons enabled)

These four distinct states can be represented using various combinations of just two conditions:

- Are there any records preceding the current record?
- Are there any records following the current record?

Our application uses these two states, which we'll name *prev* and *next* (lines 13–14), to represent the four distinct application states. As we create each component, we register it with the *StateMonitor* using the `activate` method (line 41). In this example, we only need to associate each button with a single state. For more complex applications, we could call `activate` more than once with the same component.

```
01: import java.awt.event.*;
02: import java.util.*;
03: import javax.swing.*;
04:
05: public class ListViewer extends JFrame
06: implements ActionListener
07: {
08:     Vector data;
09:     int element;
10:     JPanel buttons;
11:     StateMonitor sm;
12:
13:     private static String PREV_ELEMENTS = "prev";
14:     private static String NEXT_ELEMENTS = "next";
15:
16:     public ListViewer (Vector data)
17:     {
18:         this.data = data;
19:         sm = new StateMonitor();
20:
21:         buttons = new JPanel();
22:         addButton ("First",    PREV_ELEMENTS);
23:         addButton ("Previous", PREV_ELEMENTS);
24:         addButton ("Next",     NEXT_ELEMENTS);
25:         addButton ("Last",     NEXT_ELEMENTS);
26:         getContentPane().add (buttons);
27:
28:         if (data.size() > 1)
29:             sm.addState (NEXT_ELEMENTS);
30:         actionPerformed
31:             (new ActionEvent (this, 0, "First"));
32:         pack();
33:         show();
34:     }
35:
36:     void addButton (String label, String state)
37:     {
38:         JButton btn = new JButton (label);
39:         btn.setEnabled (false);
40:         btn.addActionListener (this);
41:         sm.activate (btn, state);
42:         buttons.add (btn);
43:     }
44:
45:     public void actionPerformed (ActionEvent e)
```

```
46:     {
47:         String cmd = e.getActionCommand();
48:         int size = data.size();
49:
50:         if (cmd.equals ("First"))
51:             element = 0;
52:         else if (cmd.equals ("Previous"))
53:             element—;
54:         else if (cmd.equals ("Next"))
55:             element++;
56:         else if (cmd.equals ("Last"))
57:             element = size - 1;
58:
59:         if (element == 0)
60:             sm.removeState (PREV_ELEMENTS);
61:         else
62:             sm.addState (PREV_ELEMENTS);
63:         if (element == size - 1)
64:             sm.removeState (NEXT_ELEMENTS);
65:         else
66:             sm.addState (NEXT_ELEMENTS);
67:
68:         setTitle ((element + 1) + " of " + size);
69:     }
70:
71:     public static void main (String[] args)
72:     {
73:         Vector v = new Vector();
74:         for (int i = 0; i < 3; i++)
75:             v.add (new Object());
76:         new ListViewer (v);
77:     }
78: }
```

In our application's `actionPerformed` method, we determine the status of our two conditions and call either `addState` or `removeState`, as appropriate. The *StateMonitor* does all the rest of the work. As we use the buttons to navigate through the list, they become enabled and disabled appropriately, as shown in Figure 37.1.

Adaptive Sensitization

Sometimes, for efficiency, it's just not practical to determine the validity of every button on your application. For example, a Web browser *could* check the status of every embedded hyperlink when it loaded a page and then disable the ones that were not accessible. But the cost of checking (in terms of time) would be too high, and the cost of not checking is minor. You'll need to resolve similar trade-offs for your applications.

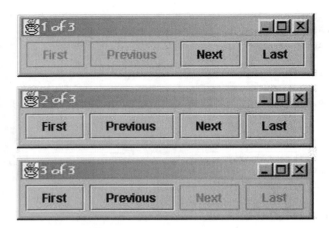

Figure 37.1   List viewer.

One compromise you should consider is adaptive sensitization. This means that you don't waste any time checking the validity of the operation until the user tries to execute it. Then, if it's not valid, your application can adapt itself appropriately. You can remove the component entirely, disable it, or just change its appearance.

For the browser example, you might just change the appearance of the hyperlink because it might only be temporarily invalid because of an intermittent network failure. But if your component represented a file name in a history list of recently accessed files, you might want to remove it entirely once you determined the file no longer exists. Another option to consider is to use a *lazy-loading* technique and disable the components in a background thread.

Item 38: Use Threads in Event Handlers to Avoid Freezing Your GUI

I am sure that at some point in your computer career you have used a search program and that once you initiated the search, you had no control over the GUI until the search was completed. This can be quite frustrating if the act of searching takes upwards of 30 seconds or more. Of course, this behavior is not just limited to search programs. Numerous types of actions could take a long time for a program to complete for which you would rather not have to wait. Some examples include downloading and displaying Web pages, compiling programs, performing backups, and so forth.

It is easy for a Java programmer to fall into the trap of producing this unfriendly behavior when writing GUI programs. Java event handling is, by default, single threaded. This means that when a user causes an event to occur (such as clicking a button), all of the event-handling code behind that event must be finished executing before the Java event-handling mechanism receives any more events. Let's look at an example of this behavior.

The following code listing lists the *BasicSearch* class, which, as its name implies, allows for a basic search to be performed. When the program is run and some text is entered for it to search on, it performs a search through its limited word list and displays matches on the screen. As it searches through the word list a delay of one second has been inserted to simulate a slow search. Once the Search button is clicked, the Cancel button is enabled and the search logic begins. If you try to click the Cancel button while the search logic is executing your clicking will be in vain. Because only one thread is allocated to do all event processing, user actions that would normally produce an event are ignored until the event-handling thread becomes idle. If you were to search on "ice" you would see the screen depicted in Figure 38.1 after waiting for approximately 12 seconds.

```
01: import java.awt.*;
02: import java.awt.event.*;
03:
04: public class BasicSearch extends Frame implements ActionListener
05: {
06:     Label         searchLabel = new Label("Find:");
07:     TextField     searchTextField = new TextField(20);
08:     Label         resultsLabel = new Label("Results:");
09:     List          results = new List();
10:
11:     Button        searchButton = new Button("Search");
12:     Button        cancelButton = new Button("Cancel");
13:
14:     static String[] words = { "ace", "race", "mace", "pace",
15:                               "chase", "rice", "splice", "mice",
16:                               "diced", "price", "lime", "dime" };
17:
18:     public BasicSearch (String title)
19:     {
20:         super(title);
21:
22:         // ...layout search form...
23:
24:         searchButton.addActionListener(this);
25:         cancelButton.addActionListener(this);
26:         cancelButton.setEnabled(false);
27:
28:         this.setSize(300,300);
29:         this.setVisible(true);
30:     }
31:
```

```
32:      public void actionPerformed (ActionEvent evt)
33:      {
34:          Object source = evt.getSource();
35:          boolean cancel = false;
36:
37:          if (source == searchButton)
38:          {
39:              searchButton.setEnabled(false);
40:              cancelButton.setEnabled(true);
41:              results.removeAll();
42:              String searchText = searchTextField.getText();
43:
44:              for (int i = 0; i < words.length; i++)
45:              {
46:                  try
47:                  {
48:                      if (Thread.interrupted())
49:                          throw new InterruptedException();
50:
51:                      Thread.sleep(1000);
52:                      if (words[i].indexOf(searchText) != -1)
53:                          results.add(words[i]);
54:                  }
55:                  catch (InterruptedException ie)
56:                  {
57:                      break;
58:                  }
59:              }
60:          }
61:          else if (source == cancelButton)
62:          {
63:              Thread.currentThread().interrupt();
64:          }
65:
66:          searchButton.setEnabled(true);
67:          cancelButton.setEnabled(false);
68:      }
69:
70:      public static void main (String args[])
71:      {
72:          new BasicSearch("Basic Search");
73:      }
74: }
```

Implementing an Effective Cancel with Threading

The Cancel button event-handling code in line 63 was rendered useless due to the single-threaded Java event handler. The way to solve this problem is to have another thread perform the search, so the Java event-handling thread is freed

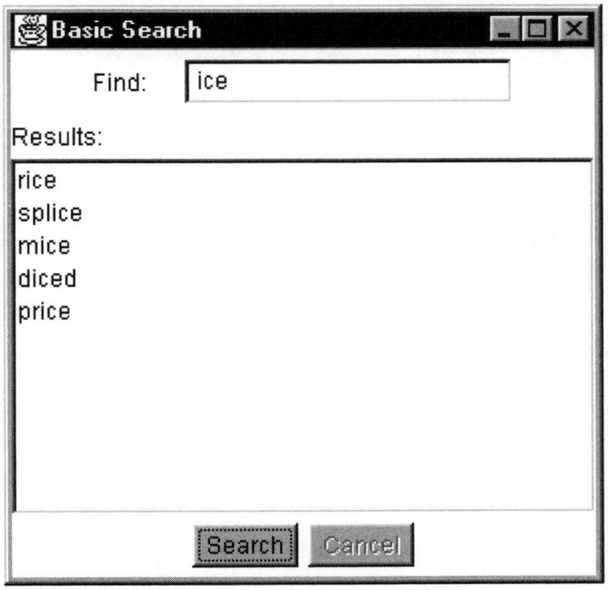

Figure 38.1   Basic Search with ineffective Cancel.

up to handle other user requests. We do this by creating another class that extends *Thread* that performs the same logic that is currently being performed by the `actionPerformed(...)` method. Our class will be called *SearchWorker*; to make its job easy we have passed a reference of *BasicSearch* to it.[1] Here is the code:

```
01: class SearchWorker extends Thread
02: {
03:     BasicSearch  basicSearch;
04:     String       searchText;
05:
06:     public SearchWorker (BasicSearch basicSearch)
07:     {
08:         this.basicSearch = basicSearch;
09:     }
10:
11:     public void doSearch (String searchText)
12:     {
13:         this.searchText = searchText;
14:         this.start();
15:     }
```

[1]Note that *SearchWorker* has to be in the same package as *BasicSearch* in order to have access to *BasicSearch*'s package-level variables.

```
16:
17:     public void cancelSearch ()
18:     {
19:         interrupt();
20:     }
21:
22:     public void run ()
23:     {
24:         for (int i = 0; i < basicSearch2.words.length; i++)
25:         {
26:             try
27:             {
28:                 if (Thread.interrupted())
29:                     throw new InterruptedException();
30:
31:                 Thread.sleep(1000);
32:                 if (basicSearch.words[i].indexOf(searchText) != -1)
33:                     basicSearch.results.add(basicSearch.words[i]);
34:             }
35:             catch (InterruptedException e)
36:             {
37:                 break;
38:             }
39:         }
40:
41:         basicSearch.searchButton.setEnabled(true);
42:         basicSearch.cancelButton.setEnabled(false);
43:     }
44: }
```

In order for *BasicSearch* to take advantage of *SearchWorker* the following two lines must be added and the `actionPerformed(...)` method must be changed.

```
SearchWorker    searchWorker;               // add after line 12
searchWorker = new SearchWorker(this);      // add after line 20
```

Here is the new `actionPerformed(...)` method for *BasicSearch*:

```
public void actionPerformed (ActionEvent evt)
{
    Object source = evt.getSource();

    if (source == searchButton)
    {
        searchButton.setEnabled(false);
        cancelButton.setEnabled(true);
        results.removeAll();
        searchWorker.doSearch(searchTextField.getText());
    }
}
```

```
        else if (source == cancelButton)
        {
            searchWorker.cancelSearch();
            searchButton.setEnabled(true);
            cancelButton.setEnabled(false);
        }
    }
```

Now when the Search button in our screen is pushed, the *Thread* associated with *SearchWorker* gets started and performs the searching task for us. You can see this if you look at the new `actionPerformed(...)` method. When the Search button is pushed the `searchWorker.doSearch(...)` method is called, which in turn starts the thread. Because the searching logic is now executing in a separate thread, the Java event-handling thread is now available to handle other user-generated events. The Cancel button can now be clicked while the search is being performed. Clicking the Cancel button results in a call to the `searchWorker.cancelSearch()` method, which sends an interrupt to the *searchWorker* thread. When the interrupt is received the search loop breaks and the thread exits cleanly. Doing the same search on "ice" and pressing the Cancel button before the search is done results in a screen similar to Figure 38.2.

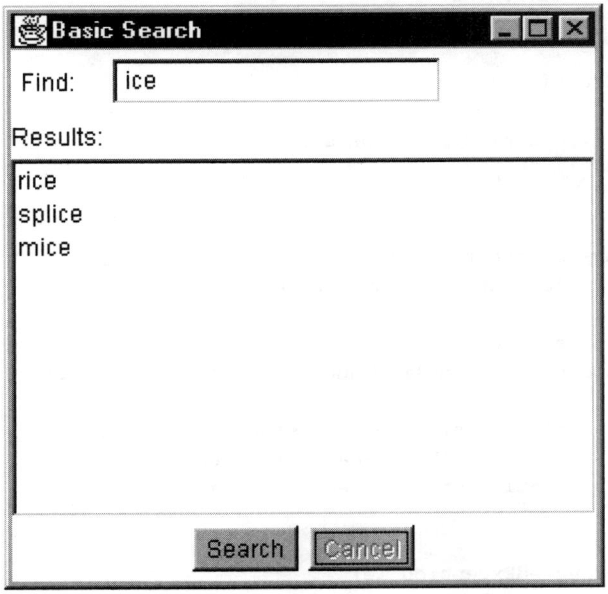

Figure 38.2   Basic Search with effective Cancel.

Implementing an Effective Cancel with SwingWorker

For those of you who use Swing, a new class *SwingWorker* is available that encapsulates a worker thread to simplify adding threading support to your application. In addition, it provides a method for getting a return value from a worker thread. As of this writing, the *SwingWorker* class is not part of the javax.swing package, but it can be downloaded at java.sun.com/products/jfc/tsc/articles/threads/threads2.html (the source for *SwingWorker* is listed in Item 38). To use the *SwingWorker* class you write a subclass and provide an implementation for the construct() method and optionally for the finished() method. To modify the initial *BasicSearch* example to use the *SwingWorker* thread we have to add the *SearchWorker* class, which subclasses *Swing-Worker*. Here is the code for the new *SearchWorker* class:

```
01: class SearchWorker extends SwingWorker
02: {
03:     BasicSearch  basicSearch;
04:     String       searchText;
05:
06:     public SearchWorker (BasicSearch basicSearch,
07:                                      String searchText)
08:     {
09:         this.basicSearch = basicSearch;
10:         this.searchText = searchText;
11:     }
12:
13:     public Object construct()
14:     {
15:         for (int i = 0; i < basicSearch.words.length; i++)
16:         {
17:             try
18:             {
19:                 if (Thread.interrupted())
20:                     throw new InterruptedException();
21:
22:                 Thread.sleep(1000);
23:                 if (basicSearch.words[i].indexOf(searchText) != -1)
24:                 {
25:                     DefaultListModel model = (DefaultListModel)
26:                                     basicSearch.results.getModel();
27:                     model.addElement(basicSearch.words[i]);
28:                 }
29:             }
30:             catch (InterruptedException ie)
31:             {
32:                 return ("Interrupted");
```

```
33:                }
34:            }
35:            return ("Done");
36:        }
37:
38:        public void finished()
39:        {
40:            basicSearch.searchButton.setEnabled(true);
41:            basicSearch.cancelButton.setEnabled(false);
42:        }
43: }
```

This implementation of the *SearchWorker* class is very similar to our vanilla implementation that extended *Thread*. Basically, the information that was in the run() method of our vanilla implementation has been put into the construct() method. The finished() method has been implemented to make the necessary changes to button availability when the worker thread exits. In order for the initial *BasicSearch* to take advantage of *SearchWorker* the following line must be added and the actionPerformed(...) method must be changed.

```
SearchWorker    searchWorker;            // add after line 12
```

Here is the new actionPerformed(...) method:

```
public void actionPerformed (ActionEvent evt)
{
    Object source = evt.getSource();

    if (source == searchButton)
    {
        searchButton.setEnabled(false);
        cancelButton.setEnabled(true);
        results.removeAll();
        searchWorker =
            new SearchWorker(this, searchTextField.getText());
    }
    else if (source == cancelButton)
    {
        searchWorker.interrupt();
    }
}
```

Now when the Search button gets clicked a new *SearchWorker* is created every time. The *SearchWorker* class performs the searching logic. When the Cancel button is clicked, we call the interrupt() method to interrupt the thread and stop its execution. Running the *BasicSearch* class with these modifications produces the same behavior as the vanilla *Thread* implementation.

Using a *Thread* in this manner isn't too much extra effort to provide the user with a more responsive GUI. As a programmer, you will have to make judgments as to whether your event-handling code will cause a significant enough performance delay to warrant using this technique.

Item 39: Model View Controller and JTree

My plan seemed rather simple at the time. I was working on a parser, and I wanted to display the parsed messages to determine if they were parsed correctly. The messages contained a hierarchy of information. Each message contained sets and fields. Some messages contained groups of sets called segments. The parser tokenized the messages into a tree, which it then traversed to insert specific fields into database tables. I wanted a view of the tokenized message before it was inserted into the database so I could verify that the tokenizer code was working properly. My JTree experience was about to begin.

I created a *TestOutput* class, which listened for parsed message events. The parsed message events contained the root TreeNode of the tokenized message tree. Each parsed message node was added to the containing root node and displayed in the JTree. Well, that was the idea anyway.

Take a look at TestOutput.java and see if you can tell what's wrong:

```
01: public class TestOutput implements ParserListener
02: {
03:     private DefaultMutableTreeNode root;
04:
05:     public TestOutput()
06:     {
07:        root  = new DefaultMutableTreeNode("Parsed Messages");
08:        JTree tree = new JTree(root);
09:        JFrame frame = new JFrame("ParserOut");
10:        JScrollPane scroller = new JScrollPane();
11:        scroller.getViewport().add(tree);
12:        frame.getContentPane().add("Center", scroller);
13:        frame.setSize(300, 300);
14:     }
15:
16:     public void Show()
17:     {
18:        frame.show();
19:     }
20:
21:     public void processEvent( ParsedMsgEvent event)
22:     {
23:        MutableTreeNode msgNode = event.getMessageNode();
24:        root.add(msgNode);
```

```
25:      }
26:
27:      public static void main(String[] args)
28:      {
29:        TestOutput output = new TestOutput();
30:        output.show();
31:      }
32: }
```

After parsing two messages and clicking on the Parsed Messages root node the GUI looked like the one shown in Figure 39.1.

It looked good at first, but unfortunately as I fed the parser messages, the GUI looked exactly the same. When I double-clicked on the root node, the message nodes for the messages that had parsed up to that point appeared. When I collapsed and expanded the tree after more messages had parsed, the subsequent message nodes were not added to the root node in the display. At first I suspected I was having repaint problems. I explored different ways to refresh my GUI, but I still had the same problem. After having no success with repaint, I took a closer look at each object as it fits into the Model-View-Controller paradigm.

The root node created on line 7 is the model, and the JTree created on line 8 is the view. When the model is modified, the view is supposed to reflect the changes. The problem was that the view was not reflecting the changes to the model. Or was that the problem? I read the Javadoc pages again and looked at the source code for JTree some more. That's when I realized I was only partly correct. When the model is modified, the view is supposed to reflect the changes. That part is correct. The incorrect part is that I was not modifying the model. Because the JTree class has a constructor that takes a Default-MutableTreeNode, I assumed that the root node was the model. It made sense at the time, and I do know what they say about making assumptions. I knew the root node was the object that held the tree data, and I knew that the JTree object was the view of the data. What I didn't know was that the JTree object actually took the DefaultMutableTreeNode and added it to a DefaultTreeModel object, which was actually the model.

Figure 39.1 Parsed Messages in a JTree.

The magic behind the scenes of the Model-View-Controller concept isn't really magic at all. The view adds itself as a listener for model events. When the model changes, it fires events to all its listeners and notifies them of the changes. Let's modify the *TestOutput* class a bit so that we can simulate new messages being parsed.

```
01:  public class TestOutput
02:  {
03:      private DefaultMutableTreeNode root;
04:      private DefaultTreeModel model;
05:
06:      public TestOutput()
07:      {
08:        root  = new DefaultMutableTreeNode("Parsed Messages");
09:        model = new DefaultTreeModel(root);
10:        JTree tree = new JTree(model);
11:        … //set up the scroll pane and the frame
12:      }
13:
14:      public void Show()
15:      {
16:        frame.show();
17:       }
18:
19:      public void processEvent(DefaultMutableTreeNode node,
20:                               int index)
21:      {
22:        model.insertNodeInto(node, root, index);
23:      }
24:
25:      public static void main(String[] args)
26:      {
27:        int count = 0;
28:        TestOutput output = new TestOutput();
29:        output.show();
30:        while(true)
31:        {
32:          output.processEvent(new DefaultMutableTreeNode("New node"),
33:                              root, count++);
34:          try { Thread.sleep(5000) }
35:          catch (Exception e) { e.printStackTrace() };
36:        }
37:    }
38:  }
```

The major change in the TestOutput class is on line 22. We are now actually modifying the model. When the insertNodeInto(...) method is called, a TreeModelEvent is fired to each TableModelListener that has added itself to

DefaultTreeModel. This is different from the first *TestOutput* class because then we were adding new nodes to the root node. The DefaultMutableTree-Node, however, does not update the JTree of its changes. The Default-TreeModel does. The DefaultTreeModel and the JTree classes take care of the details. Now that we are adding new nodes through the model our GUI will be updated automatically and will show each new node.

We don't have to understand all the underlying details, but we do have to understand which object is the model and which object is the view, and how they interact. So, if the DefaultMutableTreeNode does not update the JTree of its changes but the DefaultTreeModel does, why did the root node in the JTree in the first example have any child nodes since we were not adding the new nodes through the model? Theoretically, it should not have any child nodes displayed in the view because we did not add the new nodes through the model. I sent e-mail to Sun and its response was that behavior is unspecified if you change the model without notifying the listeners. Because we did not go through the model to update the root node the model listeners were not notified of the changes and we got unspecified results. Whether you agree with this response or not, the bottom line is that you must make changes through the model and update the listeners of these changes.

Item 40: How to Data Transfer Something Other Than Text

That feeling of true integration has been missing from your Java application. While all of the other native applications play together nicely, copying and pasting images, RTF, HTML, and more, your Java application sits in the corner ashamed because all it can do is copy and paste text. Just plain old vanilla text. It's time for something more.

This item begins with a quick overview of the java.awt.datatransfer package. Following that we discuss the three different scenarios for copying and pasting, and we discuss the different approaches for copying nontext in each scenario.

Data Transfer Overview

The *java.awt.datatransfer* package contains the classes necessary for implementing data transfer. The term *data transfer* is used because it encompasses copying, pasting, and drag and drop. To data transfer something a couple of things are needed: the data you want to transfer, a place to store the data, and a place to fetch the data. The data you want to transfer must be exposed through the *Transferable* interface. The place where you put the *Transferable* object is on a *Clipboard* object. The *Clipboard* object is very simple, and it consists of these methods:

getName (). Gets the name of the clipboard.

setContents (...). Sets the contents of the clipboard. The contents must implement the *Transferable* interface.

getContents (...). Gets the contents of the clipboard. The returned object implements the *Transferable* interface.

The *Transferable* interface is also fairly simple. One of the concepts behind the *Transferable* interface is that data needing to be transferred may have different representations of itself. These representations are called "flavors" and are identified by the *DataFlavor* class. Here are the *Transferable* methods:

getTransferData (...). This method accepts a *DataFlavor* object as an argument and returns an object, allowing the caller to get to the data in the correct format. If the *DataFlavor* is not supported, the *Unsupported-FlavorException* will be thrown.

getTransferDataFlavors (...). This method returns an array of *DataFlavor* objects.

isDataFlavorSupported (...). This method accepts a *DataFlavor* object and argument and returns true or false depending on whether the flavor is supported.

The different types of "flavors" a *Transferable* object can have are represented by MIME types. The *DataFlavor* class is used to encapsulate these MIME types along with some other supporting information (such as the Java class associated with the MIME type, the human name of the MIME type, and other MIME type attributes). The java.awt.datatransfer package already has a defined set of MIME types it supports, most of which are included as static members of the *DataFlavor* class. Two of these are the *plainTextFlavor* and *stringFlavor*. The data transfer package contains a class called *StringSelection* that supports both the *plainTextFlavor* and *stringFlavor*.

The *Clipboard* class within the data transfer package can be created and used to store or fetch a *Transferable* object within the same JVM. If you want to communicate to your operating system's clipboard you will have to get a reference to the system *Clipboard* object. This reference can be obtained with the following call:

```
Toolkit.getDefaultToolkit().getSystemClipboard()
```

Using the system *Clipboard* object allows you to place things on the operating systems *Clipboard* when you call `Clipboard.setContents (...)`.

Three Types of Data Transfer

The three types of data transfer that can occur are these:

Intra-JVM. Transferring data within the same JVM.

Inter-JVM. Transferring data from one JVM to another JVM.

Native-JVM. Transferring data from a JVM to a native application or vice versa.

In the Intra-JVM scenario, the handling of *Transferable* objects is done within the JVM. If you are using the system *Clipboard*, the data will be copied to the operating system clipboard, but it doesn't need to be for this scenario. In the Inter-JVM scenario and the Native-JVM, the data must be copied to the system clipboard and retrieved from the system clipboard for a successful transfer to take place. No matter which of the three scenarios you are using, both the data producer and the data consumer must have at least one agreed-upon format of the data, so that an understanding exists on how the data is to be processed.

The system *Clipboard* is a key element for making successful transfers in the Inter-JVM and Native-JVM scenarios. The system *Clipboard* object is specific to the JVM you are using. Your JVM contains a system *Clipboard* implementation that is written to work with the operating system you are using. Before we go any further, I would like to point out that Java versions (1.3 beta and before) provided by Sun (both for Solaris and Windows) support the transfer of text only when using the system *Clipboard*. This doesn't mean that they won't support non-text transfers it in the future, but the 1.3 beta implementation does not support it. What this means to us is that we have to use another method besides the system *Clipboard* to successfully transfer nontext.

Let's go ahead and look at an example of transferring nontext in the Intra-JVM scenario first. After we look at the example we will explore the alternatives for transferring nontext in the other two scenarios and see an example of one of the alternatives.

Intra-JVM Example

The most common type of nontext data to transfer is probably image data. The code in this example focuses on transferring an image from one component to another inside the same JVM. For the example we have created a class called *ImageCanvas* that displays an *Image* object. The *ImageCanvas* class accepts the following key strokes: Ctrl+A for copy and Ctrl+B for paste. Here is the code listing:

```
001: import java.awt.*;
002: import java.awt.event.*;
```

```
003:  import java.awt.datatransfer.*;
004:
005:  public class ImageCanvas extends Canvas
006:                          implements ClipboardOwner, KeyListener
007:  {
008:      Clipboard       clipboard;
009:      Image           img;
010:      MediaTracker    tracker = new MediaTracker(this);
011:
012:      public ImageCanvas ()
013:      {
014:          addKeyListener(this);
015:          clipboard = getToolkit().getSystemClipboard();
016:      }
017:
018:      public void setImage (Image img)
019:      {
020:          tracker.addImage(img, 0);
021:          try
022:          {
023:              tracker.waitForAll();
024:          }
025:          catch (Exception e)
026:          {
027:              System.out.println("Error loading image: " +
028:                                          e.getMessage());
029:              return;
030:          }
031:
032:          if (tracker.isErrorAny())
033:          {
034:              System.out.println("Error loading image.");
035:              return;
036:          }
037:
038:          this.img = img;
039:          repaint();
040:      }
041:
042:      public void paint (Graphics g)
043:      {
044:          if (img != null)
045:          {
046:              Dimension d = this.getSize();
047:              g.setColor(Color.white);
048:              g.fillRect(0,0, d.width, d.height); // blank background
049:              g.drawImage(img, 0, 0, img.getWidth(this),
050:                              img.getHeight(this), this);
051:          }
052:      }
053:
```

```
054:    public void keyPressed (KeyEvent evt)
055:    {
056:       if (evt.isControlDown())
057:       {
058:          if (evt.getKeyCode() == KeyEvent.VK_A)   // copy
059:          {
060:             try
061:             {
062:                clipboard.setContents(
063:                        new TransferableImage(img), this);
064:             }
065:             catch (Exception e)
066:             {
067:                System.out.println(
068:                   "Error copying data. Error: " + e.getMessage());
069:             }
070:             evt.consume();
071:          }
072:          else if (evt.getKeyCode() == KeyEvent.VK_B) // paste
073:          {
074:             Transferable clipboardData = clipboard.getContents(this);
075:
076:             if (clipboardData != null)
077:             {
078:                try
079:                {
080:                   DataFlavor flavor =
081:                   new DataFlavor("image/gif;class=java.awt.Image");
082:
083:                   if (clipboardData.isDataFlavorSupported(flavor))
084:                   {
085:                      this.setImage((Image)
086:                            clipboardData.getTransferData(flavor));
087:                   }
088:                }
089:                catch (Exception e)
090:                {
091:                   System.out.println(
092:                      "Error pasting data. Error: " + e.getMessage());
093:                }
094:             }
095:             evt.consume();
096:          }
097:       }
098:    }
099:
100:    public void keyReleased (KeyEvent evt)   {    }
101:    public void keyTyped (KeyEvent evt)      {    }
102:
103:    public void lostOwnership(Clipboard clipboard,
104:                              Transferable contents) {    }
```

```
105:
106:     public static void main (String args[])
107:     {
108:         Frame f = new Frame("Image Copy");
109:         f.setLayout(new GridLayout(0,1));
110:
111:         ImageCanvas canvas1 = new ImageCanvas();
112:         ImageCanvas canvas2 = new ImageCanvas();
113:
114:         canvas1.setImage(
115:           Toolkit.getDefaultToolkit().getImage("images/cloud.gif"));
116:         canvas2.setImage(
117:           Toolkit.getDefaultToolkit().getImage("images/sun.gif"));
118:
119:         f.add(canvas1);
120:         f.add(canvas2);
121:
122:         f.setSize(300,300);
123:         f.show();
124:     }
125: }
```

Before we continue the code listing let's take a look at the bolded lines in the source listing. Line 6 specifies that our *ImageCanvas* class implements the *ClipboardOwner* interface. When placing items on the *Clipboard* with the setContents(...) method we must specify a *ClipboardOwner*. Lines 103 and 104 list our *null* implementation of the lostOwnership(...) method, which is the only method required to implement the *ClipboardOwner* interface. In line 8 we declare the clipboard variable as *Clipboard*, and in line 15 we set it to the system *Clipboard* object.

When the Ctrl+A or Ctrl+B key is pressed the keyPressed(...) method is called. The implementation of keyPressed(...) looks for these key combinations and does a copy or paste, respectively. When doing a copy we create a new instance of the *TransferableImage* class and call setContents(...) to place this item on the clipboard (lines 62 and 63). The *TransferableImage* class is defined in the next source listing.

When doing a paste we first have to get the *Transferable* object off the clipboard and make sure it is not *null*. We can get the *Transferable* object from the clipboard by calling getContents(...) (line 74). Once we have the object we want to make sure it supports a *DataFlavor* that we support. In this case, we support only the *DataFlavor* with the MIME type "image/gif". So, first we create a *DataFlavor* with MIME type "image/gif" and attribute "class= java.awt.Image" (lines 80 and 81). To make sure the *Transferable* object we got from the clipboard has the flavor we are looking for, we must check to see if it supports the "image/gif" flavor. We do this by calling isDataFlavorSupported(...) (line 83). If the flavor is supported we request the data in the "image/gif" flavor from the *Transferable* object and use it to set the image of our component (lines 85 and 86).

The next listing shows the code for the *TransferableImage* class. This class implements the *Transferable* interface and is used to place objects of type *Image* on the clipboard.

```
127: class TransferableImage implements Transferable
128: {
129:     DataFlavor  imageFlavor;
130:     Image       img;
131:
132:     public TransferableImage (Image img) throws Exception
133:     {
134:         this.img = img;
135:         imageFlavor =
136:             new DataFlavor("image/gif;class=java.awt.Image");
137:     }
138:
139:     public Object getTransferData(DataFlavor flavor)
140:                         throws UnsupportedFlavorException
141:     {
142:         if (imageFlavor.equals(flavor))
143:             return (img);
144:         else
145:             throw new UnsupportedFlavorException(flavor);
146:     }
147:
148:     public DataFlavor[] getTransferDataFlavors()
149:     {
150:         DataFlavor[] flavors = new DataFlavor[1];
151:         flavors[0] = imageFlavor;
152:         return (flavors);
153:     }
154:
155:     public boolean isDataFlavorSupported(DataFlavor flavor)
156:     {
157:         return (imageFlavor.equals(flavor));
158:     }
159: }
```

The implementation of the *Transferable* interface is straightforward. First, we define what *DataFlavors* are supported so we can use them in all of the other methods. We define the "image/gif" *DataFlavor* in the constructor as the only flavor supported by this class. The "image/gif" *DataFlavor* is stored in the *imageFlavor* member. In the getTransferDataFlavors() method we return a one-dimensional array of *DataFlavor* with the only element being the *imageFlavor*. In the isDataFlavorSupported(...) method all we do is check to see if the flavor passed in equals the *imageFlavor*. If it does we return true; if it doesn't we return false. And in the `getTransferData(...)` method, if the requested flavor equals *imageFlavor* we return the *Image* object we store. If the requested flavor does not equal *imageFlavor* an *UnsupportedDataFlavorException* is thrown. Running the *ImageCanvas* class produces Figure 40.1. The left side shows the Image Copy frame when it is first loaded. The right side shows the output after the bottom image is copied to the top image.

Determining What Support Is Available for Data Transfer

As I mentioned before, the system *Clipboards* provided with the Java 1.3 beta version and before do not support data transfer of nontext. Here I define support to mean a bidirectional transfer of data between two JVMs or between a JVM and a native application. There are two ways to determine this, one of which is to test different combinations until you are blue in the face and find out they do not work; the other is to look at the source code of the system *Clipboard* implementation for your JVM. Luckily, you can download the Java source code from Sun's Web site so we won't have to test until we are blue. To determine the system *Clipboard* class just use this line of code:

```
Toolkit.getDefaultToolkit().getSystemClipboard().getClass().getName();
```

Printing the result of this call on a windows installation yields this:

```
sun.awt.windows.WClipboard
```

 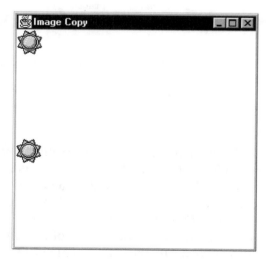

Figure 40.1   Image Copy frame before and after copy.

Looking at the code for the *WClipboard* class reveals the following two things: (1) instances of the class *StringSelection* and instances of other types of objects use different native methods when placing items on the operating system's clipboard, and (2) any items that are in the operating system's clipboard will come back either as a *StringSelection* object (if the data is of type text) or *null*. The support built into the *WClipboard* object supports only text transfers. The clipboard class for the Solaris Java implementation is the *sun.awt.motif.X11Clipboard*. This class works with the *X11Selection* class, which clearly states in the code comments that only text is supported.

Because only text can be successfully transferred across the boundary from the JVM to the operating system using the system *Clipboard* implementations, this leaves us two alternatives:

1. Convert any nontext data into text before placing it on the clipboard.

2. Use the JNI to gain access to the operating system clipboard services.

The first solution has its pros and cons. One pro is that the solution is a pure Java solution. The cons are these: (1) the data has to be converted from binary to text (could use uuencode), and (2) no native application would understand the text, which is really not text. The first solution would solve only the problem of doing Inter-JVM transfers, but not JVM-to-Native transfers.

The second solution's primary con is that it is an operating system-specific solution. The pro is that it will allow Inter-JVM transfers as well as Native-JVM transfers. While neither solution is ideal, we will implement the second solution because it provides the greatest amount of integration.

Inter-JVM and Native-JVM Example

To implement the second solution we must write JNI code to gain access to the system clipboard services. In order to minimize the impact on the applications that use the standard Java *Clipboard* object, our clipboard object will be a subclass of *Clipboard*. Because we are dealing with image data, we need to pick an appropriate data format before we place it on the clipboard. In this example, our native OS is Windows, so a Device Independent Bitmap (DIB) format is used to place the image data on the clipboard. Mapping out the work to implement this involves the following steps:

1. Create an appropriate data format for Java image data to be passed into the JNI code.

2. Create a native clipboard object with defined native methods.

3. Create a JNI implementation of the clipboard object.

To make the JNI calls more extensible, I decided that it would be best to pass the image data into the JNI routine as an array of *byte*. In order to achieve this, first we must get the pixel information about the image into an array of integers; then we can translate the integers into bytes. To make things more flexible for porting to other platforms, I modified the *TransferableImage* class to contain information about the *Image*, instead of the *Image* object itself. The *TransferableImage* class now looks like this:

```
01: import java.awt.datatransfer.*;
02:
03: public class TransferableImage implements Transferable
04: {
05:     public int     width;
06:     public int     height;
07:     public int     pixels[];
08:
09:     DataFlavor flavor;
10:
11:     public TransferableImage (int width, int height, int[] pixels)
12:                                                 throws Exception
13:     {
14:         flavor = new DataFlavor("image/raw");
15:
16:         this.width = width;
17:         this.height = height;
18:         this.pixels = pixels;
19:     }
20:
21:     public Object getTransferData(DataFlavor flavor)
22:                     throws UnsupportedFlavorException
23:     {
24:         if (flavor.equals(flavor))
25:             return (this);
26:         else
27:             throw new UnsupportedFlavorException(flavor);
28:     }
29:
30:     public DataFlavor[] getTransferDataFlavors()
31:     {
32:         DataFlavor[] flavors = new DataFlavor[1];
33:         flavors[0] = flavor;
34:         return (flavors);
35:     }
36:
37:     public boolean isDataFlavorSupported(DataFlavor flavor)
38:     {
39:         return (flavor.equals(flavor));
40:     }
41: }
```

The information it contains has been changed from storing an *Image* to storing information needed to reconstruct an *Image*. The data it contains are the *width, height,* and *pixel* data for the image. In order to successfully create an instance of *TransferableImage* from the *ImageCanvas* class, lines 62 and 63 were replaced with this code:

```
int width = img.getWidth(this);
int height = img.getHeight(this);
int[] pixels = new int[width * height];
PixelGrabber pg =
        new PixelGrabber(img, 0, 0, width, height, pixels, 0, width);
pg.grabPixels(0);

clipboard.setContents(
new TransferableImage(width, height, pixels), this);
```

This code uses the *java.awt.image.PixelGrabber* class to get the pixels of the *Image* as an integer array. Along with the *width* and *height* of the image, the *pixels* are passed in to create an instance of the *Transferable* object. We must also change the way the image paste is handled. We must now expect to get the new implementation of the *TransferableImage* class back, so we must convert the raw pixels into an *Image*. This can be accomplished by using the *java.awt.image.MemoryImageSource* class. To implement this we changed lines 80–87 to the following set of code:

```
DataFlavor flavor = new DataFlavor("image/raw");
TransferableImage ti =
   (TransferableImage) clipboardData.getTransferData(flavor);
MemoryImageSource mis =
   new MemoryImageSource(ti.width, ti.height, ti.pixels, 0, ti.width);
this.setImage(Toolkit.getDefaultToolkit().createImage(mis));
```

The only other changes made to *ImageCanvas* are to import the *java.awt. image* package and to create our own *Clipboard* object instead of the default system *Clipboard* object Java provides. These changes are reflected in code by adding the following statement after line 3:

```
import java.awt.image.*;
```

And replacing line 15 with:

```
clipboard = new NativeExtendedClipboard();
```

Now it is time to take a look at how we implemented the *NativeExtended-Clipboard* class. Before we list the code, let me mention that the basic concept behind the implementation is similar to the current Java implementation, in that we have a map of data flavors to native flavors. In our implementation, however, we map data flavors to an object that implements the *NativeClip-boardAdaptor* interface. The reason for this is that we may want to perform some preprocessing on the *Transferable* object before we send it across into the JNI code and because it will help us when we need to get data back from the operating system clipboard. The code for the *NativeClipboardAdaptor* interface is as follows:

```
01: import java.awt.datatransfer.*;
02:
03: public interface NativeClipboardAdaptor
04: {
05:     public int getFormat();
06:     public byte[] getBytes();
07:     public void setBytes(byte[] b);
08:     public Object getClipboardData();
09:     public void setTransferable(Transferable t);
10: }
```

The methods of the interface are designed to convert between a Java *Transferable* object and the information the operating system expects for placing information on the clipboard. The implementation of the *NativeExtendedClipboard* is slightly different than you might expect. In order to isolate users of this clipboard from native-specific information, it was necessary to have the *NativeExtendedClipboard* implement the *Transferable* interface. When a call to getContents(...) is made a check is made to see which native formats are available on the operating system clipboard. The results of this call are used to determine which *NativeClipboardAdaptor* objects are called to get the OS clipboard's data. Then when someone asks for the data in a particular data flavor, we already have the information available. We can find the associated *NativeClipboardAdaptor* object for the data flavor they request, and we can return the object received from the NativeClipboardAdaptor.getClipboardData() call.

When doing a setClipboardData(...) we find the *NativeClipboardAdaptor* object in our map and call NativeClipboardAdaptor.setTransferable(...). This call's purpose is to convert the format of the *Transferable* into an array of bytes. The byte information can then be retrieved by a call to NativeClipboardAdaptor.getBytes(). Here is the code for the *NativeExtendedClipboard*:

```
001: import java.awt.datatransfer.*;
002: import java.awt.Toolkit;
003: import java.io.IOException;
004: import java.util.*;
005:
006: public class NativeExtendedClipboard extends Clipboard
007:                                     implements Transferable
008: {
009:     static
```

```
010:        {
011:            System.loadLibrary("NativeExtendedClipboard");
012:        }
013:
014:    private Map          nativeFlavorMap;
015:    private Vector       nativeFlavors = new Vector();
016:
017:    public NativeExtendedClipboard ()
018:    {
019:        super("NativeClipboard");
020:        createNativeFlavorMap();
021:    }
022:
023:    private void createNativeFlavorMap ()
024:    {
025:        nativeFlavorMap = new HashMap();
026:        DataFlavor flavorImageRaw = null;
027:
028:        try
029:        {
030:            flavorImageRaw = new DataFlavor("image/raw");
031:            nativeFlavors.add(flavorImageRaw);
032:
033:            // create map of mimeType/adaptor objects
034:            nativeFlavorMap.put(flavorImageRaw.getMimeType(),
035:              Class.forName("NativeRawImageAdaptor").newInstance());
036:        }
037:        catch (Exception cnfe)
038:        {
039:            System.out.println("createNativeFlavorMap() error: " +
040:                                        cnfe.getMessage());
041:        }
042:    }
043:
044:    public Object getTransferData (DataFlavor flavor)
045:                            throws UnsupportedFlavorException
046:    {
047:        Iterator it = nativeFlavorMap.entrySet().iterator();
048:        while (it.hasNext())
049:        {
050:            //...find associated NativeClipboardAdaptor (nca)...
051:            return (nca.getClipboardData());
052:        }
053:
054:        throw new UnsupportedFlavorException (flavor);
055:    }
056:
057:    public boolean isDataFlavorSupported (DataFlavor flavor)
058:    {
059:        //search through Vector nativeFlavors to see if
060:        //flavor is supported. return true is found, false otherwise
```

```
061:        }
062:
063:        public DataFlavor[] getTransferDataFlavors()
064:        {
065:            return ((DataFlavor[]) nativeFlavors.toArray());
066:        }
067:
068:        public Transferable getContents (Object requestor)
069:        {
070:            int[] formats = getFormats();
071:
072:            Iterator it = nativeFlavorMap.entrySet().iterator();
073:            while (it.hasNext())
074:            {
075:                Map.Entry entry = (Map.Entry) it.next();
076:                NativeClipboardAdaptor nca =
077:                        (NativeClipboardAdaptor) entry.getValue();
078:
079:                for (int i = 0; i < formats.length; i++)
080:                {
081:                    if (nca.getFormat() == formats[i])
082:                    {
083:                        nca.setBytes(getBytes(formats[i]));
084:                        break;
085:                    }
086:                }
087:            }
088:
089:            return (this);
090:        }
091:
092:        public void setContents (Transferable contents,
093:                                             ClipboardOwner owner)
094:        {
095:            setNativeTransferable(contents);
096:        }
097:
098:        private void setNativeTransferable (Transferable contents)
099:        {
100:            DataFlavor[] flavors = contents.getTransferDataFlavors();
101:            String      className = "";
102:            boolean     foundIt = false;
103:
104:            Iterator it = nativeFlavorMap.entrySet().iterator();
105:            while (it.hasNext())
106:            {
107:                Map.Entry entry = (Map.Entry) it.next();
108:                String key = (String) entry.getKey();
109:
110:                // find first match and use it
111:                for (int i = 0; i < flavors.length; i++)
```

```
112:            {
113:                if (flavors[i].getMimeType().equals(key))
114:                {
115:                    NativeClipboardAdaptor nca =
116:                        (NativeClipboardAdaptor) entry.getValue();
117:                    nca.setTransferable(contents);
118:                    setNativeClipboardData(
119:                            nca.getFormat(), nca.getBytes());
120:                    foundIt = true;
121:                    break;
122:                }
123:            }
124:
125:            if (foundIt)
126:                break;
127:        }
128:    }
129:
130:    private native int[] getFormats ();
131:    private native byte[] getBytes (int format);
132:    private native void setNativeClipboardData (
133:                    int format, byte[] bytes);
134: }
```

We have already discussed how getContents(...) and setContents(...) work, so let's focus on the map creation and on the native methods. Lines 23–42 contain the code for createNativeFlavorMap(). What the code does is instantiate a *DataFlavor* object and a corresponding *NativeClipboardAdaptor* object and add them to a map. As an enhancement, you could put the information about the *DataFlavor* MIME type and the class name of the *NativeClipboardAdaptor* into a properties file. For now, we are creating one map entry between the "image/raw" *DataFlavor* and an object of class *NativeRawImageAdaptor*. The *NativeRawImageAdaptor* class implements the *NativeClipboardAdaptor* interface.

The native methods perform work to get or set information on the OS clipboard. The getFormats() call returns an array of OS-defined clipboard formats that are currently available. The getBytes(...) call retrieves the information from the OS clipboard in the requested format, and the setNativeClipboardData(...) sets the information on the clipboard using the specified format. Before we take a look at the JNI code to implement these methods, let's take a look at the source of *NativeRawImageAdaptor* to see what type of preprocessing is done on the data.

The main purpose of the *NativeRawImageAdaptor* is to take information from a Java *Transferable* object and format it so that it can be used by the OS. Basically, this involves converting the *Transferable* to an array of bytes when setting information on the OS clipboard. When information comes back from the OS clipboard, the class has to take the raw byte information and construct the appropriate *Transferable*. Here is the code:

```
01: import java.awt.datatransfer.*;
02:
03: public class NativeRawImageAdaptor implements
04:                             NativeClipboardAdaptor
05: {
06:     static int  CF_DIB = 8;
07:     static int  BYTES_PER_INT = 4;
08:     byte[]      imageData;
09:     byte[]      bytesForInt;
10:     TransferableImage  outboundCopy;
11:     DataFlavor  flavor;
12:
13:     public NativeRawImageAdaptor ()
14:     {
15:         try
16:         {
17:             flavor = new DataFlavor("image/raw");
18:         }
19:         catch (ClassNotFoundException cnfe) { }
20:     }
21:
22:     public void setTransferable (Transferable t)
23:     {
24:         TransferableImage ti = (TransferableImage) t;
25:
26:         // format we want to transfer is width, height, pixels
27:         imageData =
28:             new byte[(ti.pixels.length + 2) * BYTES_PER_INT];
29:         insertIntIntoByteArray(imageData, ti.width, 0);
30:         insertIntIntoByteArray(
31:                 imageData, ti.height, 1 * BYTES_PER_INT);
32:
33:         int offset = 2 * BYTES_PER_INT;
34:         for (int i = 0; i < ti.pixels.length; i++)
35:         {
36:             insertIntIntoByteArray2(imageData,
37:                             ti.pixels[i], offset);
38:             offset += BYTES_PER_INT;
39:         }
40:     }
41:
42:     public int getFormat ()
43:     {
44:         return (CF_DIB);
45:     }
46:
47:     public byte[] getBytes()
```

```
48:      {
49:          return (imageData);
50:      }
51:
52:      public void setBytes (byte[] b)
53:      {
54:          int width = getIntFromBytes(b, 0);
55:          int height = getIntFromBytes(b, 1 * BYTES_PER_INT);
56:
57:          int[] pixels =
58:              new int[(b.length - 2 * BYTES_PER_INT) / BYTES_PER_INT];
59:          for (int i = 0; i < pixels.length; i++)
60:              pixels[i] = getIntFromBytes(
61:                      b, 2 * BYTES_PER_INT + (i * BYTES_PER_INT));
62:
63:          outboundCopy = new TransferableImage(width, height, pixels);
64:      }
65:
66:      public Object getClipboardData()
67:      {
68:          return (outboundCopy);
69:      }
70:
71:      private int getIntFromBytes (byte[] b, int offset)
72:      {
73:
74:          int i1 = (b[offset + 3] << 24) & 0xFF000000;
75:          int i2 = (b[offset + 2] << 16) & 0xFF0000;
76:          int i3 = (b[offset + 1] << 8) & 0xFF00;
77:          int i4 = b[offset + 0] & 0xFF;
78:
79:          return (i1 | i2 | i3 | i4);
80:      }
81:
82:      private void insertIntIntoByteArray(byte[] data,
83:                                          int i, int offset)
84:      {
85:          data[offset] = (byte) (i >> 0);
86:          data[offset + 1] = (byte) (i >> 8);
87:          data[offset + 2] = (byte) (i >> 16);
88:          data[offset + 3] = (byte) (i >> 24);
89:      }
90:
91:      private void insertIntIntoByteArray2(byte[] data,
92:                                          int i, int offset)
93:      {
94:          data[offset] = (byte) (i >> 24);
95:          data[offset + 1] = (byte) (i >> 16);
96:          data[offset + 2] = (byte) (i >> 8);
97:          data[offset + 3] = (byte) (i >> 0);
98:      }
99: }
```

Most of the code is associated with converting back and forth between the byte arrays. In addition, the native format identifier this class works with is contained in the code (in our case, CF_DIB). To convert the *TransferableImage* data into an array of bytes, we must transform the *width, height,* and all *pixels* from integers into bytes. Because Windows uses the little endian format for representing integers, we take the java *int* and make its lo-byte the first byte and its hi-byte the last byte. This conversion is done in the `insertIntInto-ByteArray` (...). For converting pixels, the format can be arbitrary because we control how they are broken up in the JNI implementation. In this case, we set the hi-byte first and the lo-byte last. When data comes back from the JNI code as a byte array, the `getIntFromBytes` (...) routine is used to convert a set of bytes into an integer.

Now for the final listing—the JNI code. When discussing the JNI code I do not go into any details about how the specific JNI calls work or how to implement a native method declaration in JNI. This type of information is discussed in Item 48. The JNI code consists of the implementation of the three native methods we defined in *NativeExtendedClipboard*. After the listing of each function I point out the relevant pieces of code. Here is the (long) listing:

```
001: #include <windows.h>
002: #include "NativeExtendedClipboard.h"
003: #include "NativeExtendedTransferable.h"
004:
005: #define PALETTE_SIZE    256
006:
007: typedef struct _JavaBitmapData
008: {
009:    int       width;
010:    int       height;
011:    int       pixels[1];
012: } JavaBitmapData;
013:
014: UINT    newRegisteredFormat = 0;
015:
016: BOOL APIENTRY DllMain( HANDLE hModule,
017:                        DWORD  ul_reason_for_call,
018:                        LPVOID lpReserved
019:                      )
020: {
021:    return TRUE;
022: }
023:
024: JNIEXPORT void JNICALL
025:    Java_NativeExtendedClipboard_setNativeClipboardData
026:      (JNIEnv *pEnv, jobject pObject, jint format, jbyteArray data)
027: {
028:    HGLOBAL    handle;
```

```
029:    char       *javaData;
030:    jboolean  isCopy = FALSE;
031:
032:    JavaBitmapData     *javaBitmapData;
033:    BITMAPINFOHEADER   *bitmapHeader;
034:    RGBQUAD            *colorTable;
035:    char               *bitmapData;
036:
037:    unsigned char      red, blue, green, alpha;
038:    int                width, height, xwidth;
039:    int                pixelIndex, alignedBitmapIndex, bitmapIndex;
040:    int                numColors = 0;
041:    BOOL               colorMatch = FALSE;
042:    int                i, j, k;
043:
044:    if (OpenClipboard(NULL))
045:    {
046:      if (format == CF_DIB)
047:      {
048:        javaData =
049:          (*pEnv)->GetByteArrayElements(pEnv, data, &isCopy);
050:        javaBitmapData = (JavaBitmapData *) javaData;
051:
052:        width = javaBitmapData->width;
053:        height = javaBitmapData->height;
054:        if (width % sizeof(DWORD) == 0)
055:          xwidth = width;
056:        else
057:          xwidth = width + (sizeof(DWORD) -
058:                            (width % sizeof(DWORD)));
059:
060:        handle = GlobalAlloc(GMEM_MOVEABLE | GMEM_DDESHARE,
061:          (xwidth * height) + sizeof(BITMAPINFOHEADER) +
062:          (PALETTE_SIZE * sizeof(RGBQUAD)));
063:        bitmapHeader = (BITMAPINFOHEADER*) GlobalLock(handle);
064:        bitmapHeader->biSize = sizeof(BITMAPINFOHEADER);
065:        bitmapHeader->biWidth = javaBitmapData->width;
066:        bitmapHeader->biHeight = javaBitmapData->height;
067:        bitmapHeader->biPlanes = 1;
068:        bitmapHeader->biBitCount = 8;
069:        bitmapHeader->biCompression = BI_RGB;
070:        bitmapHeader->biSizeImage = 0;
071:        bitmapHeader->biXPelsPerMeter = 0;
072:        bitmapHeader->biYPelsPerMeter = 0;
073:        bitmapHeader->biClrUsed = 0;
074:        bitmapHeader->biClrImportant = 0;
075:
076:        // set up pointers into allocated memory
077:        colorTable = (RGBQUAD*) (((char*)bitmapHeader) +
078:                                 sizeof(BITMAPINFOHEADER));
079:        bitmapData = (char*) (colorTable + PALETTE_SIZE);
```

```
080:
081:         // create color table and assign bitmap data
082:         // make a fixed 256 color table
083:         for (i = 0; i < height; i++)
084:         {
085:             for (j = 0; j < width; j++)
086:             {
087:             pixelIndex = (i * width) + j;
088:             alignedBitmapIndex = (i * xwidth) + j;
089:             red = (char) (javaBitmapData->pixels[pixelIndex] >> 8);
090:             green = (char) (javaBitmapData->pixels[pixelIndex] >> 16);
091:             blue = (char) (javaBitmapData->pixels[pixelIndex] >> 24);
092:             alpha = (char) (javaBitmapData->pixels[pixelIndex]);
093:
094:             colorMatch = FALSE;
095:             for (k = 0; k < numColors; k++)
096:             {
097:               if ((colorTable + k)->rgbBlue == blue &&
098:                   (colorTable + k)->rgbGreen == green &&
099:                   (colorTable + k)->rgbRed == red)
100:                 {
101:                 bitmapIndex = alignedBitmapIndex +
102:                         xwidth * (height - (1 + (2 * i)));
103:                 bitmapData[bitmapIndex] = (char) k;
104:                 colorMatch = TRUE;
105:                 break;
106:                 }
107:             }
108:
109:             if (!colorMatch)
110:             {
111:               bitmapIndex = alignedBitmapIndex +
112:                       xwidth * (height - (1 + (2 * i)));
113:               bitmapData[bitmapIndex] = (char) numColors;
114:               (colorTable + numColors)->rgbBlue = blue;
115:               (colorTable + numColors)->rgbGreen = green;
116:               (colorTable + numColors)->rgbRed = red;
117:               (colorTable + numColors)->rgbReserved = 0;
118:               numColors++;
119:             }
120:           }
121:         }
122:         (*pEnv)->ReleaseByteArrayElements(pEnv, data,
123:                                     javaData, JNI_ABORT);
124:         GlobalUnlock(handle);
125:
126:         EmptyClipboard();
127:         SetClipboardData(format, handle);
128:         CloseClipboard();
129:       }
130:   }
131: }
```

Lines 7–12 define the *JavaBitmapData* structure. This structure is defined to help us get access to the byte array that will be passed in. This structure mirrors the data definition of the *TransferableImage* class. In line 48 we get the byte array with a JNI call. On line 50 we cast the byte array to *JavaBitmapData** data type. This provides easy access to the elements. After retrieving the height and width, lines 54–57 are used to determine the *DWORD* aligned width. This is a requirement for the Windows DIB format we are using. All this means is that the width must be a multiple of *sizeof(DWORD)*, even if no pixel information exists at the end of the line. In lines 60–62 we allocate the necessary memory to create the DIB format. This consists of enough room for the bitmap header, enough room for the color table, and enough room for the bitmap data. In lines 63–74 we set up the bitmap header information to the correct values. Lines 76–121 perform the actual work of converting the pixel information in the byte array into the DIB format. As we go through each pixel, we determine if we have the color value for the pixel in the color table already. If not, we add it to the color table. The value of the bitmap data for the pixel is then set to the index of the color in the color table. After the pixels have been transformed into the DIB format, we free the memory and set the contents of the DIB to the clipboard. The `SetClipboardData`(...) call in line 127 actually sets the information to the OS clipboard.

You may have noticed the funky indexing going on in order to set the index of the bitmap data. The DIB format expects the origin of the image data to be in the lower-left corner and to proceed from bottom to top. We pass in the information starting at the upper-left corner and proceeding from top to bottom. The index calculations make the necessary conversions. In addition, we take into account that we have to *DWORD* align each row.

```
133: JNIEXPORT jintArray JNICALL
134:   Java_NativeExtendedClipboard_getFormats
135:   (JNIEnv *pEnv, jobject pObject)
136: {
137:   jintArray  returnFormats;
138:   int        localFormats[100];
139:   int        numFormats = 0;
140:   int        previousFormat = 0;
141:
142:   if (OpenClipboard(NULL))
143:   {
144:     while (TRUE)
145:     {
146:       localFormats[numFormats] =
147:           EnumClipboardFormats(previousFormat);
148:       if (localFormats[numFormats] == 0)
149:         break;
150:
151:       previousFormat = localFormats[numFormats];
```

```
152:           numFormats++;
153:         }
154:         returnFormats = (*pEnv)->NewIntArray(pEnv, numFormats);
155:         (*pEnv)->SetIntArrayRegion(pEnv, returnFormats, 0,
156:                                   numFormats, localFormats);
157:         CloseClipboard();
158:
159:         return (returnFormats);
160:       }
161:     else
162:       return (NULL);
163: }
```

This function opens up the Windows clipboard and gets all formats for the data currently placed on the clipboard. The *EnumClipboardFormats* (line 147) actually does the work of getting the formats. When we have a complete listing, we allocate a Java integer array and return it to the caller.

```
165: JNIEXPORT jbyteArray JNICALL Java_NativeExtendedClipboard_getBytes
166:   (JNIEnv *pEnv, jobject pObject, jint format)
167: {
168:   HGLOBAL       handle;
169:   jbyteArray    returnData = NULL;
170:   int           BYTES_PER_INT = 4;
171:
172:   BITMAPINFOHEADER  *bitmapHeader;
173:   int               colorTableSize = 0;
174:   RGBQUAD           *colorTable;
175:   unsigned int      colorTableIndex = 0;
176:   RGBQUAD           currentNativePixel;
177:   char              *bitmapData;
178:   int               width, height, xwidth;
179:   int               numPixels;
180:   int               pixelIndex, alignedBitmapIndex, bitmapIndex;
181:   int               i, j;
182:   unsigned char     alpha;
183:
184:   if (OpenClipboard(NULL))
185:   {
186:     handle = GetClipboardData(format);
187:     if (handle != NULL)
188:     {
189:       if (format == CF_DIB)
190:       {
191:         bitmapHeader = (BITMAPINFOHEADER *) GlobalLock(handle);
192:         if (bitmapHeader->biSize == sizeof(BITMAPINFOHEADER))
193:         {
194:           width = bitmapHeader->biWidth;
195:           height = bitmapHeader->biHeight;
196:
```

```
197:            if (width % sizeof(DWORD) == 0)
198:              xwidth = width;
199:            else
200:              xwidth = width + (sizeof(DWORD) -
201:                           (width % sizeof(DWORD)));
202:
203:            numPixels = width * height;
204:
205:            // get information on color table
206:            colorTable = (RGBQUAD*) (((char*)bitmapHeader) +
207:                              sizeof(BITMAPINFOHEADER));
208:            colorTableSize = 1 << bitmapHeader->biBitCount;
209:
210:            bitmapData = (char*) (colorTable + colorTableSize);
211:            returnData = (*pEnv)->NewByteArray(pEnv,
212:                           sizeof(JavaBitmapData) +
213:                           (numPixels - 1) * sizeof(int));
214:
215:        (*pEnv)->SetByteArrayRegion(pEnv, returnData,
216:                           0, BYTES_PER_INT, (char*)&width);
217:        (*pEnv)->SetByteArrayRegion(pEnv, returnData,
218:           1 * BYTES_PER_INT, BYTES_PER_INT, (char*)&height);
219:
220:            pixelIndex = 2 * BYTES_PER_INT;
221:            alpha = 255;
222:            for (i = 0; i < height; i++)
223:            {
224:              for (j = 0; j < width; j++)
225:              {
226:                alignedBitmapIndex = (i * xwidth) + j;
227:                bitmapIndex = alignedBitmapIndex + xwidth *
228:                                    (height - (1 + (2 * i)));
229:
230:                colorTableIndex =
231:                    (unsigned int) bitmapData[bitmapIndex];
232:                currentNativePixel = colorTable[colorTableIndex];
233:                (*pEnv)->SetByteArrayRegion(pEnv, returnData,
234:                           pixelIndex + 3, 1, (char*)&(alpha));
235:                (*pEnv)->SetByteArrayRegion(pEnv, returnData,
236:                           pixelIndex + 2, 1,
237:                           (char*)&(currentNativePixel.rgbRed));
238:                (*pEnv)->SetByteArrayRegion(pEnv, returnData,
239:                           pixelIndex + 1, 1,
240:                           (char*)&(currentNativePixel.rgbGreen));
241:                (*pEnv)->SetByteArrayRegion(pEnv, returnData,
242:                           pixelIndex, 1,
243:                           (char*)&(currentNativePixel.rgbBlue));
244:                pixelIndex += BYTES_PER_INT;
245:              }
246:            }
247:        }
```

```
248:        else
249:        {
250:          // unknown bitmap flavor
251:          return (NULL);
252:        }
253:      }
254:      else
255:      {
256:        return (NULL);
257:      }
258:    }
259:    CloseClipboard();
260:  }
261:  return (returnData);
262: }
```

In the *Java_NativeExtendedClipboard_getBytes* function we perform the reverse functionality of the *Java_NativeExtendedClipboard_setNativeClipboardData* function. First we get the height and width of the DIB by looking at the header (lines 194–195). We allocate enough bytes through a JNI call to pass back the *width*, *height*, and *pixel* information of the DIB (line 211). Lines 215–218 actually set the *width* and *height* into the Java byte array. Lines 220–246 perform the reverse translation from DIB format into the pixel information we are expecting. Each element of the bitmap is looked up in the color table, and the color values for that color table entry are used to construct the pixel. After we have all of the data, we close the clipboard and return.

Using this code, you should have no problem performing Inter-JVM transfers or Native-JVM transfers. Figure 40.2 shows the result of copying both images into a painting program, combining them into one image, and copying a piece of the new image back.

The best solution for supporting all three types of transfers is to use JNI to gain access to the operating system clipboard. This solution takes a lot of work (especially to build it for multiple platforms), but the result is increased interoperability with other applications.

Item 41: A KeyListener That Doesn't Listen?

A *KeyListener* that doesn't listen? I have a two-year-old daughter who doesn't listen, but from what I read that is to be expected. If I add a *KeyListener* to a component, however, I expect it to listen.

If I add a *KeyListener* to a *JComboBox*, I expect it to listen to keystrokes when the *JComboBox* is active. The *JComboBox* actually already does this with certain keystrokes but does not work with the keys that I am adding. When the up-arrow key is pressed, the items will scroll down so you can see the previous item. Similarly, when the down-arrow key is pressed the items will scroll up so

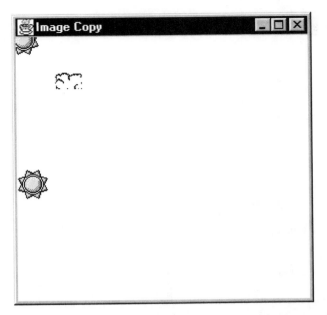

Figure 40.2   Result of copying image between native application and Java application.

you can see the next item in the list. The *JComboBox* even listens for character keystrokes. When an "a" through "z" character is pressed, the *JComboBox* tries to select an item that begins with that character. All of this functionality is great, but suppose we have a *JComboBox* that has a list of 100 items. If the user does not know the first letter of the item he wants, he must use the scroll bar, or the up- and down-arrow keys to scroll through the items. It would be nice if the user could press the page-up key and the page-down key to look through the list. In order to get this functionality you must extend the *JComboBox* class and add your own *KeyListener*. The *KeyListener* would listen for page-up and page-down keystrokes and adjust the viewable portion of the list accordingly. Suppose you are looking at a *JComboBox* that displays 10 items at once. When the list is first displayed, you would see items 0 through item 9. After you press the page-down key, you would see items 10 through item 19. Let's give it a try.

Here is the code to add the new *KeyListener*:

```
01:  public class EJComboBox extends JComboBox
02:  {
03:    public EJComboBox(ComboBoxModel aModel)
04:    {
05:      super(aModel);
06:      addExtraKeyListener();
07:    }
```

```
08:
09:    public EJComboBox(final Object[] items)
10:    {
11:        super(items);
12:        addExtraKeyListener();
13:    }
14:
15:    public EJComboBox(Vector items)
16:    {
17:        super(items);
18:        addExtraKeyListener();
19:    }
20:
21:    public void addExtraKeyListener()
22:    {
23:        addKeyListener(new ExtraKeyListener());
24:    }
25:
26:    public class ExtraKeyListener extends KeyAdapter
27:    {
28:        public void keyPressed(KeyEvent e)
29:        {
30:            ... // code to handle page-up and page-down keystrokes
31:        }
32:    }
33:  }
```

Notice that each constructor first calls super(...) and then calls the addExtraKeyListener() method. Each constructor calls its super(...) constructor so the *EJComboBox* will still get all of the functionality of the *JComboBox*. The call to the addExtraKeyListener(...) method adds the new key listener, which is listening for page-up and page-down keys to be pressed. Therefore, the *EJComboBox* will be listening for character key presses, up-arrow key presses, down-arrow key presses, page-up key presses, or page-down key presses. We get all of this functionality because we get our super classes key listeners as well as the new key listener that we just added.

To test the new *EJComboBox* class we can add a main method, which pops up a frame with an *EJComboBox* in it. When we create the *EJComboBox* we send it a list of all of the tables in our database. Let's say there are 50 tables in our database. When the *EJComboBox* comes up, we should be able to click on the combo box and press the page-down key. What do you think will happen after the page-down key is pressed? The obvious answer is, "You will see table 10 through table 19 in the list." Unfortunately, that may be the obvious answer, but it is also the wrong answer. If we display the *EJComboBox* and click on it, then press the page-down key, nothing happens at all. You can still press a character key, the up-arrow key or a down-arrow key. The functionality of the

JComboBox still works. The only problem is that the *ExtraKeyListener* that we added in the *EJComboBox* class does not listen. Let's review what we did. We created an *EJComboBox* class, which extends *JComboBox*. Each constructor calls its super classes constructor and then adds the new key listener. The new key listener listens for page-up and page-down key presses. We display the GUI, we click on the *EJComboBox*, which is listening for the page-up and page-down key presses, and nothing happens. So, if the *EJComboBox* is listening for key events, why doesn't it hear anything?

The reason is that we are not clicking on the *EJComboBox*. I don't mean that your mouse skills are poor and you are actually clicking on something else. What I mean is this: The *JComboBox* is a container object that is made up of several components. The *JComboBox* is made up of a *JButton*, a *CellRenderer*, and if the *JComboBox* is editable it also has an editor component. The component that is clicked on is the *JButton* component or the editor component if the *JComboBox* is editable. Actually, the specific component you are clicking on depends on which look and feel you are using. If you are using the metal look and feel, the component is really a *MetalComboBoxButton*, which extends *JButton*. If you are using a different look and feel, the *ComboBoxButton* specific to that UI is the component that is being clicked on. You may have guessed it. If the *JButton* component is the active component, and if our listener is listening to the *EJComboBox* component, then our listener is not going to hear anything. We have to add the *ExtraKeyListener* to the *MetalComboBoxButton* component instead of the *EJComboBox* component. If you are having trouble visualizing this, think of it this way. A *JPanel* can have many components added to it. If a *KeyListener* is added to the *JPanel*, that does not mean that the *KeyListener* gets added to every component of the *JPanel*. The *JComboBox* acts the same way. If you add a *KeyListener* to the *JComboBox* it does not automatically get added to all of the components of the *JComboBox*. Fortunately, the solution is relatively simple.

The *addExtraKeyListener* in the previous example must be modified to add the *ExtraKeyListener* to the components contained in the *JComboBox*.

```
01:  public void addExtraKeyListener()
02:  {
03:      Component[] components = getComponents();
04:      ExtraKeyListener keyListener = new ExtraKeyListener();
05:      for (int i = 0; i<components.length; i++)
06:      {
07:          if (components[i] instanceof JComponent)
08:              components[i].addKeyListener(keyListener);
09:      }
```

The addExtraKeyListener() method gets all of the components of the *EJComboBox* (line 3) and adds the *ExtraKeyListener* to each component (line

8). Now when you click on the *MetalComboBoxButton* and press the page-down key, the page-down key press is heard and the list automatically scrolls down to the next page of items.

It is important to understand the reason why the initial *EJComboBox* did not work. You may think you do not have to worry about this problem because you will never want to add a *KeyListener* to a *JComboBox*. This problem, though, applies to other situations as well. Remember, the *ExtraKeyListener* did not listen because the component being listened to was the *EJComboBox*, but the active component was actually the *MetalComboBoxButton*. You must add the listeners to the proper component. Another situation in which you run into the same problem occurs when you want to add a tool tip to a container object. If you call `setToolTipText(...)` on the *JComboBox* component, what do you think would happen? If you said, "Nothing," you are absolutely correct. The tool tip works on a mouse-over. To listen for the mouse-over you must set the tool tip text on the component that is being moused-over. In order to see the tool tip for the *JComboBox* we must set the tool tip on the *MetalComboBoxButton* component, exactly the same way we added the *ExtraKeyListener*. Give it a try.

Item 42: Printing Text, HTML, and Images in a JEditorPane

Since the inclusion of Java2D in the Java platform, printing capability has been available. This printing capability is made possible by using the classes contained in the java.awt.print package. The printing APIs included in the java.awt.print package are straightforward and easy to use—most of the work to perform printing comes from drawing to the *Graphics* object. One way to get around implementing extra code for drawing to the printer *Graphics* object is to reuse the code for drawing to the screen *Graphics* object. This is the tact taken by *JComponent*, the *superclass* of all Swing components. When the *JComponent*'s `print(...)` or `printAll(...)` method is called, the result is a call to the `paint(...)` method (after setting some flags). When using these print methods to perform printing you definitely get something printed out, but it most certainly won't be what you expect.

This item focuses on printing content available in the *JEditorPane*. The *JEditorPane* is a flexible Swing class that supports the display and editing of standard text, HTML, and RTF. For our examples we load the *JEditorPane* with HTML containing images. Before we get started let's take a look at some of the classes we will use from the *java.awt.print* package.

PrinterJob. This class is the main class for controlling printing. It can display print dialogs to adjust settings, and it can manage the print process. Information to be printed can be added by calling the `setPrintable(...)`

or `setPageable(…)` methods. To start the print job the `print()` method is used.

PageFormat. This class represents formatting characteristics of a piece of paper. This includes information about the paper, paper orientation, and the current preferred bounding rectangle for printing (x, y, width, height). The preferred bounding rectangle is computed by taking into account the paper size, orientation, and the margins. These methods can be used to obtain the rectangle's bounds: `getImageableX()`, `getImageableY()`, `getImageableWidth()`, and `getImageableHeight()`. Note that even though these methods return the coordinates of the desired rectangle, nothing prevents you from printing outside the rectangle. This may be desirable if you need to print a header or footer.

Printable. This interface contains one method, `print(…)`, which takes three arguments: a *Graphics* object, a *PageFormat* object, and an integer representing the *pageIndex*. In addition to the `print(…)` method the *PAGE_EXISTS* and *NO_SUCH_PAGE* constants are defined. An object that wishes to be printed implements this interface. When the print(…) method is called the component is expected to print itself on the specified *Graphics* object using the constraints in the *PageFormat* object. This method is called continuously until *NO_SUCH_PAGE* is returned. The component is expected to draw only the contents of the page specified by *pageIndex*. When the specified page is rendered a return of *PAGE_EXISTS* indicates success.

Pageable. This interface represents a collection of *Printable* objects in some format. Each page can potentially have its own *PageFormat* and *Printable* object. This interface is not used in this item.

Now that we have a basic understanding of these print classes, let's put them together. The following code lists the *JEditorPaneFrame* class. This class loads up a URL in a *JEditorPane* and displays it in a *JFrame*. Printing support has been added by creating a subclass of *JEditorPane* called *MyEditor* and making it implement the *Printable* interface. Here is the code:

```
01: import javax.swing.*;
02: import java.net.*;
03: import java.awt.event.*;
04: import java.awt.print.*;
05: import java.awt.*;
06: import java.io.*;
07:
08: public class JEditorPaneFrame extends JFrame
09:                              implements ActionListener
10: {
11:     JMenuItem print = new JMenuItem("Print");
```

```
12:         JMenuItem exit = new JMenuItem("Exit");
13:         MyEditor editor;
14:
15:         public JEditorPaneFrame (String title)
16:         {
17:             super(title);
18:
19:             try
20:             {
21:                 print.addActionListener(this);
22:                 exit.addActionListener(this);
23:                 JMenu file = new JMenu("File");
24:                 file.add(print);
25:                 file.add(exit);
26:                 JMenuBar menuBar = new JMenuBar();
27:                 menuBar.add(file);
28:                 setJMenuBar(menuBar);
29:
30:                 URL url =
31:                     new URL("file:/d:/jdk1.3/docs/guide/2d/index.html");
32:                 editor = new MyEditor(url);
33:
34:                 JScrollPane sp = new JScrollPane(editor);
35:
36:                 editor.setEditable(false);
37:                 getContentPane().add("Center", sp);
38:             }
39:             catch (Exception e)
40:             {
41:                 System.out.println("Error: " + e.getMessage());
42:                 System.exit(1);
43:             }
44:
45:             setSize(400,400);
46:             setVisible(true);
47:         }
48:
49:         public void actionPerformed(ActionEvent evt)
50:         {
51:             if (evt.getSource() == print)
52:             {
53:                 PrinterJob job = PrinterJob.getPrinterJob();
54:                 job.setPrintable(editor);
55:                 try
56:                 {
57:                     job.print();
58:                 }
59:                 catch (PrinterException pe)
60:                 {
61:                     System.out.println("Printer Error: " +
62:                                                     pe.getMessage());
```

```
63:              }
64:          }
65:          else if (evt.getSource() == exit)
66:          {
67:              this.dispose();
68:              System.exit(1);
69:          }
70:      }
71:
72:      public static void main (String args[])
73:      {
74:          new JEditorPaneFrame("Test JEditor Pane Print");
75:      }
76: }
77:
78: class MyEditor extends JEditorPane implements Printable
79: {
80:      public MyEditor (URL url) throws IOException
81:      {
82:          super (url);
83:      }
84:
85:      public int print (Graphics graphics, PageFormat pageFormat,
86:                                              int pageIndex)
87:      {
88:          if (pageIndex == 0)
89:          {
90:              printAll(graphics);
91:              return (Printable.PAGE_EXISTS);
92:          }
93:          else
94:              return (Printable.NO_SUCH_PAGE);
95:      }
96: }
```

When the code is executed Figure 42.1 is produced. If you select the *Print* menu item the block of code between lines 53 and 63 (inclusive) is executed. In line 53 we get a *PrintJob* so we can use it for printing. In line 54 we set the content to be printed, and in line 57 the actual print execution occurs. When the PrintJob.print() method is invoked, our *Printable* object starts getting its print(...) method invoked. In the example our *Printable* object is the *MyEditor* class, and its implementation prints its contents on a single page of paper. The printed output can be seen in Figure 42.2.

Looking at the printed output you can see several things are immediately wrong with the document.

- The left side of the text is cut off.
- The top side of the text is cut off.

Figure 42.1   JEditorPaneFrame.

- The text does not take up the full width provided.
- The font looks too big.
- Only one piece of paper is printed (this was done intentionally for now, but it will have to be fixed later on).

Using `printAll(...)` by itself is not going to work if we want a reasonable set of printed output. This leaves us with the a couple of options: (1) duplicate the printing/painting code of *JEditorPane* and modify it to ensure correct printing or (2) use translations and techniques to perform better printing without modifying the printing/painting routines. Option 1 could certainly turn out to be

■ contact us

s to help you navigate the Wiley Web
site

al
ng
:h

Search for book titles, authors, or ISBNs in the the Wiley
Catalog database
Quick Search:

Search

Go to the catalog home page

ite
:h

Search the pages on the Wiley Web site.
Quick Search:

Search

:h	analog AND	*find all documents containing both*
les	digital	*"analog" and "digital"*
	analog OR	*find all documents containing either*
	digital	*"analog" or "digital"*
	analog*	*find all documents containing "analog,"*
		"analogue," "analogy," etc.

Figure 42.2   First try of printing HTML from JEditorPane.

a daunting task, even with the help of the existing code to guide you. The
Option 1 approach will be a lot of work, and it will be hard to maintain. Given
enough time and effort, though, it could probably do everything you want it to
do. Option 2 will be a lot less work and it will be easier to maintain because it
will still use the *JEditorPane*'s existing `printAll (...)` routine. We choose
Option 2 to fix the problem.

Upon further analysis and reflection of the situation we determine that the
following tasks need to be done:

- Translate between printer coordinates and screen coordinates.

- Observe the bounding rectangle passed in by the *PageFormat*.

- Make the component paint to the full width of the bounding rectangle.

- Calculate number of pages.

The *Graphics* object that is passed into the `print(...)` function uses points instead of pixels as its coordinate system. In order for us to effectively translate the printer coordinates into screen coordinates we have to do a conversion. Each point represents 1/72 of an inch. Depending on your monitor resolution, the ratio of pixels per inch may vary. Luckily for us, the *Toolkit* class provides the `getScreenResolution()` method, which returns the number of pixels per inch for the screen. To convert printing coordinates to screen coordinates we use this formula:

```
screen_coor = printer_coor * 72 / toolkit.getScreenResolution()
```

To observe the bounding rectangle of the *PageFormat* object, we simply check the values of the *PageFormat* methods: `getImageableX()`, `getImageableY()`, `getImageableWidth()`, and `getImageableHeight()`. This returns the coordinates of the bounding rectangle in printer coordinates. Because we want screen coordinates we use this formula to convert printer coordinates to screen coordinates. To make sure these are observed during printing, the `Graphics.setClip(...)` method is used to clip the area to be printed to the newly calculated coordinates. This call will look like this:

```
graphics.setClip(newX, newY, newWidth, newHeight)
```

where graphics is an instance of *Graphics* and the <new> parameters are the translated coordinates.

The unfortunate thing about making these transformations from printer to screen coordinates is that our *Graphics* object is still point based. So when we draw according to the new screen coordinates, we are drawing outside of the desired bounding rectangle (if (72 / screen_res) > 1). We can fix this problem by scaling the information on the *Graphics* object back down to fit within the bounding rectangle. Because the *Graphics* object passed into print is really a *Graphics2D* object, we simply call the `Graphics2D.scale(...)` method to scale it back to size. The actual call will be:

```
graphics.scale(toolkit.getScreenResolution() / 72,
toolkit.getScreenResolution() / 72)
```

in which graphics is an instance of *Graphics2D* and toolkit is an instance of *Toolkit*. With these two fixes we have observed the *PageFormat* bounding rectangle and have successfully done a conversion from points to pixels, so now when we print, the size of the output looks correct, but the text is not taking up the full extent of the page width, and the left side is still cut off. There are still a few more problems to fix. To prevent the left side of the document from being cut off, we must translate the drawing origin of the *Graphics* object to *newX*, *newY* so we don't clip the regions to the left and top of these coordinates. To do this we use the `Graphics.translate(...)` method like this:

```
graphics.translate(newX, newY)
```

This call translates the origin of the paint calls such that painting to point 0, 0 actually results in painting to *newX, newY*. Now that the translation solves the problem of transforming the origins we must correct the setClip(...) call to not start at *newX, newY*. The modified call is this:

```
graphics.setClip(0, 0, newWidth, newHeight)
```

The last problem to solve is how to print the content so that the available page width is used correctly. Currently the component prints itself as it is being displayed on screen. To fix this problem we can temporarily change the width and height of the component to match the size of the *PageFormat*'s bounding rectangle and after printing set it back to its original size. This is accomplished by calling:

```
editor.setSize(newWidth, newHeight)
```

After printing setSize(...) is called again to restore the original values. This solves all of the problems accept for multipage printing, so let's take a look at the modified MyEditor.print(...) routine with these changes included. The code for determining the number of pages is also included and will be explained after the listing.

```
01: public int print (Graphics graphics, PageFormat pageFormat,
02:                                              int pageIndex)
03: {
04:     int screenResolution = getToolkit().getScreenResolution();
05:     double pixelsPerPoint = (double) screenResolution / 72d;
06:
07:     int keepWidth = getSize().width;
08:     int keepHeight = getSize().height;
09:
10:     if (pageIndex == 0)
11:     {
12:         // first time through - lets calculate num pages
13:         pageWidth = (int) (pageFormat.getImageableWidth() *
14:                                             pixelsPerPoint);
15:         pageHeight = (int) (pageFormat.getImageableHeight() *
16:                                             pixelsPerPoint);
17:
18:         setSize(pageWidth, pageHeight);
19:         Graphics temp = graphics.create();
20:
21:         printAll(temp); // recalculate our preferred height
22:
23:         temp = null;
24:
```

```
25:             int newHeight = getPreferredSize().height;
26:             if (newHeight % pageHeight == 0)
27:                 numPages = newHeight / pageHeight;
28:             else
29:                 numPages = newHeight / pageHeight + 1;
30:         }
31:     else if (pageIndex >= numPages)
32:     {
33:         return (Printable.NO_SUCH_PAGE);
34:     }
35:
36:     // make translation between pixels and points
37:     int newXOrigin = (int) (pageFormat.getImageableX() *
38:                                             pixelsPerPoint);
39:     int newYOrigin = (int) (pageFormat.getImageableY() *
40:                                             pixelsPerPoint);
41:
42:     setSize(pageWidth, pageHeight);
43:
44:     if (graphics instanceof Graphics2D)
45:     {
46:         Graphics2D graphics2D = (Graphics2D) graphics;
47:         graphics2D.scale(1 / pixelsPerPoint, 1 / pixelsPerPoint);
48:     }
49:
50:     graphics.translate(newXOrigin,
51:                   newYOrigin - (pageIndex * pageHeight));
52:     graphics.setClip(0,(pageIndex * pageHeight),
53:                                     pageWidth, pageHeight);
54:
55:     printAll(graphics);
56:
57:     setSize(keepWidth, keepHeight);
58:     return (Printable.PAGE_EXISTS);
59: }
```

On lines 4 and 5 we calculate the multiplier to be used for converting from points to pixels. On lines 13–16 and 37–40 we use the information about the bounding rectangle from *PageFormat* and convert it into the screen coordinates: *newXOrigin*, *newYOrigin*, *pageWidth*, *pageHeight*. Lines 18–29 handle the calculations needed to print multiple pages. This will be discussed in a few moments. On line 42 we resize the component to *pageWidth* and *pageHeight* so the component will print according to this size instead of the size in which it is displayed on the screen. On line 47 we perform the scaling to convert screen coordinates into printer coordinates. Lines 50–53 do the necessary translation and clipping to print out the current page. Now that everything is set up correctly, line 55 is called to actually perform the printing to the *Graphics* object. After it returns, we set the component size back to its original values (line 57) and return *PAGE_EXISTS* (line 58) to indicate a successful page has been printed. Printing the contents of the *JEditorPaneFrame* with the new code results in the output shown in Figure 42.3.

In order to support multipage printing we must accurately determine the number of pages that will be printed based on the current *PageFormat*. Lines 18–29 show how this is done. After calculating the *pageWidth* and *pageHeight* of the *PageFormat* bounding rectangle we set the component size equal to the size of the bounding rectangle. In line 19 we create a temporary *Graphics* object to be used for printing. On line 21 the `printAll(...)` method is called, which will force the recalculation of the component's preferred height. This is really what we are after, but it does not get calculated when you call `set-Size(...)`. You must actually paint the component before this value will be recalculated. Now that the preferred height has been recalculated we discard the temporary *Graphics* object (line 23). The number of pages required is the value of the newly calculated preferred height divided by the *pageHeight*. If the result of the division is not exact, we want to make sure we have a page allocated to print the content of the partial page. Lines 25–29 show the calculation of the number of pages. Because the number of pages is computed we can use this value to determine when there are no more printable pages. Line 31 performs this check. In order to properly print pages beyond the first page we must make sure the translation and clipping are done properly. Lines 50 and 52 use the product of *pageIndex* * *pageHeight* to perform the proper calculations.

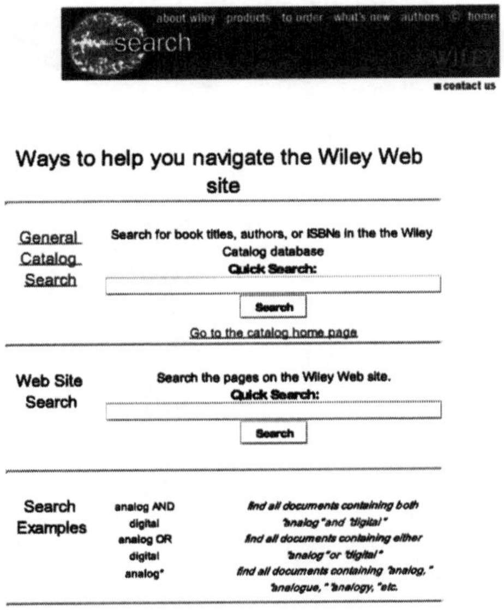

Figure 42.3 Correct output of printing HTML from JeditorPane.

Using the translations and techniques shown previously produces accurate printed output. Unfortunately, it is so accurate that lines can be broken across multiple pages. This is something you will have to live with unless you want to go back and implement option 1.

This item showed that you can get good printed output by reusing the JEditorPane's printAll(...) method if you perform the necessary translations/transformations. This methodology is not specific to *JEditorPane*—it can be applied to all *Swing* components and possibly all components if the printAll(...) method is not already overridden to perform this printing logic. Using the available printAll(...) method on a component gives you a good, immediate solution, but it may not solve all of your printing problems such as lines breaking across pages.

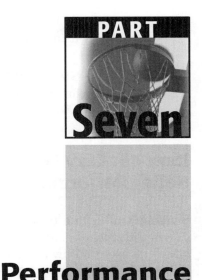

PART

Seven

Performance

We should forget about small efficiencies, say about 97% of the time: premature optimization is the root of all evil.

—DONALD KNUTH, "AN EMPIRICAL STUDY OF FORTRAN PROGRAMS"

Java performance has always been a good news/bad news proposition. The good news is that "performance is improving." The bad news is that "it's still not quite there." So, while we should follow Donald Knuth's advice, and the situation is improving (from both a hardware and a software perspective), these items will assist you in improving your code if optimization is necessary. There are five items in this part:

Item 43, "Lazy Loading Our Way to Better Performance," examines the lazy-loading design pattern to improve performance. This item is especially useful for improving the startup time of graphical user interfaces.

Item 44, "Using Object Pools for Excessive Object Creation," demonstrates and analyzes the use of object pools to recycle objects. It also compares object pools to caching.

Item 45, "Performance Watch: Array versus Vector," benchmarks the use of *Vectors* versus arrays. This item also discusses when Vectors are appropriate and the use of the ArrayList collection.

Item 46, "Avoid Using Temporary Arrays for Dynamic Array Growth," benchmarks using temporary arrays versus *System.arraycopy* for array growth.

Item 47 "Use StringBuffer Instead of '+' for Concatenation inside a Loop," benchmarks using *StringBuffer* versus '+' for String concatenation in a loop. *StringBuffer* wins big.

Item 43: Lazy Loading Our Way to Better Performance

Suppose you have a task to create a drawing package for your system. The drawing package will consist of several different drawing tools. These tools will allow the user to draw circles, squares, free-hand lines, text, images and much more. This drawing package will be used in a Command and Control System. The Command and Control System may be used to keep track of rescue troops during an earthquake in Turkey or perhaps keep track of a rescue operation for an airplane crash in the middle of the ocean. The system will have prebuilt palettes. One palette may contain all of the drawing tools for the different shapes, while another palette may contain the icons of salvage boats. The user will also be able to create his or her own palette with any clip art images he or she wants. The capability to create custom palettes will be very important because it may be one user's job to plot the location of each piece of the airplane wreckage that has been found; it may be another user's job to plot the current weather picture. Each user will want to have a custom palette that holds the drawing tools and images that are specific to that job.

Because the Command and Control System will be running on laptop computers we will have limited hardware resources. We cannot preload all of the palettes in the drawing package when the system is initializing because we may run out of memory. In this case, we must take advantage of a design pattern called lazy loading, or lazy instantiation. Of course, the disadvantage of this design pattern is that the user will have to wait for the palette to be loaded when he or she selects it. It's a difficult balance that must be achieved in order to get the best performance from the system. This balance is certainly system dependent as well as hardware dependent.

Let's look at a quick example to illustrate the lazy-loading design pattern.

```
01: public class SystemGui
02: {
03:    PreferenceGui preferenceGui = new PreferenceGUI();
04:    public ControlFrame()
05:    {
```

```
06:    // set up and display the main system GUI
07:    }
08:
09:    public preferenceMenuItemCallback()
10:    {
11:     preferenceGui.show();
12:    }
13:    // rest of class …
14: }
```

In this example, we have a main GUI class that is responsible for creating and displaying the system GUI. On line 3 we instantiate a *PreferenceGui* object that allows the user to change the preferences for the system. The *PreferenceGui* has check boxes and sliders and combo boxes. When the user selects the "Preferences" menu item the `preferenceMenuItemCallback()` method will eventually get called and the preference GUI will be displayed. So what's the problem with the code? Well, what if the user never clicks on the "Preferences" menu item? In this case, we have wasted plenty of memory storing an object that never gets used. Because the instantiation of the *PreferenceGui* object is recursive, we are also storing all of the objects that *PreferenceGui* itself instantiates, and so on. The main idea behind lazy loading is simple: Do not instantiate an object until it is needed. The *PreferenceGui* object is not needed until the user selects the "Preferences" menu item. Let's modify the code a bit to illustrate this point.

```
01: public class SystemGui
02: {
03:    PreferenceGui preferenceGui = null;
04:    public ControlFrame()
05:    {
06:     // set up and display the main system GUI
07:    }
08:
09:    public preferenceMenuItemCallback()
10:    {
11:     if (preferenceGui == null)
12:       preferenceGui = new PreferenceGUI();
13:     preferenceGui.show();
14:    }
15:    // rest of class …
16: }
```

In this example we set the *preferenceGui* object equal to *null* on line 3. When the user selects the "Preferences" menu item, the `preferenceMenuItemCallback()` method on line 9 eventually gets called, at which point the *preferenceGui* object gets instantiated if it is has not been created already. In this design, the *preferenceGui* object does not get created until it is needed. If it is not needed, we do not waste memory storing it.

To apply this concept to our palette problem, we can display a tree of palette names, but we do not actually load any palettes until the user selects one. When the user selects a specific palette, it is lazy loaded. Once the palette is loaded it is displayed showing the appropriate drawing tools or images. Once again, the disadvantage is that the user must wait for the palette to load the first time it is selected. If the user needs only one or two of the palettes for the specific job we will not be wasting memory by having them all preloaded. We may be able to improve the design by compromising a bit. We can allow the user to set a "favorite" palette preference. We can use that preference to initialize the user's favorite palette during the system initialization, while continuing to lazy load the remaining palettes. Once again, this depends on the system requirements. If the drawing tools are a major part of the system and are almost certainly going to be used, it may be a good idea to load up the user's favorite palette during system initialization. This way there will be no delay time when the user chooses his or her favorite palette.

We have discussed a few different ways to load our palettes. We can load all of the palettes during the system initialization, we can lazy load the palettes, or we can combine the two and preload only a specific palette while lazy loading the remaining palettes. The first way may not be such a good idea if we have limited memory resources, but suppose we have plenty of memory and we can load in all of the palettes during initialization. This sounds like a good idea, but why should we make the user wait for all of the palettes to be preloaded at startup if the user is going to use only a handful? The answer certainly depends on the user's requirement and the hardware constraints. If the user will most likely be using all of the palettes, then it may be a good idea. Another possible solution is stealthy loading. In this design pattern we assume that we have enough memory to load all of the palettes, but we do not necessarily want the user to have to wait a long time for the system to spin up. What we can do is kick off a low-priority thread at start-up time. If the system is dormant this thread will kick in and start loading the palettes. If the system is busy the thread will sleep. This way the user does not have to wait for the palettes to be loaded during initialization. With any luck, the palette will be loaded by the low-priority thread by the time the user selects it.

Even though no design pattern is perfect, it is important to be aware of the different techniques that can be used to achieve the balance necessary for your system to perform well. Some related design patterns such as the Proxy, Virtual Proxy, Facade, and the Double-checked Locking pattern can be found in the "Patterns in Java Volume 1" and "Patterns in Java Volume 2" books by Mark Grand (Wiley 1998, 1999).

Item 44: Using Object Pools for Excessive Object Creation

Abstraction is one of the key benefits of object-oriented languages, but it can also lead to subtle problems. Coding in a language like C forces you to have a very good idea about what resources your program requires. Java allows you to design and develop at a more abstract level. Although abstraction is clearly helpful in most cases, it does mean many developers are less aware of the internals.

How much space does an object actually require? Usually, developers just don't care. The first time you notice a problem is when your program throws an OutOfMemoryException or when your users complain that your application is sometimes sluggish and unresponsive. In some cases, this behavior is caused by excessive object creation.

Each object created takes up quite a bit of memory, at least compared to primitive data types. And the garbage collector has to deal with every object instantiated, either to release it or to determine that it's still referenced by an active program.

A common example of this occurs when *String* objects are used carelessly. Unlike in C, *Strings* in Java are objects. There's overhead associated with each one. Even simple operations like text processing can be very slow when *Strings* are used too much. The solution usually involves using *StringBuffer* objects instead, as we discuss in Item 47. The key to the solution is that using *StringBuffers* allows a program to use fewer objects. And that is the primary purpose of *object pools*.

Object Recycling

Object pools allow you to recycle objects. The benefits of real-world recycling are well known today; every aluminum can recycled means one less can that has to be produced and one less can that has to be disposed of. But, also like recycling, it's not easy. Quite a bit of special handling is required to make it work.

Like most performance-enhancing techniques, object pools must be used judiciously. Object pools have a lot of drawbacks. This section will help you avoid, or at least mitigate, these where possible.

A Comparison to Caching

In order to understand when to use object pooling, let's compare it to caching. Using a cache is sort of like using valet parking: It's a faster way to get access to your car. Using an object pool is like hailing a taxi. You get to ride in it for a while, but you have to give it back when you're done.

Object pools share some characteristics with caching; both techniques can be applied to solve similar problems. But there are important differences. Cache implementations allow you to retrieve *particular* instances of a class. Object pools provide access to objects that can be used interchangeably.

Caches typically involve a simple trade-off: Give up memory to get faster performance. Object pools require tougher decisions. You can improve performance and gain better control over certain resources at the cost of adding complexity to your code.

Performance is the most common reason for using object pools: Objects that are recycled avoid instantiation and garbage collection. Memory usage can go either way. Object pools do require memory and the overhead to manage it, but they can be used to save space by controlling the quantity of objects in use at any given time.

Here are some questions to ask when you think object pools might solve your memory, performance, or control issues:

- Are your objects reusable? In other words, can any instantiation of the class serve equally well, or you do you need a particular one?

- Are your objects complex or slow to create? Or will you be creating and disposing of them frequently? Are there a lot of them?

- Can you count on well-behaved clients? Will they return the objects they borrow when they're finished?

- Do you anticipate needing to improve performance?

- Do you need to limit access to a resource?

- Do you need to reduce or control memory requirements?

- Are any of these issues important enough that you're willing to complicate your implementation?

Implementation

Object pools tend to be fairly complex. For the purposes of this discussion, we provide a simple, extensible abstract *ObjectPoolAdapter* class that can serve as the basis for custom implementations. It's not likely, though, that this generic solution will be sufficient to satisfy your particular needs; just use it as an example.

```
01: import java.util.*;
02:
03: public abstract class ObjectPoolAdapter
04: {
05:   private Stack pool;
06:
07:   ObjectPoolAdapter()
```

```
08:    {
09:      pool = new Stack();
10:    }
11:
12:    synchronized Object borrow() throws Exception
13:    {
14:      Object obj;
15:      if (pool.size() > 0)
16:        obj = pool.pop(); // recycle
17:      else
18:        obj = construct();
19:      return (obj);
20:    }
21:
22:    synchronized void release (Object obj)
23:    {
24:      pool.push (obj);
25:    }
26:
27:    abstract Object construct() throws Exception;
28:  }
```

Note that the `borrow` and `release` methods are synchronized, to support multiple concurrent clients. The `construct` method is abstract of course, so any implementation must call the appropriate constructor.

Usually, performance optimization is one of the last steps in the development process. This is true for several reasons, but mostly because delaying this activity allows you to focus your resources where they will have the most benefit. Unfortunately, object pools do not lend themselves to an ad hoc approach—you can't just plug them in transparently. Your client programs will have to change. Therefore, it's much better to plan on using an object pool up front in the design phase, rather than trying to force it in later.

When designing your object pool, it helps to predict the usage rates. Sporadic spikes in these rates can wreak havoc on your pool. Depending on your implementation, spikes can result in significant quantities of unused objects cluttering up your pool or in long delays while clients wait for an object to be returned.

Sometimes there just aren't any taxis around when you need one. What happens when your pool is empty? You have two choices: Create more objects, or wait until one is returned. Unless you must limit the number of objects created in order to comply with certain system constraints, it's generally better to instantiate a new object when a request comes in and your pool is empty. Otherwise, clients will need to handle unpredictable delays and potentially complex thread synchronization issues.

A better alternative is to limit the size of the pool itself, without limiting the number of objects you create. If you choose this approach, then simply discard any objects that get released instead of returning them to a pool that is already full.

Whether you limit the size of the pool will influence how you handle released objects. The simplest approach is to just ignore them and leave them in the pool. In many cases, however, you'll want the object pool to periodically remove stagnant objects. Deciding which objects to remove should be left up to the implementation. The decision may depend on factors such as object age, number of free objects in the pool, number of requests for new objects expected, and so forth.

For convenience, your abstract adapter class can provide a separate thread that invokes a method such as `performMaintenance`. This thread can sleep for an implementation-dependent interval, or it can be triggered whenever some condition is met, such as a certain number of free objects in the pool. The `performMaintenance` method can be abstract, or you may want to provide a default *null* implementation.

The Good

Object pools provide a way to manage and share resources. Object pools usually support the sharing of objects between multiple clients running simultaneously. Classic examples include connections to remote servers, especially databases.

A sophisticated implementation could even schedule the creation of objects in order to prepare for an expected demand, like taxis lining up at the theater. This is a form of *lazy instantiation*. A simpler approach would be to have the pool manager create another object in a background thread, whenever there are no objects in the pool. This ensures that the next request for an object will be satisfied as quickly as possible. This is a simple technique that can improve perceived performance.

The Bad

What happens when a client fails to return an object to the pool? This is one of the more serious problems with many object pool implementations. In this case, the object can never be garbage collected because the pool still maintains a reference. And it certainly can't be recycled because it might still be in use.

One workaround is to simply abandon the object. Your pool can decide (generally based on some configurable setting) that enough time has passed and the object isn't coming back. At that point, just cut your losses and have the object pool discard its reference to the object. This will at least allow it to be freed if the client program ceases to reference it.

In our simple implementation, we don't even bother tracking the objects that are in use (borrowed by a client). Our object pool is acting as a recycling center, not a library. It's happy to accept any donations, but it's not going to fine you when you fail to return a book.

The JavaSpaces Technology solves this problem in a much more sophisticated way: by requiring clients to *lease* objects for a specific period of time. When the lease expires, clients can renew it, or the object goes back into the pool. This interface adds extra complexity for the client, but in some cases it's a necessary evil. This solves the problems of client processes that die or simply fail to release the shared resource. It also allows the object pool to have more control over the limited resources. Even well-behaved clients might be denied a lease extension if other clients are waiting for their turn.

The Ugly

Most caching techniques can be implemented in a way that is transparent to the clients using them. This is not true of object pools because each client must explicitly release the object when finished using it. This results in code that resembles classic C/C++ functions: Allocate, use, then free. It is possible to avoid this requirement using Java's weak references, but that approach doesn't usually work well with the problem domains typically addressed by object pool solutions.

One way you can simplify use for clients is to provide some static interfaces that act like the actual constructors (see the code that follows). Because some object constructors need to throw exceptions, the getInstance method can be declared to throw the same exceptions the constructor does. In order to implement this generically, the object pool's construct method is declared to throw *Exception*. The getInstance method can catch *Exceptions* and then cast them to the appropriate type as they are propagated to the client.

```
01: public class MyPool extends ObjectPoolAdapter
02: {
03:   static MyPool pool; // singleton
04:
05:   private MyPool() { }
06:
07:   public static MyPool getPool()
08:   {
09:     if (pool == null)
10:       pool = new MyPool();
11:     return (pool);
12:   }
13:
14:   public static MyObject getInstance()
15:     throws MyException
16:   {
17:     try
18:     {
19:       return((MyObject)MyPool.getPool().borrow());
20:     }
```

```
21:     catch (Exception e)
22:     {
23:       throw ((MyException) e);
24:     }
25:   }
26:
27:   Object construct() throws Exception
28:   {
29:     return (new MyObject());
30:   }
31:
32:   public static void main (String[] args)
33:   {
34:     // sample usage
35:     MyPool pool = MyPool.getPool();
36:     MyObject obj = null;
37:     try
38:     {
39:       obj = pool.getInstance();
40:       // use object
41:     }
42:     catch (MyException e)
43:     {
44:       // handle exception normally
45:     }
46:     finally
47:     {
48:       if (obj != null)
49:         pool.release (obj);
50:     }
51:   }
52:}
```

Object pools can be useful, but they should not be considered as a simple modification to solve a single problem, even performance. If your situation involves several of the problems discussed previously, you may want to consider them. Otherwise, try other solutions first. Redesign to use fewer objects or primitive data types instead. Use caching or other performance tricks.

Item 45: Performance Watch: Array versus Vector

What is the biggest knock on the Java language? Yes, indeed, it is slow. Entire books have been written on optimizing your Java code. This item focuses on the performance drawbacks of using *Vectors* compared to arrays.

A *Vector* is basically a thread-safe array that grows dynamically to allow for added elements. The beauty of using a *Vector* object is that the *Vector* class hides all the underlying work needed to make sure that there is enough space allocated to safely add a new element. The programmer simply needs to call the add() method passing in the object to be added; the *Vector* class handles the rest. Along with the ability to dynamically resize itself, the *Vector* class offers a handful of useful methods to make your programming task easier. Retrieving an object from a *Vector* at a specific index is accomplished by calling the get (...) method passing in the index of the object to be retrieved. A *Vector* gives you the added capability of removing all the elements it contains with a call to the clear() method. Also, several new elements can be added to a vector at once by calling the addAll() method passing in a Collection. (If you are interested in seeing the remaining methods that the *Vector* class has to offer, take a quick look at the Javadoc pages on Sun's Web site.) Because a *Vector* gives you all the capabilities of an array and more, the question that needs to be asked is "Why should I ever use an array when I can use a *Vector*?" The answer is performance. Using a *Vector* is substantially slower than using an array. Take a look at the following examples to see the performance difference between an array and a *Vector*. Each example loads 500,000 elements and iterates through them. These examples demonstrate the performance of an array compared to the performance of a *Vector*.

> **NOTE** The output times of the following benchmark tests vary depending on the system architecture on which they are running.

This example shows a benchmark test using an array:

```
01: public class ArrayBenchMark
02: {
03:  private Object[] objectArray;
04:  public void loadArray(int count)
05:  {
06:    objectArray = new Object[count];
07:    long begin = System.currentTimeMillis();
08:    for (int i=0; i<count; i++)
09:      objectArray[i] = new Object();
10:    long end = System.currentTimeMillis();
11:    System.out.println("The total time to load the array is" +
12:            (end - begin) + " milliseconds. ");
13:  }
14:  public void iterateThroughArray()
15:  {
16:    long begin = System.currentTimeMillis();
17:    for (int i=0; i < objectArray.length; i++)
18:    {
19:     Object o = objectArray[i];
20:    }
21:    long end = System.currentTimeMillis();
```

```
22:     System.out.println("The total time to iterate " +
23:             "through the array is " +
24:             (end - begin) + " milliseconds. ");
25:   }
26:   public static void main(String[] args)
27:   {
28:     int count = Integer.parseInt(args[0]);
29:     ArrayBenchMark bm = new ArrayBenchMark();
30:     bm.loadArray(count);
31:     bm.iterateThroughArray();
32:   }
33: }
```

The output from running java *ArrayBenchMark* 500000 is as follows:

- The total time to load the array is 2030 milliseconds.

- The total time to iterate through the array is 60 milliseconds.

Compare the output from the array example above to this example, which shows a benchmark test using a *Vector*:

```
01: public class VectorBenchMark
02: {
03:  private Vector container = new Vector();
04:  public void loadContainer(int count)
05:  {
06:   long begin = System.currentTimeMillis();
07:   for (int i = 0; i < count; i++)
08:    container.add(new Object());
09:   long end = System.currentTimeMillis();
10:   System.out.println("The total time to load the vector is " +
11:           (end - begin) + " milliseconds.");
12:  }
13:  public void iterateThroughContainer()
14:  {
15:   Iterator i = container.iterator();
16:   long begin = System.currentTimeMillis();
17:   while (i.hasNext())
18:   {
19:    Object o = i.next();
20:   }
21:   long end = System.currentTimeMillis();
22:   System.out.println("The total time to iterate through " +
23:           "the vector is " + (end - begin) +
24:           " milliseconds.");
25:  }
26:  public static void main(String[] args)
27:  {
28:   int count = Integer.parseInt(args[0]);
29:   VectorBenchMark bm = new VectorBenchMark();
```

```
30:    bm.loadContainer(count);
31:    bm.iterateThroughContainer();
32:  }
33: }
```

The output from running java *VectorBenchMark* 500000 is as follows:

- The total time to load the *Vector* is 2640 milliseconds.

- The total time to iterate through the *Vector* is 440 milliseconds.

Comparing the output from the array benchmark test with the output from the Vector benchmark test demonstrates that loading the elements of an array is approximately 30 percent faster than loading the elements of a Vector. The performance drop associated with iterating through a Vector is even greater. Iterating through the elements of an array is approximately seven times faster than iterating through the elements of a Vector.

Now that we have demonstrated the performance cost associated with using a Vector as opposed to an array, what can we do about it? The key to avoiding the performance hit demonstrated in the array and the Vector benchmark tests is understanding why a Vector is so much slower than an array. Understanding the cause of the performance cost will help you determine if you can avoid the performance hit by using a different type of container object that is not as slow.

Why is a Vector so much slower than an Array?

The underlying data structure that contains the elements of a Vector is an *Object* array. If the underlying data structure of a Vector is an array, why is a *Vector* so much slower than an array? The *Vector* class is thread-safe, which means it is synchronized. Virtually all of the performance cost associated with using a *Vector* is due to the synchronization overhead. To see the effect that synchronization has on performance we will modify our *ArrayBenchMark* class and make it synchronized.

```
01: public class SlowArrayBenchMark
02: {
03:  private Object[] objectArray;
04:  public synchronized Object get(int index)
05:  {
06:   return objectArray[index];
07:  }
08:  public void loadArray(int count)
09:  {
10:   objectArray = new Object[count];
11:   for (int i=0; i<count; i++)
12:   objectArray[i] = new Object();
```

```
13:  }
14:  public void iterateThroughArray()
15:  {
16:   long begin = System.currentTimeMillis();
17:   for (int i=0; i < objectArray.length; i++)
18:   {
19:    Object o = get(i);
20:   }
21:   long end = System.currentTimeMillis();
22:   System.out.println("The total time to iterate through " +
23:           "The slow array is " +
24:           (end - begin) + " milliseconds.");
25:  }
26:  public static void main(String[] args)
27:  {
28:   int count = Integer.parseInt(args[0]);
29:   SlowArrayBenchMark bm = new SlowArrayBenchMark();
30:   bm.loadArray(count);
31:   bm.iterateThroughArray();
32:  }
33: }
```

The output from running java SlowArrayBenchMark 500000 is as follows:

- The total time to iterate through the slow array is 330 milliseconds.

On line 19 of the SlowArrayBenchMark example, the `iterateThroughArray()` method has been changed to call a `get()` method instead of retrieving the array element directly. Notice on line 4, the `get()` method is synchronized. This means that we get a performance hit from the synchronization overhead for every object that we retrieve from the *Vector*. As you can see from the output, the total time to iterate through 500,000 objects is 330 milliseconds. This is more than five times slower than the original array benchmark test that was not synchronized.

When should I use a Vector?

The fact that a *Vector* grows and shrinks dynamically is one benefit. The second benefit is that the *Vector* class is synchronized, which makes it thread-safe. You should only use a *Vector* when you are taking advantage of both of these benefits. If you are running in a multithreaded environment then you are paying the performance price, but you are also enjoying the benefit of being thread-safe.

There may be a case where you are running in a multithreaded environment but need only a static snapshot of the *Vector*. In this case, a call to the `toArray(...)` method returns an *Object* array containing the current elements of the *Vector*. You can iterate through this array much faster than iterating through the *Vector* because you do not have the synchronization overhead. It is important to note, however, that the returned array is a completely separate object from the *Vector's* container array. The caller of the *toArray (...)* method is free to modify the contents of the array without effecting the elements in the *Vector*.

The disadvantage of using a *Vector* is that you are forced to pay the performance price caused by the synchronization overhead even if you are not enjoying the benefits of thread-safety. If your program is not multithreaded then you are needlessly paying the performance cost without reaping any of the benefits. What are you supposed to do if you need a dynamically growing container but are not running in a multithreaded environment? As of Java 2, the *Collection* classes offer several alternatives. By default most of the *Collection* classes are not synchronized so you are not forced to pay the performance cost for the synchronization overhead. The *Vector* class has been updated in Java 2 and is included in the *Collection* classes. *Vector* now extends the *AbstractList* class. *ArrayList* is another one of the *Collection* classes that extends the *AbstractList* class. *ArrayList* is the most obvious alternative to using a *Vector* when you need a dynamically growing array in a nonthreaded environment.

The ArrayList Class

The *ArrayList* class is basically a nonsynchronized *Vector*. Like the *Vector* class, the *ArrayList* class supports all the optional methods of the *List* interface. Although the *ArrayList* class is not synchronized by default you can simply use the synchronization wrapper method to make your *ArrayList* synchronized. The synchronization wrapper method is a static factory method in the *Collection* class. You simply call Collection.synchronizeList(new ArrayList()) to create a synchronized version of an *ArrayList*. An *ArrayList* is faster than a *Vector* and is also cleaner to use because it does not have to support the legacy methods that the *Vector* class supports. If you are running Java 2, it is recommended that you stick to only using the *List* interface methods of the *Vector* class. Of course, the advantage of using the *List* interface methods is that you can easily change your container object to any other container object that implements the *List* interface. We can modify the *VectorBenchMark* class from earlier in this item to create an *ArrayListBenchMark* class by replacing the *Vector* with the *ArrayList*.

This example shows a benchmark test using an *ArrayList*:

```
01: public class ArrayListBenchMark
02: {
03:   private ArrayList container = new ArrayList();
04:   public void loadContainer(int count)
05:   {
06:     for (int i=0; i<count; i++)
07:       container.add(new Object());
08:   }
09:   public void iterateThroughContainer()
```

```
10:    {
11:      Iterator i = container.iterator();
12:      long begin = System.currentTimeMillis();
13:      while (i.hasNext())
14:      {
15:       Object o = i.next();
16:      }
17:      long end = System.currentTimeMillis();
18:      System.out.println("The total time to iterate " +
19:              "through the arrayList is " +
20:              (end - begin) + " milliseconds. ");
21:    }
22:    public static void main(String[] args)
23:    {
24:      int count = Integer.parseInt(args[0]);
25:      ArrayListBenchMark bm = new ArrayListBenchMark();
26:      bm.loadContainer(count);
27:      bm.iterateThroughContainer();
28:    }
29: }
```

The output from running java *ArrayListBenchMark* 500000 is as follows:

- The total time to iterate through the *ArrayList* is 220 milliseconds.

As you can see from the output, iterating through the elements of an *ArrayList* is twice as fast as iterating through the elements of a *Vector*.

This item demonstrated that a *Vector* is considerably slower than an Array mostly because of the *Vector*'s synchronization overhead. The two benefits of a *Vector* are the ability to dynamically grow and shrink as well as the fact that a *Vector* is thread-safe. For performance reasons, you should not use a *Vector* unless you are running in a multithreaded environment. If you are not running in a multithreaded environment consider using an *ArrayList* instead of using a *Vector*. An *ArrayList*, by default, is not thread-safe but is faster than a *Vector*. An *ArrayList* can be thread-safe if it is constructed using the synchronization wrapper.

Item 46: Avoid Using Temporary Arrays for Dynamic Array Growth

Performance is such a key issue in Java. Because Java programs are executed on the Java Virtual Machine (JVM) instead of directly on the physical hardware, an extra layer of processing takes place that makes Java programs slower than natively compiled programs. Some JVM technologies such as Just-in-Time compilers (JITs) and the new Hotspot technology try to mitigate the performance issue by compiling performance-sensitive areas into native code and/or providing adaptive optimization. Although these technologies make Java programs run faster, several programming techniques can be employed by a savvy Java programmer to increase performance in Java programs. This item discusses one technique to avoid—using temporary arrays for dynamic array growth—and offers an alternative method that produces the same end result, yet increases performance by orders of magnitude.

Arrays are used to store a set of elements that are of the same data type. Each element in the array has an index that is used to access the stored element. Arrays provide the fastest access method possible (see Item 45) when performing iterations through a set of elements or a subset of elements, or even accessing a single element. One of the reasons why arrays are fast is that once an array is created its size is fixed. In many programming situations, however, the size of an array needs to change after its initial size has already been allocated. For instance, if you wanted to store the lines of a text file in an array, you probably would not know how many lines the file contains at compile time. Even at runtime, when you first open the file you still will not know. You will have to read each line of the file and count as you read in the lines to determine the number of lines in the file. You could then size the array properly, but you would then have to go back and read through the file again to store the lines of text into a corresponding array element. To avoid this behavior the array needs to be sized dynamically. Because the size of an array is fixed when it is created, the only way to "grow" the array is to keep allocating bigger arrays and copying the existing array into the new, bigger array. The example that follows demonstrates this behavior, but when it allocates a new array, it only increases its size by 1.

```
01: import java.awt.*;
02: import java.util.*;
03:
04: public class Item46
05: {
06:   private static int listSize;
07:   private static long elapsedTime;
08:
09:   public static void main (String args[])
10:   {
11:     listSize = Integer.parseInt(args[0]);
12:     displayLookupList(loadLookupData());
13:   }
14:
15:   private static void displayLookupList (String items[])
16:   {
17:     //...display code...
18:   }
19:
20:   private static String[] loadLookupData ()
```

```
21:   {
22:       Enumeration preloadedData = getPreloadedData();
23:       String[] lookupData = null;
24:       String[] temp = null;
25:       int   index = 0;
26:
27:       Date startTime = new Date();
28:       while (preloadedData.hasMoreElements())
29:       {
30:         if (index > 0)
31:         {
32:           temp = lookupData;
33:           lookupData = new String[lookupData.length + 1];
34:           for (int i = 0; i < temp.length; i++)
35:             lookupData[i] = temp[i];
36:         }
37:         else
38:           lookupData = new String[1];
39:
40:           lookupData[index] = (String) preloadedData.nextElement();
41:           index++;
42:       }
43:       Date stopTime = new Date();
44:       elapsedTime = stopTime.getTime() - startTime.getTime();
45:       System.out.println("Elapsed time: " + elapsedTime + " ms");
46:       return (lookupData);
47:   }
48:
49:   private static Enumeration getPreloadedData ()
50:   {
51:       int preloadedDataSize = listSize;
52:       Vector v = new Vector(preloadedDataSize);
53:       for (int i = 0; i < preloadedDataSize; i++)
54:         v.addElement("Item " + i);
55:
56:       return (v.elements());
57:   }
58: }
```

In the preceding load loadLookupData() method the bolded area demonstrates how the array is grown to handle a dynamic number of elements. To demonstrate the concept of having an unknown number of elements without adding a (significant) performance delay, an *Enumeration* was used to hold the preloaded data. The *while()* loop transfers the data from the *preloadedData* Enumeration into the *lookupData* array. The *lookupData* array was grown dynamically with the help of the *temp* array. You can see in using this technique that line 35 contained in the *for()* loop gets called (n–1)! times. That is for a given number of items, n, line 35 is executed the number of times equal to the factorial of n–1. The *for()* loop and the allocation of a new array every time (line 33) through the while loop make this a slow process.

One way to speed this up is to replace the *for()* loop with an array copy method that results in faster execution. Java provides a call that uses a native operation to copy one array to another. The `System.arraycopy()` method provides this operation. If you replace lines 34 and 35 in the previous code listing with the following line you will increase the performance of copying one array to another.

```
System.arraycopy(temp,0,lookupData,0,temp.length);
```

The performance benefits by using `System.arraycopy()` versus the previous code is shown in Table 46.1.

In order to really speed up the "growing" of the array, we must reduce the number of times the array is resized and the number of times we copy existing array elements into the new array. We could do this by resizing the array by more than one element each time. This could be done by writing some more code, but an existing Java class, *Vector*, already does this. The *Vector* class by default will start with an array of 10 elements, and each time it exceeds its current capacity it will double its size. The *Vector* class has several methods to change this behavior, but let's use it as-is and see what performance improvements occur. If you replace lines 24–42 in the first code listing with the following code segment, you will see a drastic performance improvement.

```
Vector   temp = new Vector();

Date startTime = new Date();
while (preloadedData.hasMoreElements())
{
  temp.addElement((String) preloadedData.nextElement());
}
lookupData = new String[temp.size()];
temp.copyInto(lookupData);
```

Table 46.1 Performance Comparison Results for Alternative Methods of Dynamic Object Array Growth

# ITEMS	GROW ARRAY W/ TEMP ARRAY	GROW ARRAY W/TEMP ARRAY USING SYSTEM.ARRAYCOPY	CREATE ARRAY USING VECTOR
100	10 ms	0 ms	0 ms
500	20 ms	20 ms	0 ms
1000	70 ms	50 ms	0 ms
5000	1442 ms	590 ms	20 ms
10000	7991 ms	2403 ms	30 ms

Tests were performed on a 333 MHz Pentium II processor computer, running Windows NT 4.0 SP 3 and using java build 1.3 beta-O.

By looking at Table 46.1 you can see the improvement over the previous two alternatives. Depending on the number of items read into the array, you can see that the *Vector* solution is 30 to 250 times faster than the other solutions. For large sets of data it is essential to use the *Vector* approach or a similar approach.

The previous examples used arrays of *String* to demonstrate array growth. Because instances of *String* are objects, we were able to use the *Vector* class to store the elements. If we were dealing with primitive data types we would not be able to use *Vector* without first converting the primitive to an object. And when you were done, more work would need to be performed to convert the array of objects back into an array of primitives. In this scenario, we have to choose between the trade-off of doing the object/primitive conversions or writing your own array "growth" algorithm that does for primitives what *Vector* does for objects. If we modify the initial code example[1] and replace the load-LookupData() method with the method listed in the code that follows we will be operating on *ints* instead of objects. In this example, we have chosen to implement the object/primitive conversions.

```
01:   private static int[] loadLookupData ()
02:   {
03:     IntEnumeration preloadedData = getPreloadedData();
04:     int[] lookupData = null;
05:     Vector  temp = new Vector();
06:
07:     Date startTime = new Date();
08:     while (preloadedData.hasMoreElements())
09:     {
10:       temp.addElement(new Integer((int)
11:           preloadedData.nextElement()));
12:     }
13:     int iNumElements = temp.size();
14:     lookupData = new int[iNumElements];
15:     for (int i = 0; i < iNumElements; i++)
16:       lookupData[i] = ((Integer)temp.elementAt(i)).intValue();
17:     Date stopTime = new Date();
18:     elapsedTime = stopTime.getTime() - startTime.getTime();
19:     System.out.println("Elapsed time: " + elapsedTime + " ms");
20:     return (lookupData);
21:   }
```

To implement the other method, writing our own array "growth" algorithm, lines 8–16 should be replaced with these lines:

---

[1]The example was also modified to define the *IntEnumeration* class, which enumerates integers as opposed to the *Enumeration* class, which enumerates objects. Other statements were changed to perform operations on *ints* instead of *Strings*.

```
01:     while (preloadedData.hasMoreElements())
02:     {
03:       if (index == capacity)
04:       {
05:         temp = lookupData;
06:         lookupData = new int[lookupData.length * 2];
07:         capacity = lookupData.length;
08:         System.arraycopy(temp,0,lookupData,0,temp.length);
09:       }
10:       lookupData[index] = preloadedData.nextElement();
11:       index++;
12:     }
13:     // trim array
14:     temp = lookupData;
15:     lookupData = new int[index];
16:     System.arraycopy(temp,0,lookupData,0,lookupData.length);
```

In this code segment, we are implementing the same functionality that *Vector* does for objects. We start with an initial capacity of 10 and double it every time the capacity needs to be increased. In the former example, we used *Vector* but had to continually convert between *ints* (primitives) and *Integers* (objects). The performance results are listed in Table 46.2. As you can see, our own array growth algorithm blows the doors off the *Vector w/ object/primitive conversions* solution.

Based on the information presented in this item, you should use the *Vector* class for dynamically storing a set of objects. If you choose to grow an array your performance will suffer, unless you implement a *Vector*-like algorithm for expanding the existing array. If you are dealing with primitives, it makes sense to implement a *Vector*-like growth algorithm as opposed to performing object/primitive conversions.

Table 46.2 Performance Comparison Results for Alternative Methods of Dynamic Integer Array Growth

# ITEMS	VECTOR W/ OBJECT/PRIMITIVE CONVERSIONS	ARRAY GROWTH W/ VECTOR-LIKE GROWTH ALGORITHM
5000	20 ms	10 ms
10000	40 ms	10 ms
20000	60 ms	20 ms
40000	110 ms	30 ms
80000	320 ms	50 ms

Item 47: Use StringBuffer Instead of '+' for Concatenation inside a Loop

One of the first Java skills learned is to use the plus operator (+) for easy *String* concatenation. For example:

```
01: String first = "Michael";
02: String last = "Daconta";
03: String fullName = first + " " + last;
```

Concatenating strings is a very common operation in programming. We use it when formatting output, constructing in-memory text buffers, and creating numerous varieties of strings. If we follow our initial impulse when constructing in-memory text buffers by choosing the plus operator for concatenation, we pay an enormous performance penalty. Let's use an example of concatenating all noncomment *Strings* from a data file. The comments in the data file are identified by a pound ('#') character at the start of the line. Here is a snippet of code that uses the plus operator for concatenation:

```
01: String buf = "";
02: String line = null;
03: while ( (line = br.readLine()) != null)
04: {
05:  if (line.startsWith("#") == false)
06:    buf += (line + "\n");
07: }
```

The variable *br* in line 3 is an instance of a *BufferedReader* created from a *FileReader*. Line 6 in the snippet is so easy to type and understand that you hardly recognize you are producing code with an exponential growth rate as the size of the input increases. Table 47.1 lists the running time in milliseconds for the preceding code on three different input files.[1]

Table 47.1   Plus Operator Performance

METHOD	2,000-LINE FILE	10,000-LINE FILE	20,000-LINE FILE
Concatenation with '+'	12,800 ms	229,210 ms	819,270 ms

[1]Tests were performed on a 550 MHZ Pentium III processor computer, running Windows NT 4.0 SP5 and using java build 1.2.2.

the whole system. A better solution is to create a *DebugManager* class that allows you to set a debug flag based on certain classes or applications. You may also still want the capability to turn on debugging messages for the entire system. Suppose you are working on a mapping system. Your mapping system allows you to plot units, display backgrounds, and measure distance between units. In some cases, you may want to see debugging statements only for the Plot Units application. In other cases, you may want to see debugging statements for the entire system. To handle this the *DebugManager* may look something like this:

```
01:  public class DebugManager
02:  {
03:    public static final String SYSTEM_DEBUG_KEY = "system.Debug";
04:    public static final boolean debug;
05:    static
06:    {
07:      debug = toBoolean(SYSTEM_DEBUG_KEY);
08:    }
09:    private static boolean toBoolean(String key)
10:    {
11:      String sDebug = System.getProperty(key);
12:      if (sDebug != null && sDebug.equalsIgnoreCase("true"))
13:        debug = true;
14:      else
15:        debug = false;
16:    }
17:    public static boolean getSystemDebug()
18:    {
19:      return debug;
20:    }
21:    public static boolean getSystemDebug(String applicationKey)
22:    {
23:      if (debug || debugToBoolean(applicationKey))
24:        return true;
25:      else
26:        return false;
27:    }
28:  }
```

Using the *DebugManager* an application would simply make a call like this: *boolean debug = DebugManager.getSystemDebug(applicationkey);*. To set the debug flag for the plot tool we would invoke the mapping system like this: *java –DplotTool.Debug=true MapSystem*. The application key for the *PlotTool* application would be *plotTool.Debug*. The application key for the background could be *backgroundLoader.Debug* and the entire system debug key is *system.Debug*. By using the *DebugManager* you can turn debugging on and off for specific applications without modifying any source code. You can also turn debugging on for the entire system. This is a rather simple approach, but it can be easily extended. You can add a GUI to the debug manager so that you can modify the debugging flags for each application on the fly instead of on the command line. You can also turn the *DebugManager* into a logging manager by adding methods that will tee the debug statements to the screen as well as to a log file. Or you can write code that has no bugs!

Item 49: Encapsulating JNI Calls through Interfaces

I am sure on at least one occasion you have had the need (or the temptation) to cross the barrier from the safety and comfort of the Java world into the dark netherworld of your operating system. Your desire to plunder the resources of the operating system—whether it be to reuse code, speed up a process, or perform seamless integration—has left you feeling guilty that your Java application is no longer cross-platform. Feel guilty no more, for through the power of interfaces and dynamic class loading you will not have to compromise cross-platform support in order to reap the benefits of native code.

This item discusses and demonstrates how to isolate JNI calls through an interface, allowing the Java application to access native code, but not preventing it from also being a pure Java solution. During the discussion we briefly review the concepts surrounding interfaces and dynamic class loading. When we begin the discussion of the native implementation of our interface, we cover the basics of creating a native method in Java and implementing it using JNI, plus how to asynchronously call a Java program from native code using JNI. But before we get started, I must apologize to those who use Solaris, Macintosh, or another non-Windows operating system because the JNI examples discussed here are implemented in Windows. Any detailed discussion of Windows code will be isolated from the main discussion.

Discussion of Concept

The trick for having an application be both a pure Java solution and an OS-dependent solution is to have multiple implementations of the same interface. Depending on the configuration of the Java application, the native implementation could be loaded, or the pure Java solution could be loaded. Figure 49.1 depicts the isolation of the Java application from the implementations of the interface.

On the left of Figure 49.1 we have the pure Java solution, in which all of the code runs inside the Java Virtual Machine. The Java application is the thing we want to isolate from JNI calls, so anywhere we might need to access JNI code

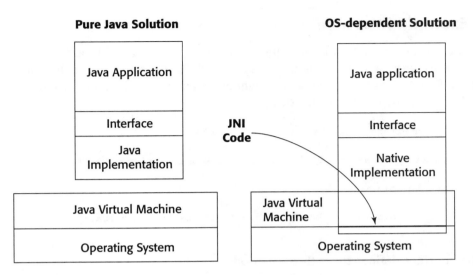

Figure 49.1   Pure Java solution versus OS-dependent solution.

an interface is created to isolate it from the Java application. On a platform on which we do not want to take advantage of native code, the Java application loads the pure Java implementation of the interface. This creates a pure Java solution that can be run by any JVM. Looking at the right side we have an OS-dependent solution. The code of the Java application has not changed, but it can take advantage of the JNI code by loading up the native implementation of the interface. Using the interface[1] approach isolates the Java application from having to worry about native code.

An interface is a type that defines constants and abstract methods. An interface does not contain any implementation code. Instead, classes that want to implement the interface provide code to implement the abstract method declarations of the interface. Interfaces are very powerful when used with dynamic class loading. Dynamic class loading provides the ability for a class to be loaded up at runtime instead of having to be known at compile time. This can be done using the `Class.forName(...)` method, which returns an object whose class is *Class*. Using the `Class.newInstance()` method creates an instance of the class that was dynamically loaded, but returns this instance back to the calling program as type *Object*. The program can cast the returned object into a defined type to gain access to its methods. By having the calling program use an interface for this defined type, many different implementations can be loaded without having to change the code of the calling program.

---

[1]Interfaces are an effective, clean way of isolating implementation code from the methods declarations that are exposed, but the same effect can be achieved if the Java application uses a superclass definition and dynamically loads subclasses for the implementation.

An Example Interface

Let's look at an example. In our example we want to define an interface that allows us to notify a user with some message and allows us to remove the notification. Its intent is to be used as an asynchronous notification, such as those used for new e-mail. Here is the code:

```
01: public interface NotifyUser
02: {
03:     public void addNotify (String iconFileName, String message);
04:
05:     public void removeNotify ();
06:
07:     public void installNotifyCallback(NotifyCallback callback);
08: }
```

The interface defines these three methods:

addNotify. Allows specification of an image file name and a message to present to the user.

removeNotify. Removes the notification if it exists.

installNotifyCallback. Allows the user of the interface to define a callback, such that when the user addresses the notification, the callback method is invoked.

The *NotifyCallback* interface is defined as follows:

```
01: public interface NotifyCallback
02: {
03:     public void restoreApplication();
04: }
```

Now let's take a look at the program that uses the interface to perform its notifications. This program presents a simple frame with two buttons: Add Notify and Remove Notify. When Add Notify is clicked the `Notify-User.addNotify(...)` method gets called. When Remove Notify is clicked the `NotifyUser.removeNotify()` method is called. In the listing below the calls on the interface and those that perform dynamic class loading are bolded.

```
01: import javax.swing.*;
02: import java.awt.event.*;
03: import java.awt.*;
04: import java.util.Properties;
05: import java.io.FileInputStream;
06:
07: public class TestNotifyUser extends JFrame implements
08:                                 ActionListener, NotifyCallback
```

```
09: {
10:     JButton     btnAddNotify = new JButton("Add Notify");
11:     JButton     btnRemoveNotify = new JButton("Remove Notify");
12:     NotifyUser  notifyUser;
13:     String      iconFileName;
14:
15:     public TestNotifyUser ()
16:     {
17:         super("Test Notify User");
18:         getContentPane().setLayout(new FlowLayout());
19:         getContentPane().add(btnAddNotify);
20:         getContentPane().add(btnRemoveNotify);
21:
22:         btnAddNotify.addActionListener(this);
23:         btnRemoveNotify.addActionListener(this);
24:
25:         try
26:         {
27:             FileInputStream fis =
28:                     new FileInputStream("TestNotifyUser.properties");
29:             Properties p = new Properties();
30:             p.load(fis);
31:             String className = p.getProperty("NotifyUserImpl");
32:             iconFileName = p.getProperty("IconFileName");
33:             fis.close();
34:
35:             Class c = Class.forName(className);
36:             notifyUser = (NotifyUser) c.newInstance();
37:             notifyUser.installNotifyCallback(this);
38:         }
39:         catch (Exception e)
40:         {
41:             System.out.println("Error: " + e.getMessage());
42:             System.exit(1);
43:         }
44:
45:         setSize(300,150);
46:         setVisible(true);
47:     }
48:
49:     public void actionPerformed (ActionEvent evt)
50:     {
51:         if (evt.getSource() == btnAddNotify)
52:             notifyUser.addNotify(iconFileName, "You have new mail.");
53:         else if (evt.getSource() == btnRemoveNotify)
54:             notifyUser.removeNotify();
55:     }
56:
57:     public void restoreApplication()
58:     {
59:         this.setState(Frame.NORMAL);
```

```
60:            notifyUser.removeNotify();
61:        }
62:
63:        public static void main (String args[])
64:        {
65:            new TestNotifyUser();
66:        }
67: }
```

On line 8 we define our class as implementing the *NotifyCallback* interface. This will allow it to be called when the user addresses the notification. Line 12 is where we declare the *NotifyUser* variable, *notifyUser*. Because we are declaring an interface type, we have to assign an instance of a class that implements the interface to the variable. Lines 31–36 show the dynamic class loading. We retrieve the name of the class from a properties file, then load the class using `Class.forName(...)`. After the class is loaded we create an instance of it by calling `Class.newInstance()` and cast it to the *NotifyUser* interface type. On lines 37, 52, 54, and 60 we make calls to *notifyUser*. Any calls to *notifyUser* are handled by the class we loaded dynamically.

Pure Java Implementation

Now that we have defined the interface, we need to implement the interface. The *SwingNotifyUser* class is the pure Java implementation of the *NotifyUser* interface. Here is the code for the *SwingNotifyUser* class:

```
01: import javax.swing.*;
02: import java.awt.*;
03: import java.awt.event.*;
04:
05: public class SwingNotifyUser implements NotifyUser
06: {
07:     SwingNotifyFrame f;
08:     NotifyCallback    callback;
09:
10:     public void addNotify (String iconFileName, String message)
11:     {
12:         f = new SwingNotifyFrame("Notify", message, iconFileName);
13:         f.installNotifyCallback(callback);
14:     }
15:
16:     public void removeNotify ()
17:     {
18:         if (f != null)
19:             f.dispose();
20:     }
21:
22:     public void installNotifyCallback (NotifyCallback callback)
```

```
23:     {
24:          this.callback = callback;
25:          if (f != null)
26:              f.installNotifyCallback(callback);
27:     }
28: }
29:
30: class SwingNotifyFrame extends JFrame implements ActionListener
31: {
32:     JButton viewMailButton = new JButton("View Mail");
33:     JButton cancelButton = new JButton("Cancel");
34:     NotifyCallback  callback;
35:
36:     SwingNotifyFrame (String frameTitle, String message,
37:                                       String iconFileName)
38:     {
39:          super(frameTitle);
40:
41:          //...do layout stuff...
42:
43:          pCenter.add(new JLabel(new ImageIcon(iconFileName)));
44:          pCenter.add(new JLabel(message));
45:
46:          pButtons.add(viewMailButton);
47:          pButtons.add(cancelButton);
48:
49:          viewMailButton.addActionListener(this);
50:          cancelButton.addActionListener(this);
51:
52:          //...do more layout stuff...
53:
54:          setVisible(true);
55:     }
56:
57:     public void actionPerformed (ActionEvent evt)
58:     {
59:          if (evt.getSource() == viewMailButton)
60:          {
61:              if (callback != null)
62:                  callback.restoreApplication();
63:          }
64:          else
65:              this.dispose();
66:     }
67:
68:     void installNotifyCallback (NotifyCallback callback)
69:     {
70:          this.callback = callback;
71:     }
72: }
```

The *SwingNotifyUser* class implements the methods defined in the *NotifyUser* interface. The previous listing also defines the *SwingNotifyFrame* that serves as the GUI for our notification. When the `SwingNotifyUser.addNotify(...)` method is called the *SwingNotifyFrame* gets created (and displayed). When the `SwingNotifyUser.removeNotify()` method is called the *SwingNotify-Frame* gets destroyed. And when the `SwingNotifyUser.installNotify-Callback(...)` method is called, we use it to install a callback on the *SwingNotifyFrame*. When the *SwingNotifyFrame's* View Mail button is clicked, it calls the `NotifyCallback.restoreApplication()` method.

The properties file used in the *TestNotifyUser* class is defined as:

```
NotifyUserImpl=SwingNotifyUser
IconFileName=images/mail.gif
```

Running the *TestNotifyUser* class with these properties results in the *Swing-NotifyUser* class being loaded as the *NotifyUser* implementation. If you click the Add Notify button on the Test Notify User frame you will see the output shown in Figure 49.2. If you click the Remove Notify button, the Notify frame will disappear. If you were to click the View Mail button of the Notify frame, this results in a callback to the *TestNotifyUser* class. If the Test Notify User frame was minimized it will restore the frame. Next it will call `NotifyUser.removeNotify()`, which causes the Notify frame to disappear.

Native Implementation

The Java code for the native implementation is very simple. It consists of declaring the `NotifyUser` methods with the native keyword and loading the native library *NativeNotifyUser*. The implementation of these methods is done through native code.

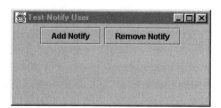

Figure 49.2   Pure Java implementation of NotifyUser.

```
01: public class NativeNotifyUser implements NotifyUser
02: {
03:     static
04:     {
05:         System.loadLibrary("NativeNotifyUser");
06:     }
07:
08:     public native void addNotify (String iconFileName,
09:                                         String message);
10:
11:     public native void removeNotify ();
12:
13:     public native void installNotifyCallback (NotifyCallback
14:                                         callback);
15: }
```

To write the native C code so that the *NativeNotifyUser* class can call it, we must first create the C function declarations. This can be accomplished by running the javah utility on the compiled class file like this:

```
javah -jni NativeNotifyUser
```

This produces the NativeNotifyUser.h file that contains the C function declarations. We need to use these function declarations to write our code. Here is the listing of the C code that implements the functions defined in Native-NotifyUser.h with the Windows-specific code taken out (it will be covered later).

```
01: #include <string.h>
02: #include "NativeNotifyUser.h"
03:
04: JavaVM      *m_vm;
05: jobject     m_pNotifyCallbackObject;
06: jmethodID   m_method_id;
07:
08: JNIEXPORT void JNICALL Java_NativeNotifyUser_addNotify
09:   (JNIEnv *pEnv, jobject pObject,
10:    jstring iconFileName, jstring message)
11: {
12: const char  *cc_iconFileName;
13: const char  *cc_message;
14: charcaBuffer[256];
15:
16: cc_iconFileName = (*pEnv)->GetStringUTFChars(pEnv, iconFileName, 0);
17: cc_message = (*pEnv)->GetStringUTFChars(pEnv, message, 0);
18:
19: //...perform windows calls to add to windows tray...
20:
21: //...install SysCallbackHandler in OS
22:
23: (*pEnv)->ReleaseStringUTFChars(pEnv, iconFileName, cc_iconFileName);
```

```
24:    (*pEnv)->ReleaseStringUTFChars(pEnv, message, cc_message);
25: }
26:
27: JNIEXPORT void JNICALL Java_NativeNotifyUser_removeNotify
28:    (JNIEnv *pEnv, jobject pObject)
29: {
30:    //...perform windows calls to remove from windows tray...
31:
32:    //...remove SysCallbackHandler from OS
33: }
34:
35: JNIEXPORT void JNICALL Java_NativeNotifyUser_installNotifyCallback
36:    (JNIEnv *pEnv, jobject pObject, jobject pNotifyCallbackObject)
37: {
38:    jclass pNotifyCallbackClass;
39:
40:    (*pEnv)->GetJavaVM(pEnv, &m_vm);
41:
42:    m_pNotifyCallbackObject =
43:        (*pEnv)->NewGlobalRef(pEnv, pNotifyCallbackObject);
44:
45:    pNotifyCallbackClass =
46:        (*pEnv)->GetObjectClass(pEnv, pNotifyCallbackObject);
47:
48:    m_method_id = (*pEnv)->GetMethodID(pEnv, pNotifyCallbackClass,
49:                               "restoreApplication", "()V");
50: }
51:
52: // SysCallbackHandler ()
53: // {
54: //     jint       returnCode;
55: //     JNIEnv    *pEnv;
56: //
57: //     returnCode =
58: //         (*m_vm)->GetEnv(m_vm, (void**) &pEnv, JNI_VERSION_1_2);
59: //
60: //     (*pEnv)->CallVoidMethod(pEnv, m_pNotifyCallbackObject,
61: //                                 m_method_id);
62: //
63: // }
```

First, let's take a look at the *Java_NativeNotifyUser_addNotify* function. Because this declaration was copied from the NativeNotifyUser.h file, all we had to do was specify names for the functions' arguments. The arguments are defined as follows:

JNIEnv *pEnv. This is the interface pointer that allows access to the JNI functions.

jobject pObject. This is the pointer to "this" (the object that defines the native JNI method).

jstring iconFileName. This is the first parameter of the `addNotify` method.

jstring message. This is the second parameter of the `addNotify` method.

Each of these arguments is valid only within the scope of the current function call. In lines 16 and 17 we use the `GetStringUTFChars(...)` JNI call to make the Java string available as a C string. We then use the C strings during the body of the function, but we have to release them after we are done by calling `ReleaseStringUTFChars(...)`.

The code for the *Java_NativeNotifyUser_installNotifyCallback* function is slightly more complicated. The goal here is to obtain a reference to the `restoreApplication()` method of the *NotifyCallback* interface and keep it around beyond the context of the current function call. To do this we are going to need to capture references for everything we need to do a *CallVoidMethod* (line 60). This involves capturing an interface pointer, storing the pointer to the *NotifyCallbackObject*, and storing the reference to the `restoreApplication()` method. Unfortunately, there is no way to persist the interface pointer so it can be used between calls. If you have the pointer to the current JVM you can create a new interface pointer at your leisure. Therefore, we have to capture the pointer to the JVM instead of to the interface pointer.

Walking through the code, you can see that line 40 is where we capture the pointer to the JVM with the `GetJavaVM(...)` call. Next we use *NewGlobalRef* on the *pNotifyCallbackObject*, so we use it after the current function call has returned (line 42). If you try to persist the pointer without adding a global reference, you will get memory access violation errors when accessing the pointer outside the context of the current call. Before we attain the method ID, we must first obtain the class of the *pNotifyCallbackObject*. This is done using the `GetObjectClass(...)` JNI call (line 45). Once we have the pointer to the class we can now obtain the method ID by calling `GetMethodId(...)` (line 48). Besides specifying the class in the call to `GetMethodId(...)`, we also need the method's name and signature. The method's name we already know to be "restoreApplication"; however, we currently do not know its signature. Java provides a tool named javap, which will let you look at the method's internal type signature. Run the javap tool on the compiled class file as follows:

```
javap -s NotifyCallback
```

The output produced is:

```
public interface NotifyCallback
    /* ACC_SUPER bit NOT set */
{
    public abstract void restoreApplication();
        /*   ()V   */
}
```

Inside the comment of the *restoreApplication* definition is the method's internal signature, '()V'. This is the value we need to pass into the `GetMethodId(...)` JNI function. The result of the `GetMethodId(...)` call is stored at the module level so we will not have to call `GetMethodId(...)` every time we need to call the `restoreApplication` method. Now that all of the module-level variables we need are captured, we need to wait for a message from the OS before we do anything.

The *SysCallbackHandler* pseudo-code represents a callback function that the OS would call when a user acknowledges the notification. The job of *SysCallbackHandler* is to call the `restoreApplication()` method. To do this it first must get an interface pointer, so we can make the JNI call `CallVoidMethod(...)`. To obtain the interface pointer we call `GetEnv(...)` (line 57), which will provide us with a valid interface pointer. After the interface pointer *pEnv* is obtained, we use `CallVoidMethod(...)` to invoke the `restoreApplication()` method.

To run the native implementation with the *TestNotifyUser* class we change the properties file to have the following values:

```
NotifyUserImpl=NativeNotifyUser
IconFileName=images/mail.ico
```

This will cause the *NativeNotifyUser* class to be loaded as the implementation of the *NotifyUser* interface. If you run *TestNotifyUser* and click the Add Notify button a mailbox icon will appear in the Windows tray, as shown in Figure 49.3. If you click the Remove Notify button the mailbox icon will disappear. When the mailbox icon is in the tray, hovering over it will display the "You have new mail" tooltip. Double-clicking on the icon will invoke the `restoreApplication()` method of *TestNotifyUser*, which will restore the Test Notify User frame if minimized and also remove the icon.

Windows Specifics

Even though this book is about Java, I would feel guilty not letting you see the Windows calls necessary to implement the native implementation. If you are not interested in looking at Windows code, just skip over this section. Here is the complete source listing of the NativeNotifyUser.c file with explanations to follow:

Figure 49.3   Native implementation of NotifyUser.

```
001: #include <windows.h>
002: #include <string.h>
003: #include "NativeNotifyUser.h"
004:
005: void replaceChar (char *, int, int);
006: LRESULT CALLBACK CallWndProc(int, WPARAM, LPARAM);
007: HWND GetTopLevelWindowHandle ();
008: BOOL CALLBACK EnumWindowsProc (HWND, LPARAM);
009:
010: HHOOK       m_hookId;
011: HWND        m_hWnd;
012: UINT        m_callbackMessage = 101;
013: HWND        m_hwndTopLevelWindow;
014: DWORD       m_dwProcessId;
015:
016: JavaVM    *m_vm;
017: jobject    m_pNotifyCallbackObject;
018: jmethodID   m_method_id;
019:
020: BOOL APIENTRY DllMain( HANDLE hModule,
021:                        DWORD  ul_reason_for_call,
022:                        LPVOID lpReserved
023:                   )
024: {
025:     return TRUE;
026: }
027:
028: JNIEXPORT void JNICALL Java_NativeNotifyUser_addNotify
029:   (JNIEnv *pEnv, jobject pObject,
030:    jstring iconFileName, jstring message)
031: {
032:     const char  *cc_iconFileName;
033:     const char  *cc_message;
034:     char        caBuffer[256];
035:     NOTIFYICONDATA tnid;
036:
037:     cc_iconFileName =
038:             (*pEnv)->GetStringUTFChars(pEnv, iconFileName, 0);
039:     cc_message = (*pEnv)->GetStringUTFChars(pEnv, message, 0);
040:
041:     tnid.cbSize = sizeof(NOTIFYICONDATA);
042:     m_hWnd = GetTopLevelWindowHandle();
043:     tnid.hWnd = m_hWnd;
044:     tnid.uID = 1;
045:     tnid.uCallbackMessage = m_callbackMessage;
046:     tnid.uFlags = NIF_ICON | NIF_TIP | NIF_MESSAGE;
047:     strcpy(caBuffer, cc_iconFileName);
048:     replaceChar(caBuffer, '/', '\\');
049:     tnid.hIcon =
050:       LoadImage(NULL, caBuffer, IMAGE_ICON, 0, 0, LR_LOADFROMFILE);
051:     lstrcpyn(tnid.szTip, cc_message, sizeof(tnid.szTip));
```

```
052:
053:        Shell_NotifyIcon(NIM_ADD, &tnid);
054:        m_hookId = SetWindowsHookEx(WH_CALLWNDPROC, &CallWndProc, NULL,
055:                          GetWindowThreadProcessId(m_hWnd, NULL));
056:        DestroyIcon(tnid.hIcon);
057:        (*pEnv)->ReleaseStringUTFChars(pEnv, iconFileName,
058:                                          cc_iconFileName);
059:        (*pEnv)->ReleaseStringUTFChars(pEnv, message, cc_message);
060: }
061:
062: JNIEXPORT void JNICALL Java_NativeNotifyUser_removeNotify
063:    (JNIEnv *pEnv, jobject pObject)
064: {
065:        NOTIFYICONDATA tnid;
066:
067:        tnid.cbSize = sizeof(NOTIFYICONDATA);
068:        tnid.hWnd = m_hWnd;
069:        tnid.uID = 1;
070:        UnhookWindowsHookEx(m_hookId);
071:        Shell_NotifyIcon(NIM_DELETE, &tnid);
072: }
073:
074: JNIEXPORT void JNICALL Java_NativeNotifyUser_installNotifyCallback
075:    (JNIEnv *pEnv, jobject pObject, jobject pNotifyCallbackObject)
076: {
077:        jclass pNotifyCallbackClass;
078:
079:        (*pEnv)->GetJavaVM(pEnv, &m_vm);
080:        m_pNotifyCallbackObject =
081:            (*pEnv)->NewGlobalRef(pEnv, pNotifyCallbackObject);
082:        pNotifyCallbackClass =
083:            (*pEnv)->GetObjectClass(pEnv, pNotifyCallbackObject);
084:        m_method_id =
085:            (*pEnv)->GetMethodID(pEnv, pNotifyCallbackClass,
086:                          "restoreApplication", "()V");
087: }
088:
089: void replaceChar (char *cpString, int charToReplace,
090:                          int replaceChar)
091: {
092:        char    *cpPosition;
093:
094:        while ((cpPosition = strchr(cpString, charToReplace)) != NULL)
095:            cpPosition[0] = replaceChar;
096: }
097:
098: LRESULT CALLBACK CallWndProc(int nCode, WPARAM wParam,
099:                          LPARAM lParam)
100: {
101:        CWPSTRUCT    *cwp;
```

```
102:      jint      returnCode;
103:      JNIEnv    *pEnv;
104:
105:      if (nCode < 0)
106:          return (CallNextHookEx(m_hookId, nCode, wParam, lParam));
107:      else
108:      {
109:          cwp = (CWPSTRUCT*) lParam;
110:          if (cwp->message == m_callbackMessage)
111:          {
112:              if (cwp->lParam == WM_LBUTTONDBLCLK)
113:              {
114:                  if (m_pNotifyCallbackObject != NULL)
115:                  {
116:                      returnCode =
117:                          (*m_vm)->GetEnv(m_vm, (void**) &pEnv,
118:                                  JNI_VERSION_1_2);
119:                      (*pEnv)->CallVoidMethod(pEnv,
120:                          m_pNotifyCallbackObject, m_method_id);
121:                  }
122:              }
123:          }
124:      }
125:
126:      return (CallNextHookEx(m_hookId, nCode, wParam, lParam));
127: }
128:
129: HWND GetTopLevelWindowHandle ()
130: {
131:      m_dwProcessId = GetCurrentProcessId();
132:      EnumWindows (&EnumWindowsProc, 0);
133:
134:      return (m_hwndTopLevelWindow);
135: }
136:
137: BOOL CALLBACK EnumWindowsProc (HWND hwnd, LPARAM pProcessId)
138: {
139:      DWORD   dwProcessId;
140:
141:      GetWindowThreadProcessId (hwnd, &dwProcessId);
142:      if (m_dwProcessId == dwProcessId)
143:      {
144:          m_hwndTopLevelWindow = hwnd;
145:          return (FALSE);
146:      }
147:      return (TRUE);
148: }
```

I am not going to go through each line of code in detail, but I will point out the interesting parts of the program. Starting with the Java_Native-

`NotifyUser_addNotify` method, our goal is to call the `Shell_Notify-`
`Icon(...)` Windows function. To get to this point, we must set up a *NOTIFYI-*
CONDATA structure with the correct values. The members of the
NOTIFYICONDATA structure are populated as follows:

cbSize. Size of *NOTIFYICONDATA* structure.

hWnd. The handle of the window to receive callback messages.

uID. Application-defined icon identifier.

uCallbackMessage. ID of message to be sent to the callback window.

uFlags. Flags indicating that we have a valid icon, tool tip, and callback message.

hIcon. The handle of the icon to display in the Windows tray.

szTip. Text of tool tip.

To get the *hIcon* and *hWnd* parameters we have to do a little work. Let's look
at *hIcon* first because this is more straightforward. We get the icon file name
passed in from the Java object, but we get it with a different file separator. To
fix this, we call the `replaceChar(...)` routine we have defined to swap the file
separator. After we have a valid file name we make a call to `LoadImage(...)` to
load up the icon. The `LoadImage(...)` function will interpret only images
defined as a Windows cursor, icon, or bitmap. In our case, we are expecting an
icon file so we pass the *IMAGE_ICON* parameter as one of the arguments to
`LoadImage(...)`.

Getting the Window handle is a little more complicated. There are several
ways of doing this, each with its own pros and cons. The way shown here oper-
ates as follows:

1. First the current process ID of this process is looked up by calling
   `GetCurrentProcessId()`.

2. Next, an enumeration of all top-level windows is performed. For every window in the enumeration our callback function `EnumWindowsProc(...)`
   gets called.

3. For the window handle that gets passed into `EnumWindowsProc(...)`, we
   grab its current process ID and compare it to the one we got from
   `GetCurrentProcessId()`. If we have a match, then the current window handle we are evaluating is the one we want.

Obviously, this approach has some problems in that if there were more than
one top-level window for the current process you might get the wrong window.
For the purposes of our example, though, all we need is any top-level window
in the process to accept the callback messages. Another way you could find the

window handle is to use the `FindWindow(...)` function, but it has the drawback of potentially returning a window handle from a different process.

Now comes the next big issue: How do we handle window messages passed to our Java window? Because it is a Java window we do not have access to the window's current message callback function. The only way we can get the messages is to stick a hook on the thread our Java window is in and intercept the messages. This is what the `SetWindowsHookEx(...)` function does. Once the hook is installed any message sent to a window running in the thread we specified will be passed to our `CallWndProc(...)` function. It is inside the `Call-WndProc(...)` function that we wait for the system to call us with the message ID we specified. If we get this message, then we use JNI to call the `restore-Application()` method on the *NotifyCallback* object.

That does it for the `Java_NativeNotifyUser_addNotify` method; now let's look at the `Java_NativeNotifyUser_removeNotify` method. The Windows calls in this routine are straightforward. First, we set up enough information in the *NOTIFYICONDATA* structure to identify the icon we created with `addNotify(...)`. Once we have enough information we call `Shell_Notify-Icon(...)` with the NIM_DELETE parameter to remove it from the Windows tray. Right before we remove the icon, we have to remove the Windows hook because we no longer will be expecting a callback from the OS.

By using interfaces to segment out JNI calls from the rest of your Java application, you will not limit yourself to supporting only one OS. Other implementations of the interface can be loaded and used whether they are pure Java implementations or native implementations for different operating systems. And don't limit your use of interfaces for just this one cause. Interfaces are powerful constructs that can be used to segment out large pieces of code or libraries from the rest of your application.

Item 50: Assertions

While some professional Integrated Development Environments are becoming quite sophisticated, many teams developing in Java still have very little support for debugging. In fact, trace statements are commonly the only technique some projects use. You can do better; one simple but effective tool you can use is *Assertions*. Even if you do use an IDE with a good debugger, coding with assertions is still a good idea.

Many programmers are already familiar with assertions and the *design by contract* approach to coding. For those who are not, a brief explanation will help. Assertions are statements about conditions that the programmer assumes are true. For example, to ensure data validity, a programmer could add a line like this (usually called a *pre-condition*):

```
assert (year.length >= 4, "Year not Y2K compliant!");
```

Similarly, if you wanted to check the effect of a method, you could specify a *post-condition* that compared the expected results with the actual results.

During the development phase, if an assertion is not true, the program typically outputs some debug information, and halts. This simple technique is very effective at finding some types of bugs early in the process, when they are easier to fix. For the production version of the system, the assertion handling is usually disabled.

Assertions in Java

Some languages (such as *Eiffel*) have support for assertions built into the language. Java does not—yet. Also, unlike C/C++, Java does not support code preprocessing. C and C++ make extensive use of preprocessing, and support for assertions is one of the most common uses. Although some third-party preprocessors do exist, the Java designers decided not to provide this ability. Preprocessing is too easily abused, and the benefits it offers can often be achieved in other ways.

However, as part of the Java Community Process, a Java Specification Request (JSR-000041) proposing the addition of an assertion facility was accepted in late 1999. You can get more details about this proposal at www .java.sun.com/aboutJava/communityprocess/jsr/jsr_041_asrt.html. In short, it proposes adding a new keyword "assert" to the language.

Typically, assertions are used only during development and then removed (by redefining the macro expanded by the preprocessor) for the production version. The Java implementation (as proposed) will have a few advantages over this approach. First, Java will support a runtime switch to enable assertions. The intent is to allow assertions to remain even in production code, with little or no impact on performance. Second, assertions may be enabled or disabled on a global, per-package or per-class basis. Third, the implementation will take advantage of Exceptions. Normally, when an assertion fails, the program is halted. Instead, the JVM will throw an *AssertionError* exception whenever an assertion fails.

Using Assertions

For the best results, you should make extensive use of assertions throughout your code. Ideally, your design should specify any assumptions that are being made. These assumptions should translate directly into assertions. Finding problems early in the process can significantly reduce the time it takes to fix them.

Assertions can discourage the propagation of errors. Without assertions, developers tend to wrap bandages around perceived problems. These hacks may work-around the problem, but they mask the real error. Worse yet, different programmers may each "fix" the same problem in multiple places, and in different ways.

It's also worth noting that you should comment any nontrivial assertions. The idea with using assertions is to save time. A simple comment explaining the condition can save hours for a developer not intimately familiar with the code.

How Not to Use Assertions

There are some risks associated with using assertions, but they are avoidable if you're aware of them. First, because assertions are conditionally executed, you do not want to embed any expressions with side effects in the actual assertions. For example, this could be dangerous:

```
assertion ((result = process(x)) > 0, "x not valid");
```

Instead, evaluate the expression first:

```
int result = process(x);
assertion (result > 0, "x not valid");
```

Assertions should not be used to validate data sent to your API. Public methods need to check their arguments. Doing this with assertions is not appropriate, again because these checks may be disabled. Using assertions to check *nonpublic* method arguments is considered a good practice.

Also, you don't want to use an assertion in a way that would hide an appropriate exception. For example, when an array index is out of bounds, throwing an IndexOutOfBoundsException is better than an *AssertionError*. Assertions should be used to detect illegal conditions, not real errors.

A subtler problem in a multithreaded environment is timing. It's possible for assertions to affect the execution timing in a way that hides a thread bug, such as a race condition. The bug may never occur until the assertions are disabled. There's no simple solution for this, just make sure you test your code with and without the assertions enabled.

Assertions can also help with complex algorithms. It's not uncommon to have to completely rewrite an algorithm in order to optimize it. Often the initial version is simple and straightforward, while the optimized version becomes complex and difficult to maintain. In these situations, consider maintaining both versions. Use the simple version in a post-condition assertion to produce the "expected" results that you compare with the actual results. Note that in this case we do want the slow version embedded inside the assertion, not before it, because we don't want to execute it when assertions are disabled.

```
Object someMethod()
{
   // complex code
   result = ...
   assert (result == simpleButSlowVersion());
}
```

Sample Implementation

If you want to start using assertions now, we'll provide a sample implementation that simulates some aspects of the JSR proposal. First, we need to allow a runtime switch. This can be done using the -D option to set a system property. Our class will ignore any assertions unless this property is set (lines 4–5). Note that unlike assertions implemented using a preprocessor, in this example the assert method will still be called. It will just return after checking the property.

The *Assert* class itself is quite simple. We need to provide two assert methods (lines 7 and 13). We'll make them static, so they're easy to use. You can test this class using either *java Assert* or *java -DASSERT Assert*. The "true" assertion (line 24) should never fail, and the "false" one should fail if and only if the *–DASSERT* property is set.

```
01: public final class Assert
02: {
03:    /** Enable assertions using -DASSERT */
04:    private static final boolean ASSERT =
05:       System.getProperty ("ASSERT") != null;
06:
07:    public static void assert (boolean assertion)
08:    {
09:       if (ASSERT && !assertion)
10:          throw new AssertionError (null);
11:    }
12:
13:    public static void assert (boolean assertion,
14:                               String message)
15:    {
16:       if (ASSERT && !assertion)
17:          throw new AssertionError (message);
18:    }
19:
20:    public static void main (String[] args) // test
21:    {
22:       try
23:       {
```

```
24:                Assert.assert (true, "never show this");
25:                Assert.assert (false, "show if -DASSERT");
26:            }
27:        catch (AssertionError e)
28:            {
29:                System.out.println (e);
30:            }
31:        }
32: }
```

The output (with the property set) should look like this:

```
> java -DASSERT Assert

Assert fail: show if -DASSERT
  source: Assert.java
  method: Assert.main
  line #: 25
```

In order to mimic the methods in the JSR proposal, we implemented an *AssertionError* class that is worth examining. The interesting part is the stackEntry method. We borrowed a trick from the Bean Development Kit's *MethodTracer* class. By instantiating an *Exception* object, we get access to a stack trace. We perform some rudimentary parsing on this text to get the source file name and line number.

We should note that the format of the stack trace output is not specified, and it may vary across JVM implementations. You may have to tweak the stack-Entry method. Also, in the proposal, the getMethod method actually returns a *Method* object. To keep it simple, our implementation is just returning the method name. The toString method is not part of the proposal; we added it to simplify the *Assert* class.

```
01: import java.io.*;
02:
03: public class AssertionError extends Error
04: {
05:     private String method;
06:     private String sourceName;
07:     private int line = -1;
08:
09:     public AssertionError (String message)
10:     {
11:         super (message);
12:
13:         String s = stackEntry().trim();
14:         int space = s.indexOf (' ');
15:         int paren = s.indexOf ('(');
16:         int colon = s.indexOf (':');
```

```
17:
18:            method = s.substring (space + 1, paren);
19:            sourceName = s.substring (paren + 1, colon);
20:            try
21:            {
22:                paren = s.indexOf (')');
23:                String ln = s.substring (colon+1, paren);
24:                line = Integer.parseInt (ln);
25:            }
26:            catch (NumberFormatException e)
27:            {
28:                System.out.println ("Bad format: " + s);
29:            }
30:        }
31:
32:    public String getMethod()
33:    {
34:        return (method);
35:    }
36:
37:    public String getSourceName()
38:    {
39:        return (sourceName);
40:    }
41:
42:    public int getLineNumber()
43:    {
44:        return (line);
45:    }
46:
47:    public String toString()
48:    {
49:        StringBuffer buf = new StringBuffer();
50:        buf.append ("Assert fail: " + getMessage());
51:        buf.append ("\n source: " + getSourceName());
52:        buf.append ("\n method: " + getMethod());
53:        buf.append ("\n line #: " + getLineNumber());
54:        return (buf.toString());
55:    }
56:
57:    private String stackEntry()
58:    {
59:        String s = null;
60:        try
61:        {
62:            StringWriter sw = new StringWriter();
63:            PrintWriter pw = new PrintWriter (sw);
64:            (new Exception()).printStackTrace (pw);
65:            String buf = sw.getBuffer().toString();
66:            StringReader sr = new StringReader (buf);
67:            BufferedReader br = new BufferedReader (sr);
```

```
68:
69:          for (int i = 0; i < 4; i++) // skip 4 lines
70:            br.readLine();   // to the calling method
71:          s = br.readLine();
72:        }
73:      catch (IOException e)
74:        {
75:          e.printStackTrace();
76:        }
77:      return (s);
78:    }
79: }
```

If you can't wait for the JSR implementation, and if you want more functionality than our example provides, you may want to check out *JaWA* (Java With Assertions) and *Jass*, online at http://theoretica.informatik.uni-oldenburg.de/~jass/.

Index